KEY FACTS KEY CASES

Constitutional & Administrative Law

KEY FACTS KEY CASES

The **Key Facts Key Cases** revision series is designed to give you a clear understanding and concise overview of the fundamental principles of your law course. The books' chapters reflect the most commonly taught topics, breaking the law down into bite-size sections with descriptive headings. Diagrams, tables and bullet points are used throughout to make the law easy to understand and memorise, and comprehensive case checklists are provided that show the principles and application of case law for your subject.

Titles in the series:

Constitutional & Administrative Law

Company Law

Contract Law

Criminal Law

English Legal System

Equity and Trusts

European Union Law

Evidence

Family Law

Human Rights

Land Law

For a full listing of the Routledge Revision range of titles, visit www.routledge.com/law

KEY FACTS KEY CASES
Constitutional & Administrative Law

Jamie Grace

LONDON AND NEW YORK

First published 2016
by Routledge
2 Park Square, Milton Park, Abingdon, Oxon, OX14 4RN

and by Routledge
711 Third Avenue, New York, NY 10017

Routledge is an imprint of the Taylor & Francis Group, an informa business

© 2016 Jamie Grace

The right of Jamie Grace to be identified as author of this work has been asserted by him in accordance with sections 77 and 78 of the Copyright, Designs and Patents Act 1988.

All rights reserved. No part of this book may be reprinted or reproduced or utilised in any form or by any electronic, mechanical, or other means, now known or hereafter invented, including photocopying and recording, or in any information storage or retrieval system, without permission in writing from the publishers.

Trademark notice: Product or corporate names may be trademarks or registered trademarks, and are used only for identification and explanation without intent to infringe.

British Library Cataloguing in Publication Data
A catalogue record for this book is available from the British Library

Library of Congress Cataloging-in-Publication Data
Grace, Jamie, author.
  Key facts key cases : constitutional & administrative law.
    pages cm. — (Key facts key cases)
  1. Constitutional law—European Union countries.
  2. Administrative law—European Union countries. 3. European Union countries—Politics and government. I. Title. II. Title: Constitutional & administrative law. III. Title: Constitutional and administrative law.
  KJE4445.G73 2016
  342.4—dc23
  2015021327

ISBN: 978-0-415-83323-3 (pbk)
ISBN: 978-1-315-76198-5 (ebk)

Typeset in Goudy
by Apex CoVantage, LLC
Printed by CPI Group (UK) Ltd, Croydon, CR0 4YY

Contents

PREFACE xiii
TABLE OF CASES xv
TABLE OF STATUTES xxvii

PART 1
THE DEVELOPMENT OF CONSTITUTIONAL AND ADMINISTRATIVE LAW IN THE UK   1

Chapter 1

CONTEMPORARY AND FOUNDATIONAL ISSUES IN PUBLIC LAW   1

1.1	What is a constitution?	2
1.2	Classifying constitutions	3
1.3	Essential elements of the UK constitution	6
1.4	Should the UK constitution be codified?	7
1.5	Legal and non-legal sources of the constitution	10
1.6	The concept of constitutional statutes	11
1.7	The continuing constitutional contribution of the common law	13
1.8	The scope of the royal prerogative today	13
1.9	The impact of distinctly European legal systems and values	14
1.10	Other sources of constitutional values and practices	15
	Key cases checklist	16

Chapter 2

THE RULE OF LAW AND A SEPARATION OF POWERS   24

2.1	A description of the rule of law	24
2.2	Dicey's formulation of the rule of law	25
2.3	Bingham's view of the rule of law	26
2.4	Examples of the rule of law as a functional element of the UK constitution	27
2.5	Reconciling a strict view of the rule of law with some legal rules in the United Kingdom today	28

2.6	Some broader interpretations of what the 'rule of law' might entail	29
2.7	The relationship between the rule of law and the 'separation of powers'	31
2.8	The actual extent of the doctrine of 'separation of powers' in the UK constitution today	32
2.9	Constitutional fusion between elements of Government in the United Kingdom	33
2.10	The impact of the Constitutional Reform Act 2005 and other issues	35
	Key cases checklist	37

Chapter 3

PARLIAMENTARY SOVEREIGNTY — 42

3.1	A brief overview of parliamentary sovereignty, or 'parliamentary supremacy'	43
3.2	Potentially unlimited legislative power for Parliament?	43
3.3	Exploring the details of legislative supremacy	44
3.4	Limitations to parliamentary supremacy	45
3.5	Limitations on parliamentary sovereignty from a European dimension?	48
3.6	Lord Hoffman's version of the 'principle of legality'	49
	Key cases checklist	51

Chapter 4

CONSTITUTIONAL CONVENTIONS — 55

4.1	Definitions of constitutional conventions	55
4.2	Examples of constitutional conventions	56
4.3	Are constitutional conventions legally binding?	57
4.4	Should constitutional conventions themselves be codified?	58
	Key cases checklist	59

Chapter 5

THE ROLE OF INTERNATIONAL LAW — 63

5.1	What is international law?	63
5.2	The development of international law	64
5.3	Sources of international law	64
5.4	Custom in international law	65
5.5	Treaties	66
5.6	International law and national law	67
5.7	The effect of international law in the UK constitution	67
	Key cases checklist	71

Chapter 6
EUROPEAN UNION LAW 72

6.1	The origins and development of EU law	72
6.2	EU Treaties	73
6.3	Institutions within the European Union	74
6.4	The Court of Justice of the European Union	75
6.5	Different EU law instruments: Treaties, Regulations and Directives	76
6.6	Supremacy of EU law and the European Communities Act 1972	78
6.7	*Factortame* and the impact on parliamentary sovereignty	81
6.8	The EU Charter on Fundamental Rights and overlaps with European human rights law	82
6.9	An ongoing relationship between the United Kingdom and the European Union?	85
	Key cases checklist	86

Chapter 7
EUROPEAN HUMAN RIGHTS LAW AND THE HUMAN RIGHTS ACT 1998 89

7.1	The European Convention on Human Rights and Fundamental Freedoms	90
7.2	Particular rights from the ECHR and its Protocols	90
7.3	Derogation	95
7.4	The proportionality principle	95
7.5	The margin of appreciation	95
7.6	The UK constitution and the impact of the Human Rights Act 1998	96
7.7	Section 2 of the Human Rights Act 1998: UK courts drawing on the case law of the ECtHR	96
7.8	Section 3 of the Human Rights Act 1998: interpreting statute in the light of the ECHR	99
7.9	Sections 4 and 10 of the Human Rights Act 1998: Declarations of Incompatibility and fast-track statutory reform	99
7.10	Section 6 of the Human Rights Act 1998: duties to be upheld by public bodies under the ECHR	101
7.11	Section 7 of the Human Rights Act 1998: cases brought by the 'victims' of rights infringements under the ECHR	102
7.12	Section 8 of the Human Rights Act 1998: remedies for the unlawful interference with rights under the ECHR	103

7.13	Possible reform of the UK human rights framework	103
	Key cases checklist	106

Chapter 8
DEVOLUTION AND INDEPENDENCE 111

8.1	Historical overview of the formation of the United Kingdom	112
8.2	Key developments in the late 20th century	114
8.3	Key legislation – an overview	116
8.4	Recent moves toward greater devolution or independence	119
8.5	Looking ahead	121

PART 2
PUBLIC LAW IN PRACTICE 125

Chapter 9
THE CONTEMPORARY ROLE AND POSSIBLE REFORM OF PARLIAMENT 125

9.1	A bicameral Parliament	126
9.2	The electoral system relevant to the 'Westminster Parliament'	127
9.3	Other electoral systems used in the United Kingdom	129
9.4	The Electoral Commission and controls on lobbying and campaigning	130
9.5	Broadcasting	132
9.6	The House of Commons	133
9.7	The House of Lords	134
9.8	The Parliament Acts	137
9.9	Parliamentary privilege	138
9.10	Parliamentary standards	140
	Key cases checklist	142

Chapter 10
THE CONTEMPORARY ROLE, SCOPE AND POWERS OF THE EXECUTIVE 146

10.1	Defining the executive: Ministers, Government departments and public bodies	147
10.2	Ministerial responsibility and accountability, and a Ministerial Code	151
10.3	Local authorities	152
10.4	Police structures	155
10.5	Different types of public body	156

10.6	Prerogative powers today: the Monarch and Ministers exercising power	157
10.7	Proper scrutiny of the executive branch of Government by Parliament	166
10.8	The work of the parliamentary committees	168
10.9	Wider controls on the power of the executive: judicial review, the media and the electorate	169
10.10	The traditional role of the Civil Service and the growth of 'special advisers' to Ministers	170
10.11	The executive, public records and freedom of information law in the United Kingdom and Europe	173
	Key cases checklist	176

Chapter 11

THE CONTEMPORARY ROLE AND POWERS OF THE COURTS — 179

11.1	The role of the courts in the UK constitution	179
11.2	The importance of the separation of powers doctrine in assigning the courts a role in the UK constitution	180
11.3	Developing the common law	180
11.4	Engaging in dialogue with Parliament, the Government and European legal structures	181
11.5	Engaging with Parliament	183
11.6	Engaging with the Government	185
11.7	Engaging with European legal structures: the European Union	186
11.8	Engaging with European legal structures: a relationship with the European Court of Human Rights	186
11.9	The growth of the landscape of administrative justice	188
11.10	A system of tribunals	188
11.11	Ombudsmen and regulators	190
11.12	Inquiries	192
	Key cases checklist	193

Chapter 12

THE CONSTITUTIONAL ROLE AND CONFIGURATION OF JUDICIAL REVIEW — 196

12.1	Defining the role of judicial review	196
12.2	A (problematic) growth in judicial review, or scrutiny of the Government we can be proud of?	197
12.3	Judicial review and the Human Rights Act 1998	198
12.4	Defining public bodies: amenability to judicial review	199
12.5	Reviewing crucial matters of policy	200

12.6	Limitations on judicial review: the concept of justiciability	201
12.7	Ouster clauses and other exclusions in relation to judicial review	201
12.8	Exhausting other processes: the importance of the availability of other remedies beyond judicial review	203
	Key cases checklist	204

Chapter 13

PROCESS, STANDING AND REMEDIES IN JUDICIAL REVIEW — 208

13.1	Procedural requirements in applying for permission for judicial review	209
13.2	The pre-action protocol in relation to claims for judicial review	210
13.3	Time limits	211
13.4	'Sufficient interest' standing	211
13.5	Standing in human rights claims	212
13.6	Representative standing	213
13.7	Prerogative remedies in judicial review – and the influence of the Human Rights Act 1998	214
13.8	Other remedies used in judicial review	215
13.9	Declaratory relief	216
13.10	Judicial deference and comity: refusal of a remedy	216
	Key cases checklist	217

Chapter 14

SUBSTANTIVE GROUNDS FOR JUDICIAL REVIEW — 220

14.1	An overview of grounds for judicial review	221
14.2	Types of illegality and the importance of statutory interpretation in deploying arguments about illegality in claiming judicial review	222
14.3	Illegality as an excess of powers (*ultra vires*)	223
14.4	Illegality as an improper purpose	223
14.5	Illegality as an error of law (or an error of fact)	224
14.6	Illegality as a failure to take into account a relevant consideration, or the taking into account of an irrelevant consideration	225
14.7	Illegality as an unlawful delegation of power in decision-making	226
14.8	Illegality as an unlawful fettering of discretion in decision-making	226
14.9	Unreasonableness and irrationality	227
14.10	*Wednesbury* unreasonableness	227

14.11	Proportionality: influenced by human rights law	228
	Key cases checklist	230

Chapter 15

PROCEDURAL GROUNDS FOR JUDICIAL REVIEW — 237

15.1	An overview of procedural grounds for judicial review	237
15.2	Natural justice	238
15.3	Bias: the rule against bias (*nemo judex in causa sua*)	239
15.4	Legitimate expectations	241
15.5	Procedural fairness	245
15.6	Procedural *ultra vires*	245
15.7	The general public sector equality duty (or duties)	246
	Key cases checklist	250

Chapter 16

HUMAN RIGHTS GROUNDS FOR JUDICIAL REVIEW — 256

16.1	An overview of human rights grounds for judicial review	256
16.2	Engaging rights: measuring lawful and unlawful interferences with rights	259
16.3	Absolute, limited and qualified rights in the language of the ECHR	259
16.4	The concept of 'positive obligations' under the ECHR	260
16.5	The concept of a margin of appreciation	260
16.6	Preventing the use of ECHR rights to undermine the rights of others	261
	Key cases checklist	262
16.7	Article 2 ECHR	263
16.8	Article 3 ECHR	263
16.9	Article 5 ECHR	265
16.10	Article 6 ECHR	266
16.11	Case law on qualified rights under the ECHR	268
16.12	Article 8 ECHR	269
16.13	Article 9 (and Article 14) ECHR	275
16.14	Article 10 ECHR	276
16.15	Article 11 ECHR	277
16.16	ECHR rights drawn from Protocols	279
16.17	Overlaps between ECHR rights and the EU Charter on Fundamental Rights	279

INDEX — 281

Preface

This new series of **Key Facts Key Cases** is built on the two well-known series, *Key Facts* and *Key Cases*. Each title in the *Key Facts* series now incorporates a 'Key Cases' section at the end of most chapters, which is designed to give a clear understanding of important cases. This is useful when studying a new topic and invaluable as a revision aid. Each case is broken down into a straightforward factual context, and the key principle that was used to decide the case, or which emerges as a result of the decision in the case. These elements of each Key Case summary are:

 Key Facts

 Key Law

Many case summaries in the Key Cases sections in this book are brought to life with some pertinent quotations from the judges who decided the case, or some key commentary that puts the decision in the case into a particular context. Sometimes a second, crucial case which highlights the point of law concerned is linked to at the end of the overview of a case. These elements of each Key Case summary will be highlighted as:

 Key Judgment

 Key Comment

 Key Link

My approach has been to feature the most prominent, newer case law from the European Court of Human Rights, and the UK Supreme Court, so that the most vital-to-appreciate issues across the UK legal system, in the field of

Constitutional and Administrative Law, are addressed in this edition of the book. In addition to a focus on the most vital case law to understand, *Key Facts Key Cases Constitutional & Administrative Law* also supplies readers with an up-to-date commentary on the key political and constitutional issues that are developing today, mainly in relation to devolution, human rights law and **EU membership**.

This book has a newer structure – featuring distinct chapters on the **incorporation of international law in the UK constitution**, and issues of **devolution** and potential independence, as well as crucial **human rights law developments**. This new structure is something that should mean that the book is as useful as possible for students approaching any one of the wide variety of curricula one might encounter.

This book is, in effect, a text which covers large bodies of UK public law, and as a result is equally balanced in the way it approaches both constitutional law, and administrative law. As such, the book is broken down into two parts: Part 1, on **the development of constitutional and administrative law in the UK** (together comprising 'public law'); and Part 2, a series of chapters on **public law in practice** (meaning a heavy focus on the principles, procedures and particularly the grounds of judicial review).

The law stated in this book is as I believe it to be on 26 May 2015. I would like to thank my wife, Sara, for her support and patience as I worked on this book.

Jamie Grace, Sheffield, May 2015

Table of Cases

A v Secretary of State for the Home Department [2004]
UKHL 56, HL 27, 37, 39
A v Secretary of State for the Home Department (No 2)
[2005] UKHL 71 .... 93, 163
A v United Kingdom [2002] ECHR 35373/97 140
Agricultural Horticultural and Forestry Industry Training
Board v Aylesbury Mushrooms Ltd (1972) 1 All ER 280 .... 246, 251
Akumah v London Borough of Hackney [2005] 1 WLR 985 223
Al-Skeini v United Kingdom (2011) 53 EHRR 18 263
Amministrazione delle Finanze dello Stato v Simmenthal
SpA (Case 106/77) [1978] ECR 629 88
Anderson v Gorrie [1895] 1 QB 668 28
Animal Defenders International v UK (2013)
57 EHRR 21 .... 133, 142, 144–5
Anisminic v Foreign Compensation Commission
[1969] 2 AC 147, HL 202, 204, 206, 224
Anufrijeva v Southwark LBC [2003] EWCA
Civ 1406 .... 103, 106, 215, 217–219
Ashbridge Investments Ltd v Minister of Housing & Local
Government [1965] 3 All ER 371 224
Associated Provincial Picture Houses v Wednesbury
Corporation [1948] 1 KB 223, CA 227–30, 244
Aston Cantlow and Wilmcote with Billesley Parochial
Church Council v Wallbank [2003] UKHL 37, HL 101–2, 200
Attorney General v de Keyser's Royal Hotel Ltd
[1920] AC 508 164
Attorney General v Fulham Corporation
[1921] 1 Ch 440 222
Attorney General v Jonathan Cape Ltd [1976]
QB 752, QBD 57, 59, 60, 150
Attorney General v National Assembly for Wales
Commission and others [2012] UKSC 53 119
Attorney General for New South Wales v Trethowan
and Others [1932] AC 526, PC 45

Attorney General of Hong Kong v. Ng Yuen Shiu,
[1983] 2 AC 629 242
Attorney-General of Trinidad and Tobago v Lennox
Phillips [1995] 1 All ER 93 162
Attorney General's Reference No.3 of 1999 [2001] 2 AC 91 246
Austin v UK (2012) 55 EHRR 14 265
AWG Group Ltd v Morrison [2006] EWCA Civ 6 240
Axel Springer AG v Germany [2012] ECHR 227 272
Barnard v National Dock Labour Board [1953] 2 QB 18 .... 226, 234
Barnsley Metropolitan Borough Council v Norton and
others [2011] EWCA Civ 834 247
BBC v Johns [1964] 1 All ER 923; [1965] Ch 32 164
Beach v Freeson [1972] 1 QB 14 139
Bellinger v Bellinger [2003] 2 All ER 593 101
Benkharbouche v Embassy of Sudan [2015] EWCA Civ 33 .... 83, 84, 279
Blackburn v Attorney General [1971] 1 WLR 1037; [1971] 2
All ER 1380, CA 46, 201
Boddington v British Transport Police [1998] 2 All ER 203 221
Bradbury v Enfield Borough Council [1967] 3 All ER 434 246
Bradlaugh v Gosset (1884) 12 QBD 271, QBD 140
Brasserie du Pêcheur SA v Federal Republic of Germany
(Cases C-46/93, C-48/93) [1996] ECR I-1029; joined with
R v Secretary of State for Transport, ex parte Factortame
Ltd (No 4) (Joined cases C-46/93 and C-48/93) [1996] 2
WLR 506, ECJ 78
British Oxygen Co v Board of Trade [1971] AC 610 .... 226, 232–233
Bromley London Borough Council v Greater London
Council [1983] 1 AC 768 222
Bulmer v Bollinger [1974] Ch 401, HC 76
Burmah Oil Company v Lord Advocate [1965]
AC 75, HL 13, 18, 29, 43, 51
Bushell's Case (1670) Jones T 13 28
Caballero v UK (2000) 30 EHRR 643 93
Campaign for Nuclear Disarmament v Prime Minister [2002]
EWHC 2777 (Admin) 163, 176–77
Campbell v Mirror Group Newspapers Ltd [2004] 2
AC. 457 .... 98, 101, 200
Carltona Ltd v Works Commissioners [1943] 2
All ER 560, CA 150, 176, 226, 234
Case of Proclamations (1611) 12 Co Rep 74; 77 ER 1352 .... 158, 165
Chahal v United Kingdom (1997) 23 E.H.R.R. 413 93
Cheney v Conn [1968] 1 All ER 779, HC 44, 51
Church of Scientology v Johnson Smith [1972] 1 QB 522 138

CILFIT S & I v Ministro della Sanita [1982] ECR 3415 76
Clark v University of Lincolnshire & Humberside
  [2000] 1 WLR 1988 197
Cook v Alexander [1974] 1 QB 279 139
Commission v UK: Re Tachographs [1979] E.C.R. 419 .... 77, 86
Costa v ENEL [1964] (Case 6/64) [1964] ECR 1125, ECJ 78, 86, 88
Council of Civil Service Unions v Minister of State for the
  Civil Service ('the GCHQ Case') [1985] AC 374, HL 14, 161–2,
          163, 176–78, 201, 204, 221, 227, 228, 231, 237, 238, 242
D v United Kingdom [1997] ECHR 25 93
Day v Savadge (1615) 86 ER 235 44
De Freitas v Benny [1976] AC 239 162
Derbyshire County Council v Times Newspapers Ltd [1993] AC 534 96
Dillenkofer v Federal Republic of Germany [1996] ECR I-4845 78
Dimes v Grand Junction Canal Co (1852) 3 HL Cas 759, HL 240, 253
Douglas v Hello! Ltd [2001] QB 967 .... 98, 101
Dr Bonham's Case (1610) 8 Co Rep 114 44
Dudgeon v United Kingdom (1981) 4 EHRR 149 94
Duncan Sandys' Case (1938) (decision of Select Committee) 138
Duport Steels Ltd v Sirs [1980] 1 WLR 142, HL 33, 37, 40
East African Asians v United Kingdom [1981] 3 EHRR 76 93
Edinburgh and Dalkleith Railway v Wauchope (1842)
  8 Cl & F 710, CA 45, 51, 52
Ellen Street Estates Ltd v Minister of Health [1934] 1 KB 590, CA 44
Entick v Carrington (1765) 19 St
  Tr 1029 .... 13, 16, 19, 25, 158, 164, 176
Evans v United Kingdom [2007] ECHR 265 93
Eweida v UK [2013] IRLR 231 275–76
Ex parte Cannon Selwyn (1872) 36 JP 54 53
Ezeh and Connors v UK [2002] 35 EHRR 28 239
Firth v United Kingdom (2014) (47784/09) 279
Francome and Another v Mirror Group Newspapers
  Ltd and Others [1984] 2 All ER 408 .... 21, 27
Francovich and Bonifaci v Italy (Cases C-6, C-9/90)
  [1991] ECR I-5357, ECJ 78
Garland v BREL [1982] ECR 359, HL 80
Ghaidan v Godin-Mendoza [2004]
  UKHL 30, HL 99, 100, 101, 106, 107
Gillan & Quinton v United Kingdom [2010] ECHR 28 94
Gillick v West Norfolk & Wisbeck Area Health Authority
  [1986] AC 112 212
Glynn v. Keele University [1971] 1 W.L.R. 487 238
Goodwin v United Kingdom (1996) 22 EHRR 123 94

Gough v United Kingdom (2015) SCCR 1 276
H and B v United Kingdom (2013) 57 EHRR 17 264–65
Hanif and Khan v United Kingdom (2012) 55 EHRR 16 268
Harper v Secretary of State for the Home Department
    [1955] Ch 238, CA 127
Hirst v UK (No 2) (2005) 16 BHRC 409,
    ECHR 104, 127, 142, 143, 261, 279
In re W (Children) (Family Proceedings: Evidence)
    [2010] UKSC 12 258
Internationale Handelsgesellschaft MbH v EVST
    (Case 11/70) [1970] ECR 1125, ECJ 78
Johnson v United Kingdom (1997) 27 EHRR 296 93
Kennedy v Charity Commission [2014]
    UKSC 20 .... 103, 184, 193, 194
Laker Airways v Department of Trade [1977] QB 643, CA 164
Lee v Bude and Torrington Junction Railway Company
    (1871) LR 6 CP 576 .... 45, 52–53
Leonesio v Ministero dell'Agricoltura [1972] ECR 287 77
Litster v Forth Dry Dock Ltd [1990] 1 AC 546 80
Local Government Board v. Arlidge [1915] A.C. 120 238
London & Clydeside Estates Ltd v Aberdeen DC
    [1980] 1 WLR 182 245–46
Lustig-Prean and Beckett v United Kingdom [1999] ECHR 71 94
M v Home Office [1994] 1 AC 377, HL 13, 16, 20, 27, 37, 215
Macarthys v Smith [1979] 3 All ER 32, CA 80
Madzimbamuto v Lardner-Burke [1969] 1 AC 645, HL 46, 57, 59, 61
Magee and others v United Kingdom (2015)
    (Applications nos. 26289/12, 29062/12 and 29891/12) 265
Malone v United Kingdom (1984) 7 EHRR 14 93
Mangold v Helm C-144/04 [2006] All ER (EC) 383 77
Manuel and Others v Attorney General [1983]
    1 Ch 77, CA 46, 57, 59, 62
Marleasing SA v La Commercial Internacional de
    Alimentacion SA (Case 106/89) [1992] 1 CMLR 305 .... 80, 86, 88
Marshall v Southampton and South West Hampshire Area Health
    Authority (No 1) (Case 152/84) [1986] QB 401, ECJ 77
Marshall and Dori v Recreb Srl (C-91/92) [1994] ECR I-3325 77
McCann v United Kingdom (1996) 21 EHRR 97 93
McDonald v UK (2014) 17 CCL Rep 187 269–70
McHugh v United Kingdom (2015) (51987/08) 279
McMichael v UK (1995) 20 EHRR 205 94
Mercury Communications plc v Customs and Excise
    Commissioners [1997] 2 All ER 366 197

Merkur Island Shipping Corp v Laughton and Others
[1983] 2 AC 570, HL 27, 37, 38
Metropolitan Properties Co (FGC) Ltd v Lannon
[1969] 1 QB 577 240
Mortensen v Peters (1906) 14 SLT 227, HC 44
Mosley v News Group Newspapers Ltd.
[2008] EWHC 1777 (QB) 98, 101
Mosley v UK (2011) 161 NLJ 703 270–71
Murray v United Kingdom (1994) 19 EHRR 193......................................93
National Union of Rail, Maritime and Transport Workers
('The RMT') v United Kingdom [2014] IRLR 467.....................277–78
NHS Trust A v M [2001] Fam 348 97
North and East Devon Health Authority, ex parte Coughlan
[2001] QB 213..244–45, 254–55
Norwood v UK (2005) 40 EHRR SE11
(Application No. 23131/03)..261
NS v Secretary of State for the Home Department
[2011] EUECJ C-411/10 and C-493/10..83
O'Hara v United Kingdom (2002) 34 EHRR 32 93
O'Reilly v Mackman [1983] 2 AC 237, HL 197
Osborn v The Parole Board [2013] UKSC 61 239
Osman v United Kingdom [1998] ECHR 101 94
Othman v United Kingdom (2012) 55 EHRR 1..............................267–68
P v Cheshire West and Chester Council [2014] UKSC 19..............259, 265
Paton v United Kingdom [1980] 3 EHRR 408..93
Perilly v Tower Hamlets Borough Council [1973] QB 9.........................224
Pickin v British Railway Board [1974] AC 765, HL 13, 16, 20, 45
Pickstone v Freemans plc [1989] AC 66 80
Poplar Housing and Regeneration Community
Association Ltd v Donoghue [2001] EWCA Civ 595........................102
Porter v Magill [2002] 2 AC 357;
[2001] UKHL 673, HL...224, 240, 253–54
Pretty v United Kingdom (2002) 35 EHRR 1...93
Prohibitions del Roy (Case of Prohibitions) (1607)
12 Co Rep 63 ....13, 16, 19, 158
R v A (Complainant's Sexual History) (2001) The
Times, 24 May, HL...99, 106, 107
R v Army Board of Defence Council exparte
Anderson [1992] QB 169 ....227, 239
R v Boundary Commission for England, ex parte Foot
[1983] QB 600, HC...127
R v Bow Street Magistrates' Court, ex parte Pinochet
Urgart (No 2) [1999] 2 WLR 272, HL 240

R v British Broadcasting Corporation, ex parte Referendum
Party (1997) The Times, 29 April, DC 132–3
R v Broadcasting Complaints Commission, ex parte Owen
[1985] QB 1153 133
R v Chaytor and others [2010] UKSC 52 .... 140, 142, 143
R v Chief Constable of North Wales Police and Others
ex parte AB and Another [1997] 3 WLR 724 227
R v Chief Constable of Sussex ex parte International
Trader's Ferry Ltd [1999] 1 All ER129 228
R v City Panel on Take-overs and Mergers, ex p Datafin
plc [1987] QB 815 .... 199, 204, 205
R v Civil Service Appeal Board ex parte Cunningham
[1991] 4 All ER 310 240
R v Cornwall CC ex parte Huntingdon [1994] 1 All ER 694 202
R v Criminal Injuries Compensation Board, ex parte A
[1999] 2 AC 330 224
R v Criminal Injuries Compensation Board and Another,
ex parte P [1994] P.I.Q.R. P400 163
R v Deputy Governor of Parkhurst Prison, ex parte
Leech [1988] A.C. 533 203
R v Director of Public Prosecutions, ex parte
Kebeline and Others [1999] 3 WLR 175 .... 99, 101, 106, 109, 243
R v DPP ex p Manning (2001) QB 330 241
R v Disciplinary Committee of the Jockey Club,
ex p Aga Khan [1993] 1 WLR 909 .... 200, 204, 205
R v Football Association Ltd, ex parte. Football League
Ltd [1993] 2 All ER 833 200
R v Gloucestershire County Council, Ex parte Barry [1997]
AC 584 226
R v Hampden (Case of Ship Money) (1637) 3
St Tr 825 158
R v Higher Education Funding Council, ex parte Institute
of Dental Surgery [1994] 1 All ER 651, [1994] 1 WLR 242 241
R v HM Inspectorate of Pollution ex parte Greenpeace
Ltd no.2 (1994) 4 All ER 329 213
R v HM Treasury, ex parte BT plc (Case C-392/93)
[1996] ECR I-1631 78
R v HM Treasury, ex parte Smedley [1985] QB 657 .... 33, 34, 37, 41, 212
R v Horncastle and Others [2009] UKSC 14 258
R v Horseferry Road Magistrates' Court, ex parte
Bennett [1994] AC 42, HL 27, 37, 38
R v Inland Revenue Commissioners, ex parte MFK
Underwriting Agents Ltd [1990] 1 WLR 1545 242

R v Inland Revenue Commissioners, ex parte National
  Federation of Self-employed and Small Businesses
  [1982] AC 617, HL 211, 217–18
R v Inland Revenue Commissioners, Ex p Preston [1985] AC 835 203
R v Lambert, Ali and Jordan [2001] 1 All ER 1014 .... 99, 100, 109
R v Liverpool Corporation ex parte Liverpool Taxi
  Fleet Operators' Association [1972] 2 QB 299 .... 213, 242
R v Liverpool Crown Court ex parte Luxury Leisure
  Limited (The Times 9 October 1998)(1999) LR 30 225
R v Lord Chancellor ex parte Witham [1998] QB 575 222–23
R v Lord President of the Privy Council, ex parte
  Page [1992] 3 WLR 1112 224
R v Medical Appeal Tribunal (ex parte Gilmore) [1957] 1 QB 574 202
R. v. Ministry of Agriculture, Fisheries and Food,
  ex parte Hamble (Offshore) Fisheries Ltd. [1995] 2 All ER 714 243
R v Minister of Agriculture ex p Padfield [1968] AC 997 .... 223, 233, 241
R v Ministry of Defence, ex parte Murray [1998] COD 134 240
R v Ministry of Defence, ex p Smith [1996] QB 517 228
R v Parliamentary Commissioner for Administration,
  ex parte Dyer [1994] 1 All ER 375 .... 201, 204, 206
R v Poole Borough Council ex parte Beebee et al [1991] 2 PLR 27 213
R v Secretary of State for Education and Employment
  exparte Begbie [2000] 1 WLR 1115 243
R v Secretary of State for Employment, ex parte Equal
  Opportunities Commission [1995] 1 AC 1 .... 81, 213
R v Secretary of State for the Environment ex parte Norwich
  City Council [1982] QB 808 223
R v Secretary of State for the Environment, ex parte
  Ostler [1977] QB 122 202
R v Secretary of State for the Environment, ex parte
  Rose Theatre Trust Co Ltd [1990] 2 WLR 186 213
R v Secretary of State for Environment, ex parte Ward [1984] 1
  WLR 834 212
R v Secretary of State for Foreign and Commonwealth Affairs,
  ex parte Everett [1989] QB 811, CA 162
R v Secretary of State for Foreign and Commonwealth Affairs,
  ex parte Rees-Mogg [1994] QB 552; [1994] 2
  WLR 115, CA 162, 176–77, 201, 212
R v Secretary of State for Foreign and Commonwealth
  Affairs, ex parte World Development Movement
  [1995] 1 All ER 611 .... 214, 217–18, 223
R v Secretary of State for Health, ex parte US Tobacco
  International Inc [1992] 1 All ER 212 .... 244, 254

R v Secretary of State for the Home Department, ex parte
Al Fayed [1997] 1 All ER 228...162, 241, 253
R v Secretary of State for the Home Department ex parte
Asif Mahmood Khan [1984] 1 WLR 1337 242
R v Secretary of State for the Home Department ex parte
Behluli [1998] COD 328...243
R v Secretary of State for the Home Department, ex parte
Bentley [1994] QB 349 162
R v Secretary of State for the Home Department, ex parte
Brind [1991] 1 AC 696, HL 96, 106, 108, 228, 229
R v Secretary of State for the Home Department,
Ex p Bugdaycay [1987] AC 514 236
R v Secretary of State for the Home Department,
Ex parte Doody [1994] 1 AC 531 ....240–41, 252–53
R v Secretary of State for the Home Department, ex parte
Fire Brigades' Union and Others [1995] 2 WLR 1, CA 33, 37, 40, 164
R v Secretary of State for the Home Department, ex parte
Hargreaves [1997] 1 All ER 397 244
R v Secretary of State for Home Department, ex parte
Hosenball [1977] 1 WLR 766..61–62
R v Secretary of State for the Home Department
Ex p. Jeyeanthan [2000] 1 W.L.R. 354...246
R v Secretary of State for the Home Department,
ex parte Khawaja [1984] AC 74 224
R v Secretary of State for the Home Department, ex parte
McWhirter (1969) The Times, 20 October 127
R v Secretary of State for the Home Department,
ex parte Northumbria Police Authority [1989] QB 26, CA 164
R v Secretary of State for the Home Department Ex p. Oladehinde.......226
R v Secretary of State for the Home Department,
ex parte Simms [1999] 3 WLR 328......................49–50, 51, 54, 227, 257
R v Secretary of State for the Home Department
ex parte Swati [1986] 1 WLR 477 203
R v Secretary of State for the Home Department
exparte Tarrant [1985] QB 251..239
R v Secretary of State for the Home Department,
ex parte Venables [1998] AC 407 ....27, 224, 225, 235
R v Secretary of State for Transport, ex parte Factortame Ltd
and Others (No 2) [1991] 1 AC 603, HL........13, 16, 21, 81, 86, 186, 193
R v Secretary of State for Transport, ex parte Factortame (No. 5) (1998)
The Times, 28 April, [2000] 1 AC 524 ....23, 81, 84
R v Secretary of State for Transport, Ex parte Pegasus Holdings
(London) Ltd. [1988] 1 W.L.R. 990; [1989] 2 All E.R. 481 238

R v Sefton Metropolitan BC ex parte Help the Aged [1997] 4
All ER 582 226
R v Somerset County Council, ex parte Fewings [1995] 3
All ER 20 225
R v Sussex Justices, Ex parte McCarthy ([1924] 1 KB 256 239–240
R v Talbot Borough Council, ex parte Jones [1988] 2 All ER 207 .. 225, 226
R (on the application of AB) v Secretary of State for the
Home Department [2013] EWHC 3453 (Admin) 83
R (Abdi & Nadarajah) v Secretary of State for the
Home Department [2005] EWCA Civ 1363 242
R (on the application of Alconbury Developments Ltd) v
Secretary of State for the Environment, Transport
and the Regions [2001] UKHL 23, HL 100, 196, 229
R (Al Haq) v Secretary of State for Foreign & Commonwealth
Affairs [2009] EWHC 1910 214
R (Anderson) v Home Secretary [2002] UKHL 46 .... 98, 100
R (Ann Summers Ltd) v Jobcentre Plus [2003] EWHC 1416 229
R (Asha Foundation) v Millennium Commission [2003]
EWCA Civ 88 241
R (Association of British Civilian Internees (Far East Region)) v
Secretary of State for Defence [2003] EWCA Civ 473 229
R (on the application of Bancoult) v Secretary of State for
Foreign and Commonwealth Affairs [2008] UKHL 61 .... 163, 176
R (BAPIO Action Ltd) v Secretary of State for the Home
Department [2007] EWCA Civ 1139 248
R (Begum) v Denbigh High School [2006] UKHL 15 98
R (Bibi) v Newham London Borough Council [2001]
EWCA Civ 607 243
R (Branwood) v Rochdale Metropolitan Borough. Council
[2013] EWHC 1024 (Admin) 249
R. (Brown) v. Secretary of State for Work and Pensions
[2008] EWHC 3158 247–28
R (Bulger) Secretary of State for the Home Department
[2001] 3 All ER 449 225
R (Cart) v Upper Tribunal [2011] UKSC 28 .... 190, 193
R. (on the application of Catt) v Commissioner of Police
of the Metropolis [2015] UKSC 9 274
R (Daly) v Home Secretary [2001] UKHL 26 .... 98, 228–29
R (Domb) v London Borough of Hammersmith and Fulham
& Ors [2009] EWCA Civ 941 248
R (Elias) v Secretary of State for Defence ([2006] 1 WLR 3213 247
R. (on the application of Evans) v Attorney General [2015]
UKSC 21 276–77

R (on the application of Gentle and Another) v Prime
Minister and Others [2008] UKHL 20 97
R (on the application of H) v Mental Health Review Tribunal
for North and East London Region [2001] EWCA Civ 415 97
R (Hajrula) v London Councils [2011] EWHC 448 249
R (HJ and HT) (Iran and Cameroon) v Secretary of State
for the Home Department [2010] UKSC 31 .... 185, 193
R (HS2 Action Alliance Ltd) v The Secretary of State for
Transport & Anor & linked cases [2014] UKSC 3 .... 184, 195
R (on the application of Hurley and Moore) v Secretary of
State for Business Innovation and Skills) [2012] EWHC
201 (Admin) 216–17, 249
R (on the application of Jackson) v Attorney
General [2005] 4 All ER 1253, HL 45, 51, 53, 137, 142
R (on the application of Julian West) v Lloyd's
of London [2004] EWCA Civ 506, CA 200
R (on the application of Kaur and Shah) v London
Borough of Ealing [2008] EWHC 2062 248
R (KB) v Mental Health Tribunal [2003] EWHC 193 98
R (Limbuela) v Secretary of State for the Home
Department [2005] UKHL 66 97
R (Meany) v Harlow District Council [2009] EWHC 559 248
R (Moseley) v Haringey London Borough
Council [2014] UKSC 56 .... 245, 251
R (N) v Secretary of State for the Home Department
[2005] UKHL 31 97
R (National Association of Health Stores) v Department
of Health [2005] EWCA Civ 154 248
R (National Farmers Union) v Secretary of State for the
Environment, Food and Rural Affairs [2003] EWHC 444 163
R (on the application of Pennington) v the Parole Board [2009]
EWHC 2296 97
R (Pham) v Secretary of State for the Home Department
[2015] UKSC 19 .... 103, 229, 235
R (on the application of Pretty) v DPP [2001] UKHL 61 97
R (on the application of Pro-Life Alliance) v BBC [2003]
UKHL 23, HL 133, 142, 144
R (Quila and another) v Secretary of State for the
Home Department [2011] UKSC 45 .... 229, 269, 272–73
R (Rashid) v. Secretary of. State for the Home Department
[2005] EWCA Civ 744 242
R(Rogers) v Swindon Primary Care Trust [2006] EWCA Civ 392 228

R (RT) (Zimbabwe) v Secretary of State for the Home
 Department [2012] UKSC 38 185
R (SG) v Secretary of State for Work and Pensions [2015]
 UKSC 16 .... 70, 71, 201
R (Sivasubramaniam) v Wandsworth County Court [2002]
 EWCA Civ 1738 203
R(Suryananda) v Welsh Ministers [2007] EWCA Civ 893 .... 213, 217
R. (on the application of T) v Secretary of State for the
 Home Department [2014] UKSC 35 273–74
R (Ullah) v. Special Adjudicator [2004] UKHL 26 .... 97, 187, 193
R (Yemshaw) v London Borough of Hounslow [2011] UKSC 3 .... 183, 193
Rabone v Pennine Care NHS Trust [2012] UKSC 2 260
Reference Re the Amendment of the Constitution
 of Canada (1982) 125 DLR (3rd) 1 .... 58, 59, 60
Re Fletcher's Application [1970] 2 All ER 527 191
Re: Parliamentary Election for Bristol South
 East [1964] 2 QB 257 140
Redfearn v United Kingdom (2012) 162 NLJ 1466 278
Ridge v Baldwin [1964] AC 40, HL 238, 246, 251–52
Roy v Kensington Family Practitioner Committee [1992] 1 AC 624 197
Royal College of Nursing v DHSS [1981] 1 All ER 545 213
S and Marper v United Kingdom [2008] ECHR 1581 259–60
Sagnata Investments v Norwich Corporation [1971] 2 QB 614 227
Salomon v Commissioners of Customs and
 Excise [1967] 2 QB 116 .... 67, 71
S.A.S. v France Application No. 43835/11 (1 July 2014) 260
Schmidt v Secretary of State for Home Affairs [1969] 2 Ch 149 212
Secretary of State for the Home Department v
 Rehman [2001] UKHL 47; [2003] 1 AC 153 229
Shaw v DPP [1962] AC 220 34
Simmenthal SpA v Commission [1979] ECR 777 .... 78, 86
South Buckinghamshire DC v Porter [2004] UKHL 33 241
Steel and Morris v United Kingdom (2005) 41 EHRR 22 94
Stefan v General Medical Council [1999] 1 WLR 1293 241
Stockdale v Hansard (1839) 9 Ad & E 1, QBD 43, 138
T and V v United Kingdom (1999) 30 EHRR 121 .... 93, 94
The Observer and The Guardian v United Kingdom (1991) 14
 EHRR 153 94
The Sheriff of Middlesex (1840) 11 Ad.&E. 273 139
The Sunday Times v United Kingdom (1979) 2 EHRR 245 94
Thoburn v Sunderland City Council [2002]
 1 CMLR 50, CA 11, 16, 17, 46–47

Trendtex Trading Corporation v Central Bank
of Nigeria [1977] 1 QB 529 .... 68, 71
Van Gend en Loos v Nederlandse Tariefcommissie
(Case 26/62) [1963] ECR 1, ECJ 76, 78, 86, 87
Vauxhall Estates Ltd v Liverpool Corporation [1932] 1 KB 733 .... 44, 51
Venables v New Group Newspapers Ltd [2001] Fam 430 101
Vidal-Hall v Google Inc. [2015] EWCA Civ 311 .... 83, 279
Vinter v United Kingdom 34 BHRC 605 263–64
Von Colson and Kamann v Land Nordrhein-Westfalen
(Case 14/83) [1984] ECR 1891, ECJ 80
von Hannover v Germany (No. 2).
Reference (2012) 55 E.H.R.R. 15 271
W and B (Children: Care Plan), Re (2002)
The Times, 15 March, HL 99
Waddington v Miah [1974] 1 WLR 683 96
Wason v. Walter (1868) L.R. 4 Q.B. 73 139
Webb v EMO Air Cargo (UK) Ltd [1992] 4 All ER 929, HL 80
West Rand Central Gold Mining Co v The King [1905] 2 KB 391 68
Wheeler v Leicester City Council [1985] AC 1054 .... 225, 233
Wilson v First County Trust Ltd (No 2) [2003] UKHL
40; [2003] 3 WLR 568, HL 100, 106, 108, 110
YL v Birmingham City Council and Others
[2007] UKHL 27, HL 102, 200, 257

Table of Statutes

Abdication Act 1936 .... 4, 43
Act of Settlement 1700 .... 10, 43
Acts of Union 1706/7 .... 10, 17, 112
Agricultural Marketing Act 1958 234
Armed Forces Act 2006 28
Bill of Rights 1689 .... 4, 10, 11, 43, 44, 47, 138, 158
   Article 9 .... 138–9, 143
British Nationality Act 1981 235
British Railways Act 1968 20
Broadcasting Act 1980 132
Canada Act 1982 62
Care Act 2014 154
Children Act 1989 154
Colonial Laws Validity Act 1865 45
Communications Act 2003 .... 142, 190
Constitutional Reform Act 2005 .... 8, 11, 31, 35
Constitutional Reform and Governance
   Act 2010 .... 12, 70, 150, 162, 173, 194
Criminal Justice Act 1988 40
Criminal Justice and Courts Act 2015 .... 135, 210
Crown Proceedings Act 1947 28
Data Protection Act 1998 .... 83, 173–5
Data Retention and Investigatory Powers Act 2014 164
Declaratory Act 1720 113
Defamation Act 1996 138
Deregulation Act 2015 138
Equality Act 2010 .... 12, 246
   S 149 246–47
European Communities
   Act 1972 .... 4, 11, 14, 17, 21–23, 47–48,
                                                        69, 72, 79–82, 117, 186
     S 2(1) 48, 76, 79
     S 2(2) 17, 79
     S 2(4) 23, 47, 79–80

S 3(1) 79
European Parliamentary Elections Act 1999 138
European Union Act 2011 .... 12, 48
Extradition Act 2003 159
Fixed-Term Parliaments Act 2011 .... 12, 133–4, 147
Freedom of Information Act 2000 .... 12, 173–5, 194
Government of Ireland Act 1914 138
Government of Ireland Act 1920 114
(Government of) Wales Act 1998 .... 6, 11, 17, 47, 114, 116, 117, 130
Government of Wales Act 2006 .... 116, 118
Greater London Authority Act 1999 130
House of Commons Commission Act 2015 12
House of Commons Disqualification Act 1975 .... 33, 127
House of Lords Reform Act 2014 137
Human Rights Act 1998 .... 8, 11, 17–18, 29, 31, 39, 47,
                49–50, 54, 69, 83–84, 103–6, 117, 121, 186–187,
                194–5, 198, 200, 211, 214–16, 221–22, 238, 257
  S 2 .... 96, 272
  S 3 .... 47, 99
  S 4 .... 99, 100, 215
  S 6 .... 101, 222, 257
  S 7 .... 102, 212–13
  S 8 .... 103, 215, 216
  S 10 99
  S 12 .... 103, 215
  S 13 96
  S19 47
Hunting Act 2004 .... 45, 53, 138
Inquiries Act 2005 192
Irish Church Act 1869 53
Laws in Wales Act 1536 112
Life Peerages Act 1958 134
Local Government Act 1972 .... 152, 153
Local Government Act 2000 .... 152, 153
Local Government and Public Involvement in Health Act 2007 152
Localism Act 2011 .... 152, 154
Magna Carta 1215 .... 10, 11, 17
Merchant Shipping Act 1988 .... 21–23, 81
Ministerial and Other Salaries Act 1975 147
Nigeria Independence Act 1960 44
Northern Ireland Act 1998 .... 6, 11, 47, 117
Overseas Development and Co-operation Act 1980 218
Parliament Act 1911 .... 4, 10, 44, 45, 53, 58, 60, 137

Parliament Act 1949..10, 44, 45–46, 53, 137
Parliamentary Commissioner Act 1967 ....191, 206
Parliamentary Standards Act 2009...141
Police Act 1964 246
Police and Criminal Evidence Act 1984..28, 166
Political Parties Elections and Referendums Act 2000..........................131
Political Parties and Elections Act 2009..131
Public Bodies Act 2011 157
Public Records Acts 1958 and 1967..173–4
Race Relations Act 1976...233
Recall of MPs Act 2015...12
Regulation of Investigatory Powers Act 2000....................................163–4
Scotland Act 1978..115
Scotland Act 1998.......................................6, 11, 17, 47, 115, 117, 121, 123, 129
Scotland Act 2012...117, 120
Sexual Offences (Amendment) Act 2000 138
Southern Rhodesia Act 1965..46, 61
Statute of Westminster 1931 ....58, 60, 62
Supreme Court Act 1981..209–211
  S 31 ....211, 214
Terrorism, Crime and Security Act 2001 ....28, 39
Theft Act 1968 140
Trade Union and Labour Relations Act 1964..40
Transparency of Lobbying, Non Party Campaigning and
  Trade Union Administration Act 2014 131–2
Treaty of Union 1706..10, 17, 112
Tribunals and Inquiries Act 1992...240
Tribunals, Courts and Enforcement Act 2007 189
Union with Ireland Act of 1800...113
(Government of) Wales Act 1998 ....6, 11, 17, 47, 114, 116, 117, 130
Wales Act 1978..114
War Crimes Act 1991..44, 138
War Damages Act 1965..13, 18, 44
Weights and Measures Act 1985..17
Welfare Reform Act 2012..70
Welsh Church Act 1914..138
Zimbabwe Independence Act 1979...44

Table of Instruments

Aarhus Convention (1998)	195
Anglo-Irish Treaty 1922	114
Belfast Agreement 1998	115
Charter of the United Nations and the Statute of the International Court of Justice (1945)	65, 66
Charter of Fundamental Rights of the European Union	73, 82–84
Constitution of the United States of America (1787)	32
Declaration of Delhi (1959)	30
European Convention on Human Rights and Fundamental Freedoms (1950) (ECHR)	28, 31, 39, 49, 69, 83, 90, 169, 186–87, 257
Article 2 ECHR	90, 93, 97, 263
Article 3 ECHR	90, 93, 97, 263–64
Article 4 ECHR	90
Article 5 ECHR	90, 93, 97, 215, 241, 265–66
Article 6 ECHR	91, 94, 98, 238, 239, 241, 258, 266–68
Article 7 ECHR	91
Article 8 ECHR	91, 94, 98, 268–74
Article 9 ECHR	91, 98, 268–69, 275
Article 10 ECHR	91, 94, 268–69, 271–72, 276–77
Article 11 ECHR	91, 277–78
Article 12 ECHR	91
Article 13 ECHR	91
Article 14 ECHR	91, 275–76
Article 17 ECHR	261
Article 1 First Protocol	92
Article 2 First Protocol	92
Article 3 First Protocol	92, 279
Article 1 Fourth Protocol	92
Article 2 Fourth Protocol	92
Article 3 Fourth Protocol	92
Article 4 Fourth Protocol	92
Sixth Protocol	92
Article 1 Seventh Protocol	92
Article 2 Seventh Protocol	92
Article 3 Seventh Protocol	92
Article 4 Seventh Protocol	92
Article 5 Seventh Protocol	92
Twelfth Protocol	92
Thirteenth Protocol	92
Fourteenth Protocol	92

EU Data Protection Directive (1995) 83, 175
Good Friday Agreement (Belfast Agreement) 1998 115
Single European Act 1986 76
St Andrews Agreement 2006 118
Treaty of Amsterdam (1997) 73
Treaty on European Union (Maastricht Treaty, TEU) (1992) 73, 74
Treaty on the Functioning of the European Union............73, 74, 75, 76, 77
Treaty of Lisbon (2007) 73, 74
Treaty of Nice (2001) 73
Treaty of Rome (1957)..72
Treaty Establishing a Constitution for Europe (2004) 73
United Nations Declaration of Human Rights 1948 90

Part 1
The development of constitutional and administrative law in the UK

1 Contemporary and foundational issues in public law

- Unitary and Devolved
- Parliamentary
- Democratic
- Monarchical
- Uncodified
- Flexible

Values

Sources and **Values** of the **UK Constitution**

Source

- Statute
- Common Law
- Convention
- Royal Prerogative
- International Law
- European Legal Frameworks

1.1 What is a constitution?

1.1.1 A basic definition of a 'constitution' would be a body of rules regulating the way in which an organisation or institution operates. However, when the term 'constitution' is used in the context of a State's constitution the definition is a little more complex.

The constitution of a State would be expected to:

- establish the **organs of government**. Traditionally, this would consist of a body responsible for legislative functions; a body responsible for executive functions; and a body responsible for judicial functions;
- **allocate power** between those institutions;
- provide for the **resolution of disputes** on the interpretation of the constitution; and
- establish procedures etc. for the **amendment of the constitution**.

1.1.2 The constitution therefore defines the relationship between the various institutions of the State (**horizontal relationship**) and that between the State and the individual (**vertical relationship**).

1.1.3 In a narrow sense, a constitution could be defined as a particular document (or series of documents) setting out the framework and principal functions of the organs of government in a particular State. Such a constitution will have, as Wade describes, 'special legal sanctity', meaning that it is the highest form of law in the State.

1.1.4 The majority of States have such a constitution, against which all other laws are measured. Should such laws fail to conform to the constitution, they may be declared unconstitutional by the courts.

1.1.5 The United Kingdom does not have a constitution that is the highest form of law since its constitutional principles can be amended by the passing of ordinary legislation – a consequence of the principle known as **parliamentary supremacy**, or parliamentary sovereignty (discussed in Chapter 3).

1.1.6 For this reason some have argued that the United Kingdom does not have a constitution. However, if we consider the wider definition of a **constitution**, which would be one that refers to **the whole system of government, including all the laws and rules that regulate that government**, we can clearly see that the United Kingdom does have a constitution.

1.2 Classifying constitutions

1.2.1 Constitutions can be classified in a number of different ways. We often talk of 'written' (**codified**) or 'unwritten' (**uncodified**) constitutions.

1.2.2 This has been the traditional way of classifying a constitution. In many examples, constitutions are described as being written or unwritten. This is too simplistic an explanation. It is more accurate to describe constitutions as codified or uncodified.

1.2.3 A codified constitution is one where the constitution is enshrined in a single document or series of documents, as, for example, in the United States.

1.2.4 An **uncodified** constitution is one where the constitutional rules exist, and indeed may be written down in legislation, but there is no one source that can be identified.

1.2.5 The United Kingdom is one of the few major countries in the world not to have a codified constitution. Consequently, the sources of the UK constitution are varied and include, for example, statute, common law and conventions.

1.2.6 In modern constitutional terms the desire to create a codified constitution will often be the result of some significant event, such as, for example:

- revolution (e.g. France 1789);
- reconstruction and/or redefinition of a State's institutions following war/armed conflict (e.g. Germany, Iraq);
- conferment of independence on a former colony (e.g. India, Australia, Canada);
- creation of a new State by the union of formerly independent States (e.g. United States, Malaysia);
- creation of a new State(s) by the break-up of a former Union of States (e.g. States created by the break-up of the former Republic of Yugoslavia).

1.2.7 The United Kingdom has suffered no major historical or political event that has necessitated the creation of a codified constitution. There have nevertheless been significant constitutional events such as, for example:

- the 1688 Revolution;
- the Union of England and Scotland (1707) and Great Britain with Ireland (1800);

- the House of Lords crisis 1910;
- the abdication of the Monarch 1936; and
- joining the European Economic Community (now known as the European Union) in 1973.

1.2.8 However, all of these events were responded to or anticipated through parliamentary means; by the passing of ordinary legislation such as, for example:

- Bill of Rights 1688/9;
- Parliament Act 1911;
- Abdication Act 1936; and
- European Communities Act 1972.

Hence the United Kingdom's constitution has **evolved over time and remains uncodified.**

1.2.9 Constitutions can also be classified as 'rigid' or 'flexible' constitutions. This way of classifying a constitution was first suggested by Lord Bryce in the late 19th century.

- A **flexible** constitution is one where all the laws of that constitution may be amended by the ordinary law-making process. The United Kingdom has a flexible constitution.
- A **rigid** constitution is one where the laws of that constitution can only be amended by special procedures. Consequently, the constitution is 'entrenched'. In other words, it is protected from being changed by the need to comply with a special procedure.

1.2.10 *For example,* the United States has a rigid constitution that cannot be amended by the passing of an ordinary piece of legislation (an Act of Congress). A special procedure has to be followed, which requires there to be:

- a two-thirds majority in each House of the Federal Congress (the legislative body), followed by:
- the acceptance (ratification) of at least three-quarters of the individual states that make up the United States.

A further example: In the Republic of Ireland, a Bill passed by both Houses of Parliament, a majority of votes in a referendum and the assent of the President are required to change the constitution.

1.2.11 A constitution can also be described as a 'unitary' or a 'federal' constitution. This description rests on the way that law-making bodies or institutions (sometimes known as 'organs of the state', 'state organs' or simply 'organs') are distributed throughout the country as a whole.

- A **federal** constitution is one where government powers are divided between central (federal) organs and the organs of the individual states/provinces that make up the federation. For example, the United States and Canada have federal constitutions. If there is to be any change in the distribution of power between the federal organs and the state organs, there must be amendment of the constitution using a special procedure.
- A **unitary** constitution is one where all government power rests in the hands of one central set of organs.

1.2.12 There are some other ways in which constitutions can be classified. Constitutions can be described as being:

- **Supreme** or **subordinate** – if the legislature cannot change the constitution by itself, then the constitution is **supreme**. If the legislature can change the constitution by itself, then it is **subordinate**.

- **Monarchical or republican:**
    (a) In a monarchical constitution, the Head of State is a King or Queen and State powers are exercised in their name.
    (b) In a republican constitution, the Head of State is a President.
    (c) This classification has become less popular since the majority of monarchies, including the United Kingdom, have, in practical terms, removed the constitutional power of the Monarch.
    (d) In the United Kingdom, for example, the majority power rests with Parliament and the executive.
    (e) In contrast, in a republican constitution, such as the United States, the Head of State, the President, has significantly more power since he or she is elected and consequently accountable to the people.

- **Fused or separated** – the latter is a constitution that adheres to the doctrine of the separation of powers. The former is one that does not, so that certain organs of the State have a range of powers. (The separation of powers is discussed in part of Chapter 2.)

- De Smith claims that constitutions can also be classified as **presidential** (e.g. the United States) or **parliamentary** (e.g. the United Kingdom).

  (a) In a **parliamentary** system the people choose representatives to form the legislature. The legislature will be responsible for scrutinising the executive and consenting to laws. There is usually a separate Head of State who formally and ceremonially represents the State but who has little political power.

  (b) In a **presidential** system the leader of the executive, the President, is elected independently of the legislature. The President appoints the rest of the executive, who are often not members of the legislature. The President is also the Head of State.

1.3 Essential elements of the UK constitution

The key aspects of the UK's constitution can be classified as:

1.3.1 **Uncodified (or unwritten)** – The United Kingdom does not have a codified constitution since there is no single document or series of documents that contain the constitution.

1.3.2 **Unitary** – The United Kingdom is a union of once separate countries but operates a unitary rather than federal system. The Parliament, sitting at Westminster, has full legislative supremacy but has granted considerable self-government through the process of **devolution** to:

- Scotland (e.g. through the Scotland Act 1998);
- Northern Ireland (Northern Ireland Act 1998); and
- Wales (Wales Act 1998).

However, the arrangements preserve the unlimited power of Parliament to legislate for the devolved regions and to override laws made by any of the devolved bodies:

- Numerous matters remain outside the authority of the devolved bodies to legislate on, for example, international relations, defence and national security, and economic and fiscal policies are reserved matters under the Scotland Act 1998.
- In addition, Parliament retains the authority, or 'sovereignty', to repeal these Acts and regain power to fully govern (see Chapter 3) – though politically this might be extremely difficult to achieve, since devolved government in Scotland, Wales and Northern Ireland is, at the time of writing, very popular.

1.3.3 **Flexible** – The constitution is flexible because technically all laws relating to it can be enacted, repealed and/or amended by Parliament using the same procedure, i.e. the passing of an ordinary Act of Parliament.

However, relatively recent modification to this traditional doctrine in the UK constitution with changes to parliamentary supremacy (also known as 'parliamentary sovereignty') should be noted.

1.3.4 **Monarchical** – The Queen is the Head of State and succession to the throne is based on the hereditary principle. However, by convention (see Chapter 4) the Queen exercises her constitutional powers only on the advice of her Ministers and, in many cases, the powers are in fact exercised by Ministers in her name.

1.3.5 **Parliamentary supremacy or 'sovereignty'** – Parliament is supreme (or 'sovereign') and can make or unmake any law and legislate on anything it wishes. In theory, no Parliament can be bound by its predecessors or bind its successors. (This principle and the limitations now imposed on it by, e.g., membership of the European Union and the European human rights law system are discussed in detail in Chapter 6 and Chapter 7 respectively.)

1.3.6 **Bicameralist** – The United Kingdom has a legislative body known as Parliament, which is composed of two chambers. These two chambers are known as the House of Commons (the lower House) and the House of Lords (the upper House).

1.3.7 **Democratic** – The House of Commons has a membership that is directly elected at least every five years. The political Party that wins the majority of seats in the House makes up the Government.

The leader of that political Party is then appointed by the Queen to be the Prime Minister, who in turn nominates the Ministers of the Government who are responsible for departmental activities and are accountable to Parliament. (The electoral system is discussed in Chapter 9.)

1.4 Should the UK constitution be codified?

1.4.1 The advantages of an uncodified constitution such as that of the United Kingdom include the following:

- the constitution is flexible and easily adaptable to change; and
- as Dicey argued, it is a strength that the UK's constitution is one embedded in the structure of the law as a whole, rather than being merely a piece of paper.

1.4.2 The disadvantages of an uncodified constitution include the following:
- because of the flexibility of the constitution, constitutional principles can change without the support of the people;
- the ease with which the constitution can change can lead to confusion and people are left unsure of the constitutional position;
- the lack of a codified constitution means that many people do not know or understand constitutional principles; and
- the courts cannot declare Acts of Parliament to be unconstitutional.

1.4.3 Since 1997 the UK's constitution has undergone the most far-reaching reform since the 19th century. The reforms, whilst not all necessarily completed, could move the United Kingdom away from a traditional unitary state with an unwritten constitution and a sovereign Parliament.

1.4.4 This is partly because the **constitution is increasingly being reduced to writing/codified**. For example:
- Lord Bingham identified that 18 statutes of constitutional importance were introduced between 1997 and 2004; and
- it is possible to identify still more 'statutes of constitutional importance' enacted under the Coalition Government between 2010 and 2015.

1.4.5 In addition to this, the **doctrine of parliamentary supremacy has been modified** by the supremacy of European Community law (see Chapter 6) and the incorporation of the European Convention on Human Rights by the Human Rights Act 1998 (see Chapter 7). In the context of the effect of membership of the European Union on the supremacy of Parliament, we can see a distinct modification of the traditional doctrine in that implied repeal no longer operates for certain important statutes. These have been called 'constitutional statutes' (see 1.6 for further discussion).

1.4.6 The **Constitutional Reform Act 2005** provides for moves towards a more formal separation of executive, legislative and judicial powers (see Chapter 2 for the 'separation of powers').

1.4.7 Also, the process of **devolution** for Scotland, Wales and Northern Ireland, whilst not formally affecting the unitary character of the constitution, has created a system that the sovereign Westminster Parliament is unable to undo in practice (see Chapter 3 on parliamentary sovereignty).

1.4.8 Whilst it may be argued that a codified constitution would ensure that important principles are consented to by the people, enshrined and subject to change only when approved by the people (entrenchment), it should be remembered that no codified constitution can ever be completely comprehensive. For example:
- a codified constitution may be vague, leading to inconsistent interpretation; and
- a codified constitution will also be reflective of the time in which it was written, and because of its rigidity be difficult to change.

1.4.9 Consequently, in a way similar to uncodified constitutions, the majority of codified constitutions are also supplemented by unwritten standards, rules, practices etc. often to fill any gaps or to allow for adjustment.

1.4.10 Finally, the actual effectiveness of a constitution against abuse of power depends on the willingness of the organs of the State to comply with it, the ability of the courts to enforce it and the people to abide by it, regardless of whether it is codified or uncodified.

1.4.11 In 2007 the Government published a Green Paper entitled 'The Governance of Britain'. The proposals in the Green Paper included discussion of ideas to:
- develop a British Bill of Rights; and
- produce a codified/written constitution.

1.4.12 The idea of a British Bill of Rights was explored further by the Joint Committee on Human Rights and was contained within a Green Paper, 'Rights and responsibilities: developing our constitutional framework' published in March 2009. However, no legislation was produced prior to the May 2010 General Election.

1.4.13 But, since the 2010 General Election, the Coalition Government of Conservatives and Liberal Democrats undertook considerable constitutional work involving considerable changes to the landscape of UK governance, though perhaps not drastic constitutional reforms. The General Election of May 2015, however, may mark a serious acceleration of constitutional change in the United Kingdom.

1.4.14 Some of the statutes introduced by the Coalition Government between 2010 and 2015 are addressed at 1.6, on the issue of the concept of constitutional statutes.

1.4.15 The idea of a codified constitution was not expanded upon in either the Constitutional Renewal White Paper published in March 2008, or the Constitutional Reform and Governance Act, which received the Royal Assent on 8 April 2010.

1.5 Legal and non-legal sources of the constitution

1.5.1 The constitution of the United Kingdom can be seen to comprise both legal and non-legal sources of constitutional values and practices. As far as legal sources of the constitutions are concerned, **statute** is traditionally considered the primary source of constitutional law in the United Kingdom and is otherwise known as an Act of Parliament. A statute can be amended only by Parliament. (The common law is also regarded as a significant source of constitutional values – see 1.7.)

1.5.2 The principal non-legal source of constitutional rules and values is what is known as constitutional conventions, which are commonly agreed-upon customs and practices in relation to the proper operation of government under the constitution. Constitutional conventions themselves are the focus of Chapter 4.

1.5.3 There are many examples of constitutionally significant statutes, including the following:

- **Magna Carta 1215** – a settlement with the Crown, protecting the rights of individuals, freedom of the Church and trial by jury;
- **Bill of Rights 1688** – altered the balance of power in favour of Parliament over the Crown. After this statute, the Crown required Parliament's consent for certain actions, such as raising taxes;
- **Act of Settlement 1700** – combined with the Bill of Rights to ensure that the Monarch could no longer govern by use of the prerogative and marked the point when Parliament became the dominant constitutional organ;
- **Treaty of Union 1706** – united England and Scotland under one Parliament.

1.5.4 Significant statutes during the 20th century and early 21st century include, for example:

- **Parliament Acts 1911 and 1949** – reducing the power of the House of Lords in the legislative process;

- **European Communities Act 1972** – providing for the United Kingdom to become a member of the European Economic Community;
- **Scotland, Northern Ireland and Wales Acts 1998** – providing for devolution;
- **Human Rights Act 1998** – providing for the domestic incorporation of the European Convention on Human Rights; and
- **Constitutional Reform Act 2005** – providing for, *inter alia*, greater separation of powers (see Chapter 2).

1.6 The concept of constitutional statutes

1.6.1 Traditionally, all statutes have been considered of equal importance, all being subject to the doctrine of implied repeal, a consequence of parliamentary supremacy (see Chapter 3). There has, though, been increasing recognition of a hierarchy of statutes, witnessed, for example, in the comments of Laws LJ in *Thoburn v Sunderland City Council* (2002).

1.6.2 In *Thoburn*, statutes were considered to be of two types: '**ordinary**' statutes and '**constitutional**' statutes. A constitutional statute would be one that would affect the legal relationship between the individual and the State in some general manner, or would enlarge or diminish the scope of fundamental constitutional rights.

1.6.3 Laws LJ was of the opinion that the following statutes were examples of constitutional Acts of Parliament:

- Magna Carta 1215;
- Bill of Rights 1688;
- Acts of Union;
- Human Rights Act 1998;
- Scotland Act 1998;
- Government of Wales Act 1998; and
- European Communities Act 1972

1.6.4 Such so-called constitutional statutes are no longer subject to implied repeal because they protect the special status of constitutional rights.

1.6.5 Consequently such statutes are subject only to express repeal and are consequently perhaps 'semi-entrenched'. (For further discussion of this in the context of the supremacy of Parliament, see Chapter 3. For further discussion of the European Communities Act 1972, see Chapter 6 and for the Human Rights Act 1998, see Chapter 7.)

1.6.6 The Conservative and Liberal Democrat Coalition Government in power in the United Kingdom between May 2010 and May 2015 placed a number of pieces of legislation on the statute book, or brought other statutes into force, which can also be seen to have constitutional features. Though only their treatment by both the courts and the current Conservative majority Government, following the General Election in May 2015, will establish to what extent, if any, these newer arrivals possess a quality of being 'semi-entrenched'.

1.6.7 Some of these newer examples of so-called constitutional statutes might be said to include:

- Equality Act 2010;
- Constitutional Reform and Governance Act 2010;
- European Union Act 2011;
- Fixed-Term Parliaments Act 2011;
- House of Commons Commission Act 2015; and
- Recall of MPs Act 2015.

1.6.8 Some statutes could be said to be politically entrenched. An example of this is the Freedom of Information Act 2000 since this statute a creates a culture of greater transparency for government in the United Kingdom, and allows closer scrutiny of the State, principally by the media for the benefit of raising awareness of issues for members of the public to consider. It is difficult to imagine a political climate where the principle of freedom of information could be completely repealed and removed entirely from the statute book.

1.6.9 Political necessity sometimes requires the enactment of a statute. For example, there is a constitutional convention (see Chapter 4) that a referendum, as a type of vote on a political issue of national significance, is empowered by a dedicated statute created by the Westminster Parliament.

1.6.10 It is also the case that constitutional convention (as well as a principle of international law) requires that an international treaty be transposed into domestic UK law by way of an Act of Parliament (see Chapter 5).

1.7 The continuing constitutional contribution of the common law

1.7.1 The common law is another legal source of the constitutional values of the United Kingdom.

1.7.2 This source is created by case law, and is also known as **precedent**. Common law is subordinate to statute in that statute on the same subject matter takes precedence because of the doctrine of parliamentary supremacy. For example, after the decision in *Burmah Oil v Lord Advocate* (1965) Parliament passed the War Damage Act 1965, which overruled the decision of the House of Lords and which, in addition, had retrospective effect. (Parliamentary supremacy, often known as **parliamentary sovereignty,** is discussed in **Chapter 3**.)

1.7.3 There are some landmark decisions in the common law which continue to have great constitutional significance, however:

- *Prohibitions del Roy* (1607) – where the court concluded that the King was not permitted to act as a judge;
- *Entick v Carrington* (1765) – where the court concluded that a general warrant for entry into private property and seizure of private property was a trespass and illegal;
- *Pickin v British Rail Board* (1974) – in which the court held that once an Act of Parliament had passed through the relevant legislative stages, no body could question its validity;
- *M v Home Office* (1994) – where it was held that the Home Secretary had committed contempt of court by disobeying a judge's order; and
- *R v Secretary of State for Transport, ex parte Factortame (No. 2)* (1989) – where it was held that directly enforceable rules of EC law overrode conflicting rules of national law, regardless of their constitutional significance.

1.8 The scope of the royal prerogative today

1.8.1 The source of law known as the royal prerogative, which gives senior Government officials, particularly Ministers of the Crown, a lawful ability to exercise powers on behalf of the Monarch, also plays a part in articulating UK constitutional arrangements.

1.8.2 This source of law derives from common law powers and is described by Dicey as 'every act which the executive Government can lawfully do without the authority of [an] Act of Parliament'. (This source of law in the constitution is discussed in further detail in Chapter 10.)

1.8.3 In this way the royal prerogative gives rise to executive 'prerogative powers'.

1.8.4 There are two main categories of prerogative powers:

1. *Prerogative powers in relation to foreign affairs*, for example:
   - the power to declare war and peace;
   - the power to deploy armed forces abroad;
   - the power to make treaties.

2. *Prerogative powers in relation to domestic affairs*, for example:
   - the power to defend the realm;
   - the power to grant mercy and pardons and reduce sentences.

1.8.5 Until the landmark judgment in *Council of Civil Service Unions v Minister for the Civil Service* (1985), the exercise of prerogative powers by the executive was not subject to judicial review.

1.9 The impact of distinctly European legal systems and values

1.9.1 The UK Parliament passed the European Communities Act 1972 and thereby agreed to implement and enforce all law of the European Union.

1.9.2 This source of law has become increasingly important, while simultaneously creating difficulties for both the courts and politicians.

1.9.3 Significant rights have been created by EU law, including those in relation to employment law, sex discrimination, free movement for EU nationals and laws regulating the free movement of goods, services and capital.

1.9.4 The primary constitutional significance of EU law is its relationship with UK domestic law, particularly since the UK's constitution operates under the traditional doctrine of parliamentary supremacy. (This is discussed in detail in Chapter 3 and Chapter 6.)

1.10 Other sources of constitutional values and practices

1.10.1 Parliament has sole jurisdiction to determine its own composition and procedure. Thus the law and custom of Parliament (e.g. parliamentary privilege) is a source of constitutional law. (Parliamentary privilege is discussed in detail in Chapter 9.)

1.10.2 The writings of eminent scholars may also be said to be a source of constitutional law, especially since the courts may refer to them. Examples of such scholars include Dicey, Blackstone and Jennings.

Key Cases Checklist

Prohibitions del Roy (1607) – where the court concluded that the King was not permitted to act as a judge.

Pickin v British Rail Board (1974) – in which the court held that once an Act of Parliament had passed through the relevant legislative stages, no body could question its validity.

Cases demonstrating key constitutional principles

Thoburn v Sunderland City Council (2002) – where it was held that a constitutional statute would be one that would affect the legal relationship between the individual and the State in some general manner, or would enlarge or diminish the scope of fundamental constitutional rights.

R v Secretary of State for Transport, ex parte Factortame (No. 2) (1989) – where it was held that directly enforceable rules of Community law overrode conflicting rules of national law, regardless of their constitutional significance.

M v Home Office (1994) – where it was held that the Home Secretary had committed contempt of court by disobeying a judge's order.

Entick v Carrington (1765) – where the court concluded that a general warrant for entry into private property and seizure of private property was a trespass and illegal.

1.6.1 *Thoburn v Sunderland City Council* [2002] 1 CMLR 50 (HC)

Key Facts

The Weights and Measures Act 1985 authorised the use of both metric and imperial measures for the purposes of trade. Subsequent regulations made under s 2(2) of the European Communities Act 1972 prohibited the use of both and gave priority to the metric system. It was argued that the 1985 Act had impliedly repealed s 2(2) of the 1972 Act and should therefore take precedence.

The court held that there was no inconsistency between the 1985 and 1972 Acts, so there was no need to discuss the doctrine of implied repeal. However, Laws LJ stated that there should be recognition of a hierarchy of statutes with there being two types – ordinary and constitutional statutes. A constitutional statute would affect the legal relationship between the individual and the State in some general, overarching manner or would enlarge or diminish the scope of fundamental constitutional rights. In his opinion, Laws LJ considered the following as examples of constitutional statutes:

Magna Carta 1215, the Bill of Rights 1688, the Act of Union, the Reform Acts extending the franchise, the Human Rights Act 1998, the Scotland Act 1998, the Government of Wales Act 1998 and the European Communities Act 1972.

Key Law

Constitutional statutes, according to Laws LJ, should not be subject to implied repeal because they protect the special status of constitutional rights. Instead, such statutes are subject only to express repeal.

Key Judgments

Laws LJ

'We should recognise a hierarchy of Acts of Parliament: as it were "ordinary" statutes and "constitutional" statutes.'

'Ordinary statutes may be impliedly repealed. Constitutional statutes may not. For the repeal of a constitutional Act or the abrogation of a fundamental right to be effected by statutes, the court would apply this test: is it shown that the legislature's actual . . . intention was to effect the repeal or abrogation? I think that this could only be met by express words in the later statute, or by words so specific that the inference of an actual determination to effect the result contended for was irresistible. The ordinary rule of implied repeal does not satisfy this test. Accordingly, it has no application to constitutional statutes.'

Key Comment

Traditionally, the UK's uncodified constitutional system has not recognised any distinction between different statutes – each is passed using the same process, so no Act of Parliament has any formal special status. In traditional constitutional terms, no Act can be entrenched in that all Acts are subject to implied repeal. However, the courts have for some time considered the European Communities Act 1972 as having a special legal status in that implied repeal does not apply to it (see Chapter 6). The passing of the significant Human Rights Act 1998 has opened up the debate as to whether other statutes are so constitutionally significant that they cannot be impliedly repealed.

1.7.2 *Burmah Oil v Lord Advocate* [1965] AC 75 HL

Key Facts

In 1942, British forces destroyed the company's oil installations in Rangoon to prevent advancing Japanese forces from gaining control of them. The British Government made an *ex gratia* payment of £4 million to the company in compensation. The company sued the Government for £31 million in compensation.

The House of Lords held that compensation was payable by the Crown for the destruction of property caused by exercise of the royal prerogative in relation to war.

The Government immediately introduced the War Damage Act 1965. This statute retrospectively nullified the effect of the decision of the House of Lords.

Key Law

This case therefore clearly demonstrates the subordination of the judiciary to Parliament because of the doctrine of parliamentary supremacy – statute overrides common law and Parliament has such legislative competence it can legislate retrospectively.

1.7.3 *Prohibitions del Roy (Case of Prohibitions) (1607) 12 Co Rep 63* (KB)

Key Facts

The King claimed the right to dispense justice in his own right. In the Resolution of the Judges, Chief Justice Coke stated that 'the King in his own person cannot adjudge any case . . . this ought to be determined . . . in some court of justice'.

Key Law

Here the Court of King's Bench concluded that the King was not permitted to act as a judge.

1.7.3 *Entick v Carrington* (1765) 19 St Tr 1029 (KB)

Key Facts

Two King's messengers, with a warrant issued by the Secretary of State, broke into Entick's house and took away papers. It was alleged that he was writing seditious material. Entick sued for trespass to his property and goods; the Government argued that the warrant was legal.

Key Law

The Court of King's Bench determined that there was no law supporting the issuing of the warrant and therefore it was illegal and void.

Key Judgment

Lord Camden CJ
'No man can set foot upon my ground without my licence, but he is liable to an action . . . If he admits the fact, he is bound to show by way of justification, that some positive law has empowered or excused him.'

Key Comment

Government according to the law means that neither the executive nor any Government official can exercise a power unless it is authorised by some specific rule of law. Dicey placed great emphasis on this case when explaining his meaning of the rule of law, namely that no person be punishable in goods or person except for a distinct breach of the law and that every person, irrespective of rank, be subject to the ordinary law of the land. It is Dicey's explanation of the rule of law that underpins traditional understanding of this constitutional doctrine.

1.7.3 *Pickin v British Rail Board* [1974] AC 765 (HL)

Key Facts

Pickin argued that he had been deprived of an interest in land by the British Railways Act 1968. He claimed that the Act was invalid because it had been passed fraudulently.

Key Law

The 'enrolled Act' rule, developed as part of the doctrine of the supremacy of Parliament, precludes the courts from investigating whether internal procedures of the House have been complied with; no court can question the validity of an Act of Parliament or disregard it.

Key Judgment

Lord Reid
'In earlier times many learned lawyers seem to have believed that an Act of Parliament could be disregarded in so far as it was contrary to the law . . . but since the supremacy of Parliament was finally demonstrated by the Revolution of 1688 any such idea has become obsolete.'

Key Comment

This is a key case in establishing the premise that all that a court can do is to 'construe and apply the enactments of Parliament'.

1.7.3 *M v Home Office* [1994] 1 AC 377 (HL)

Key Facts

M sought political asylum but his application was rejected by the Home Secretary. An injunction was issued but M was deported. The House of Lords considered whether a Government Minister or department could be found to be in contempt of court and whether an injunction could be enforced against them.

Key Law

The Home Secretary had committed contempt of court by disobeying the injunction. In addition, there was power to grant injunctions against Ministers acting in their official capacity.

Key Comment

Dicey's explanation of the rule of law included, as his second proposition, the idea that every man was subject to the ordinary law and the courts. This case is an example of the courts applying this principle, one of equality, to a Government Minister.

Key Link

The principle was also expressed by Lord Donaldson in *Francome and Another v Mirror Group Newspapers Ltd and Others* [1984] 2 All ER 408: 'Parliamentary democracy is . . . based on the rule of law. That requires all citizens to obey the law . . . There are no privileged classes to whom it does not apply.'

1.7.3 *R v Secretary of State for transport, ex parte Factortame (No. 2)* [1991] 1 AC 603 (HL)

Key Facts

Spanish fishing vessels had been registered in the United Kingdom so that they could take advantage of British fishing quotas. In 1988 the United Kingdom passed the Merchant Shipping Act 1988, which introduced a licensing system. This required applicants, *inter alia*, to have a genuine and substantial connection with the United Kingdom. The conditions made it effectively impossible for Factortame to obtain the licence.

The European Commission brought an enforcement action in the European Court of Justice (ECJ) for breach of the EC Treaty (the right to establish a company and the right to freedom from discrimination on the basis of nationality) and the ECJ ordered the United Kingdom to suspend the offending sections of the Merchant Shipping Act. Meanwhile, Factortame brought proceedings under judicial review in the English courts, requesting interim relief in the form of an injunction against the Secretary of State preventing its deregistration.

The House of Lords, following the Court of Appeal, concluded that there was no power in English law to grant interim relief, since to do so would imply that the Act was invalid, contrary to the principles of parliamentary supremacy. However, the House of Lords requested a preliminary reference as to whether it was obliged under Community law to protect Community rights and grant interim relief.

The ECJ referred to the principle that Community law must take precedence over conflicting national law and be fully and uniformly applied. The Court concluded that any principle of national law preventing interim relief should be set aside.

Key Law

In *Factortame (No. 2)* the House of Lords accepted the ECJ's ruling in that Community law must take precedence over directly conflicting national law and granted interim relief, suspending operation of Part II of the Merchant Shipping Act 1988.

Key Judgment

Lord Bridge
'If the supremacy . . . of Community law over the national law of member states was not always inherent in the EEC Treaty it was certainly well established in the jurisprudence of the Court of Justice long before the United Kingdom joined the Community. Thus, whatever limitation of its sovereignty Parliament accepted when it enacted the European Communities Act 1972 was entirely voluntary. Under the terms of the 1972 Act it has always been clear that it was the duty of a United Kingdom court . . . to override any rule of national law found to be in conflict with any directly enforceable rule of Community law.'

Key Comment

This case was the first to reach the courts where there was a direct conflict between national and Community law and which could not be rectified using other interpretative methods. The response of the ECJ was entirely consistent with its previous jurisprudence on the supremacy of Community law (see Chapter 6). The decision has implications for the traditional principles of parliamentary supremacy or sovereignty: according to the 'enrolled Act' rule, no court should be able to question the validity of statute, and under the doctrine of implied repeal, no legislation should bind a future Parliament.

The *Factortame* decision means that the courts can examine the validity of legislation, in the context of whether it breaches Community law. In addition, s 2(4) of the European Communities Act 1972 is semi-entrenched in that it extends the obligation to be consistent with Community law obligations to legislation passed in the future.

Key Link

In *R v Secretary of State for Transport, ex parte Factortame (No. 5)* (1998) *The Times*, 28 April, [2000] 1 AC 524 the House of Lords ruled that the UK's breach of Community law by passing the Merchant Shipping Act 1988 was sufficiently serious as to warrant the awarding of damages under the principle of State liability (see Chapter 6).

2 The rule of law and a separation of powers

- The law should not be secret, arbitrary or retrospective
- Every person, irrespective of rank, is subject to the ordinary law of the land and the jurisdiction of the courts
- The rule of law entails that laws should be clear, precise, transparent and accessible

The Rule of Law

The Rule of Law and the Separation of Powers

The Separation of Powers

- The **legislature** creates and promulgates the law
- The **executive** determines and administers policy based upon the law
- The **judiciary** ensures that the executive is prohibited from governing unlawfully

2.1 A description of the rule of law

2.1.1 The rule of law is capable of many definitions, based on both philosophical and political theories, and hence it is a difficult doctrine to explain definitively.

2.1.2   In basic terms, the rule of law is the supremacy of law over man. As Aristotle explained in the fourth century BC, 'the rule of law is to be preferred to that of any individual'.

2.1.3   Carroll defines the rule of law as 'neither a rule nor a law'. It is now generally understood as a doctrine of political morality which concentrates on the role of law in securing the correct balance of rights and powers between individuals and the State in free and civilised societies.

2.1.4   The rule of law can be interpreted as:

- an overarching, universal law that applies to everyone, including the executive and legislature; and
- that man-made laws should conform to a 'higher' law, the rule of law.

2.1.5   The rule of law is consequently often recognised as a means of **ensuring the protection of individual rights against governmental power.**

2.2 Dicey's formulation of the rule of law

2.2.1   In the United Kingdom, the general concept of the rule of law has become identified with Dicey's explanation of the doctrine in his 1885 text, *An Introduction to the Study of the Law of the Constitution*. According to Dicey, the rule of law was a distinct feature of the UK constitution, with three main concepts.

2.2.2   Firstly: No person is punishable in body or goods except for a distinct breach of the law (***Entick v Carrington* (1765)**). This concept attempts to ensure that law is not secret, arbitrary or retrospective, thereby limiting the discretionary power of Government. To comply with the rule of law, laws should be clear, precise, transparent and accessible.

2.2.3   Secondly: Every person, irrespective of rank, is subject to the ordinary law of the land and the jurisdiction of the courts. Dicey based this principle on the UK system as compared with those of the time in, for example, France, where disputes with Government officials were heard in administrative courts separate from the ordinary civil courts and where different rules applied.

2.2.4   Thirdly: The common law creates a system of rights and liberties superior to that offered by any declaration or Bill of Rights. This is because the common law system emphasises remedies for infringement of rights rather than merely declaring the content of those rights.

2.3 Bingham's view of the rule of law

2.3.1 Much more recently than Dicey's ideas, there has been a highly regarded dissection of the concept of the rule of law, as proffered by Sir Tom Bingham, a much-loved former Law Lord, in his text *The Rule of Law* (2010).

2.3.2 In this book, Bingham offered up his own useful, working definition of the rule of law:

> '*All persons and authorities within the state, whether public or private, should be bound by and entitled to the benefit of laws publicly made, taking effect (generally) in the future and publicly administered by the courts.*'

2.3.3 Bingham also condensed his view of the scholarship on the rule of law into eight vital principles. These serve as a sound checklist to consider before we move on to consider the extent of the operation of the rule of law in the United Kingdom today:

(1) The law must be accessible and so far as possible intelligent, clear and predictable.

(2) Questions of legal right and liability should ordinarily be resolved by the application of the law and not the exercise of discretion.

(3) The laws of the land should apply equally to all, save to the extent that objective differences justify differentiation.

(4) Ministers and public officials at all levels must exercise the powers conferred on them in good faith, fairly, for the purpose for which the powers were conferred, without exceeding the limits of such powers and not unreasonably.

(5) The law must afford adequate protection of fundamental human rights.

(6) Means must be provided for resolving, without prohibitive cost or inadequate delay, *bona fide* civil disputes which the parties themselves are unable to resolve.

(7) Adjudicative procedures provided by the State should be fair.

(8) The rule of law requires compliance by the State with its obligations in international war as in national law.

2.4 Examples of the rule of law as a functional element of the UK constitution

2.4.1 The existence of administrative law, particularly the process of **judicial review**, enables the courts to ensure power is controlled and the executive is accountable for its actions and is based on the need to ensure the rule of law.

2.4.2 Some examples of cases where the courts have referred to the significance of the doctrine in the constitution include:

- *Francome and Another v Mirror Group Newspapers Ltd and Others* (1984) – where Lord Donaldson referred to the doctrine as one underpinning parliamentary democracy and extending to all citizens;

- *Merkur Island Shipping Corporation v Laughton and Others* (1983) – where Lord Diplock commented on the need for the law to have clarity;

- *R v Home Secretary, ex parte Venables* (1997) – the Home Secretary had considered a campaign conducted in a national newspaper when determining the sentencing of convicted children, rather than basing the decision on their progress/rehabilitation in detention. The action was considered 'an abdication of the rule of law';

- *R v Horseferry Road Magistrates' Court, ex parte Bennett* (1994) – where Lord Griffiths noted that it is the responsibility of the courts to maintain the rule of law, to oversee executive action and to not permit action that threatens basic human rights or breaches the rule of law;

- *M v Home Office* (1994) – where, applying Dicey's second proposition that every person is subject to the law, the House of Lords held that the Home Secretary could be found in contempt of court by disobeying an injunction; and

- *A v Secretary of State for the Home Department* (2004) – where the House of Lords held that power to detain only foreign nationals indefinitely as suspected terrorists, without charge, under the

Terrorism, Crime and Security Act 2001 was a breach of both the European Convention on Human Rights (ECHR) and the rule of law.

2.5 Reconciling a strict view of the rule of law with some legal rules in the United Kingdom today

2.5.1 If we apply Dicey's concept of the rule of law to the modern UK constitution, we can make a number of observations.

2.5.2 The first concept, that no person may have their body or goods interfered with except for a distinct breach of the law, is in direct contrast to the provisions of some present-day statutes. For example:

- the police have powers of arrest, stop and search when they have only 'reasonable grounds' for suspecting certain facts in relation to a criminal offence, under the Police and Criminal Evidence Act 1984;
- the Government also has power to interfere with a person's goods/property without any breach of the law, for example, the exercise of compulsory purchase orders when buying land for development and building infrastructure like roads and railways.

2.5.3 The second concept formulated by Dicey was that no person is above the law. However, there are a number of contraventions of this principle in the modern constitution. For example:

- the Monarch in her personal capacity is not subject to the jurisdiction of the ordinary courts;
- the Crown is also in a privileged position in litigation (Crown Proceedings Act 1947) and cannot be sued in tort for the actions of its servants;
- no civil action may be brought in respect of the comments or actions of a judge exercising his or her judicial role (*Anderson v Gorrie* (1895)) or in relation to a jury's verdict (*Bushell's Case* (1670));
- Members of Parliament have rights and immunities beyond those granted to the ordinary citizen, such as freedom of expression and freedom from arrest in certain circumstances. Conversely, there are individuals who are subject to additional legal restraints. For example, under the Armed Forces Act 2006, members of the

armed forces are subject to additional legal codes of conduct and offences, such as desertion, and a different judicial system.

2.5.4 The third concept, that common law provides protection of individual rights in the UK constitution, remains the case today, although added protection has been provided by virtue of the Human Rights Act 1998, for example.

2.5.5 The faith Dicey had in the ability of the common law to protect rights and liberties, though, has been criticised.

- Dicey failed to appreciate that the effectiveness of the common law in offering such protection can be greatly reduced by the pre-eminence given to statute, a consequence of the supremacy of Parliament.
- Hence, while the common law may offer protection in the form of remedies for those whose rights are infringed, statute may remove that protection, as was the case in *Burmah Oil v Lord Advocate* (1965).

2.5.6 Here are some examples of specific criticisms of Dicey's view of the rule of law:

- Sir Ivor Jennings claimed that Dicey's standard of the rule of law was influenced by his political views and that the phrase could be used to describe any society where a state of law and order exists.
- Consequently, the rule of law is seen to operate 'best' in societies that meet Dicey's standards. Jennings instead claimed that the rule of law may exist in societies that do not meet Dicey's standards – in other words, that the rule of law can exist in political systems other than those based on traditional Western democratic models.

2.6 Some broader interpretations of what the 'rule of law' might entail

The rule of law as a political concept

2.6.1 Laws should exhibit particular characteristics and meet minimum standards in terms of the way they are expressed and administered. For example, Raz argues that the making of laws should be guided by the following principles:

- laws should be general (i.e. not discriminate), prospective, open and clear;
- laws should be relatively stable (i.e. should not be subject to frequent and unnecessary amendment);
- making delegated legislation should be guided by clear, stable, open general rules;
- there should be a guaranteed independent judiciary;
- the application of law should accord with the rules of natural justice (i.e. there should be no bias and there should be the right to a fair hearing);
- the courts must have the power to review law-making and administrative action to ensure it is compliant with these rules;
- the courts should be easily accessible (i.e. access to justice should not be hindered by excessive delays and expense); and
- the discretion of crime-preventing bodies should not be allowed to pervert the law (i.e. agencies such as the police should not be able to choose which laws to enforce and when).

However, Raz's approach has been criticised as placing too much emphasis on procedure as a means of protecting rights, whilst failing actually to identify the nature and extent of the rights themselves.

The rule of law as a substantive concept

2.6.2   Laws should not be morally neutral. Dworkin, for example, argues that laws should contain fundamental values, i.e. be 'morally good'. However, this interpretation is not universally agreed with because many 'values' are not capable of concrete definition, for example, the right to life versus abortion and hunting versus animal welfare.

The Declaration of Delhi 1959

2.6.3   This was issued by the International Commission of Jurists and declares that the purpose of all law should be respect for the 'supreme value of human personality'. The Declaration identified that a constitution observing the rule of law would have certain characteristics:

- **Representative government** – in the United Kingdom we have free and fair elections but there are concerns as to whether the electoral system is capable of providing a truly representative government.

- **Respect for basic human rights** – this has been enhanced with the passing of the Human Rights Act 1998.
- **No retrospective penal laws** – judicial practice is not to accept retrospective legislation generally, unless an Act expressly permits such application, in which case the courts must abide by it because of parliamentary supremacy. However, such laws would probably breach both the ECHR and EU law.
- **Ability to bring proceedings against the State** – provided by, for example, judicial review, discussed in later chapters of this book.
- **Right to a fair trial** including the presumption of innocence, legal representation, bail and the right to appeal – these characteristics apply in the English legal system, although there are criticisms of the reduction in legal aid impacting on the ability for many to pursue legal action.
- **An independent judiciary** – applicable to the English legal system and now enhanced with the passing of the Constitutional Reform Act 2005.
- **Adequate control of legislation** – there are criticisms of the ability of the executive to pass delegated legislation without sufficient checks and balances and of well-resourced bodies to procure private Bills serving their own interests.

2.7 The relationship between the rule of law and the 'separation of powers'

2.7.1 The separation of powers is an ancient political idea, which can be traced back to Aristotle and was perhaps most thoroughly explained by the French jurist, Montesquieu, who based his analysis on the British constitution of the early 18th century.

2.7.2 The doctrine is based on the notion that there are three distinct functions of Government – **legislative, executive** and **judicial** functions. According to the doctrine in its basic form, these three functions should be vested in distinct bodies so that excessive power is not concentrated in the hands of one body. To do otherwise could lead to abuse of power or what Montesquieu termed 'tyranny'.

2.7.3 This concept of the doctrine has, however, been re-interpreted by, for example, Blackstone, to mean that it is not necessary for distinct bodies to hold each power, with no influence over each other, but that what is required is a '**check and balance**' system operating between them – sometimes referred to as the theory of 'mixed government'.

2.7.4 Different constitutions have adopted different approaches to applying the separation of powers.

- In France there is not complete separation of powers but the doctrine can be witnessed, for example, in the judiciary's inability to question the validity or interfere with the functions of the legislature.

- In the United States a 'check and balance' system operates under the 1787 Constitution. Consequently, the legislature (Congress, comprising the House of Representatives and the Senate), executive (President) and judiciary (federal courts and Supreme Court) operate in a 'creative tension' whereby each can check the other. For example, the Supreme Court can declare legislation unconstitutional; the President is elected separately from Congress and neither they nor their Cabinet can sit or vote in Congress; and Congress (the Senate) must approve presidential nominations for executive office.

2.7.5 There have been a number of more modern examinations of the doctrine and its application to the British constitution. Marshall argues that the doctrine lacks any significant definition and is inconsistent. Professor Wade claims that the British constitution exhibits only one example of the doctrine, namely judicial independence.

2.7.6 However, the judiciary has repeatedly asserted the existence of the doctrine in the British constitution. Professor Munro therefore concludes that whilst the doctrine is 'rooted in constitutional tradition'; it is neither 'absolute nor a predominant feature of the British constitution'.

2.8 The actual extent of the doctrine of 'separation of powers' in the UK constitution today

2.8.1 The three organs of government do exist in the modern British constitution and to a certain extent there is separation of powers (e.g.

judicial independence and judicial refusal to intervene in legislative and executive matters such as parliamentary privilege).

2.8.2 The courts have confirmed that the British constitution features the doctrine. For example:

- In *R v Secretary of State for the Home Department, ex parte Fire Brigades Union and Others* (1995) Lord Mustill spoke of Parliament, the executive and the courts each having 'their distinct and largely exclusive domain'.

- In *Duport Steels Ltd v Sirs* (1980) Lord Denning stated that the British constitution was 'firmly based' on the doctrine, with the result that 'Parliament makes the laws, the judiciary interprets them'.

- In *R v HM Treasury, ex parte Smedley* (1985) Sir John Donaldson MR stated 'it is a constitutional convention of the highest importance that the legislature and the judicature are separate and independent of one another'.

2.8.3 There is also some separation in terms of personnel. For example, the majority of positions within the executive, such as civil servants and members of the armed forces, disqualify the holder from membership of the legislature (House of Commons Disqualification Act 1975). To some extent, each body also acts as a check on the other (e.g. judicial review).

2.8.4 However, there is also considerable overlap of functions and personnel, sometimes described as 'fusion', and ultimately the 'check and balance' system is subject to the principle that Parliament is sovereign.

2.9 Constitutional fusion between elements of government in the United Kingdom

2.9.1 The result of the British electoral system combined with the Party system produces a dominant executive that actually sits within the legislature (by convention, positions within the executive can be held only by Members of either House of Parliament).

2.9.2 This executive, through strict Party discipline and powers to control debate within the House of Commons, is capable of effectively depriving the legislature of its true function.

2.9.3 The legislature has delegated power to Ministers so that they may deal with issues through the production of statutory instruments (delegated legislation), although this is subject to some parliamentary scrutiny.

2.9.4 Ministers also have residual prerogative powers, which result in the ability to legislate without the consent of Parliament (Orders in Council). This power is to some limited extent 'checked' by the courts under the process of judicial review.

The executive and judiciary

- Members of the judiciary are appointed by the executive.
- The creation of numerous tribunals under statute has resulted in executive/administrative bodies hearing disputes between private individuals and between private individuals and Government departments (though the courts do still have oversight of these systems in their function as the constitutional 'check' on the executive in judicial review).
- There are also disputes between private individuals and executive authority that may be determined only by a Minister, in other words, a member of the executive. For example, this is the case in relation to planning permission by a local authority and challenging compulsory purchase orders. This offers a clear example of the executive performing a judicial function (though again, judicial review can provide oversight by the courts here too).

The judiciary and the legislature

- Unlike those systems with a codified constitution, there is no provision within the British constitution for a court to challenge primary legislation and declare it unconstitutional. Consequently, there is no ultimate check on the legislature from the judiciary. However, in the case of delegated legislation, the judiciary can employ judicial review: see *R v HM Treasury, ex parte Smedley* (1985).
- The judiciary is to some extent capable of creating law, which should, under the strict idea of a formal separation of powers, be a role reserved for the legislature. This occurs through the process of precedent, creating common law. This was described in *Shaw v DPP* (1962), in the context of criminal law, as a 'residual power to enforce the supreme and fundamental purpose of the law'.

Fusion of personnel

- The Prime Minister is head of the Cabinet and therefore the executive, yet under convention must be a Member of Parliament, elected to the House of Commons, and is therefore a member of the legislature.
- Ministers are often members of the Cabinet (the executive) and usually also Members of Parliament (the legislature).

2.10 The impact of the Constitutional Reform Act 2005 and other issues

2.10.1 The **Constitutional Reform Act 2005** provided for a more formal separation of executive, legislative and judicial powers and a removal of some of the fusion that had been created as a result of historical anomalies.

2.10.2 The key reforms included the following.

Judicial independence

- For the first time the Act enshrined in law a duty on Government Ministers to uphold the independence of the judiciary. They are specifically barred from trying to influence judicial decisions through any special access to judges.
- This should aid in ensuring that the rule of law is upheld.

A Supreme Court of the United Kingdom

- A major innovation of the Act was to introduce the idea of a new Supreme Court, replacing the Appellate Committee of the House of Lords, thus separating the highest court from Parliament, the legislature.
- The jurisdiction of the Supreme Court is that of the Appellate Committee, as well as the jurisdiction of the Judicial Committee of the Privy Council in respect of devolution matters.
- All existing Law Lords became justices of the court, but they remain full members of the House of Lords.
- The new court has its own building (the former Middlesex Guildhall Crown Court) and opened in October 2009.

Judicial Appointments Commission

- The Act established an independent Judicial Appointments Commission, responsible for selecting candidates to recommend for judicial appointment.

Reforming the role of the Lord Chancellor

- The office of the Lord Chancellor was considered one of the most glaring examples of the fusion of powers within the constitution. Traditionally the Lord Chancellor was a member of the executive and sat in the Cabinet. As head of the judiciary the Lord Chancellor presided over the House of Lords when exercising its judicial function. As a member of the House of Lords the position also offered membership of the legislature.

- The original Constitutional Reform Bill proposed abolition of the role of Lord Chancellor but this was rejected by the House of Lords. Instead the Act modified the role, now known as the Lord Chancellor and Secretary of State for Justice.

- In particular, the judicial functions of the Lord Chancellor were transferred to the Lord Chief Justice. The Lord Chief Justice is responsible for the training, guidance and deployment of judges and represents the views of the judiciary to Parliament and Ministers.

- The Lord Chancellor was also replaced as the Speaker of the House of Lords by the Lord Speaker.

The Attorney General

- The role of the Attorney General was discussed as part of the Governance of Britain Green Paper and the Constitutional Renewal White Paper but the conclusion was for the Attorney General to retain both legal and political powers.

Key Cases Checklist

- *Merkur Island Shipping Corporation v Laughton and Others* (1983) – where Lord Diplock commented on the need for the law to have clarity;
- *R v Horseferry Road Magistrates' Court, ex parte Bennett* (1994) – where Lord Griffiths noted that it is the responsibility of the courts to maintain the rule of law, to oversee executive action and to not permit action that threatens basic human rights or breaches the rule of law;
- *M v Home Office* (1994) – where, applying Dicey's second proposition that every person is subject to the law, the House of Lords held that the Home Secretary could be found in contempt of court by disobeying an injunction (see 1.7.3); and
- *A v Secretary of State for the Home Department* (2004) – where the House of Lords held that power to detain only foreign nationals indefinitely as suspected terrorists, without charge, under the Terrorism, Crime and Security Act 2001 was a breach of both the European Convention on Human Rights (ECHR) and the rule of law.

> Cases drawing on the Rule of Law

> **Cases drawing on the Rule of Law and the Separation of Powers**

> Cases drawing on the Separation of Powers

- In *R v Secretary of State for the Home Department, ex parte Fire Brigades Union and Others* (1995) Lord Mustill spoke of Parliament, the executive and the courts as each having 'their distinct and largely exclusive domain'.
- In *Duport Steels Ltd v Sirs* (1980) Lord Denning stated that the British constitution was 'firmly based' on the doctrine, with the result that 'Parliament makes the laws, the judiciary interprets them'.
- In *R v HM Treasury, ex parte Smedley* (1985) Sir John Donaldson MR stated 'it is a constitutional convention of the highest importance that the legislature and the judicature are separate and independent of one another'.

2.4.2 Merkur Island Shipping Corporation v Laughton and Others [1983] 2 AC 570 (HL)

Key Facts

Members of a trade union were sued for damages for losses arising from industrial action. The court was required to construe three statutes to identify whether, as a trade union, they were immune from tortuous liability.

Key Law

The court expressed concern that it was required to spend considerable time interpreting three statutes that were not clearly expressed.

Key Judgment

Lord Diplock
'Absence of clarity is destructive of the rule of law; it is unfair to those who wish to preserve the rule of law; it encourages those who wish to undermine it.'

Key Comment

One of the aspects of the rule of law is that laws should attain certain minimum standards. This includes that laws be clear, not ambiguous, vague or obscure.

2.4.2 R v Horseferry Road Magistrates' Court, ex parte Bennett [1994] 1 AC 42 (HL)

Key Facts

Bennett, a New Zealand citizen, was wanted by the police for alleged offences. He was arrested in South Africa. Even though there was no extradition treaty between the United Kingdom and South Africa, the police put him on a plane for the United Kingdom, where he was arrested. He was committed to the Crown Court for trial and challenged this decision. The Divisional Court dismissed the application on the basis that even if he had been illegally abducted his trial would still be fair.

Key Law

The House of Lords reversed the decision. Bennett had been abducted in that he had been brought back to the United Kingdom in breach of the existing extradition process, international law and the laws of South Africa. The authorities had therefore abused their power and this resulted in the entire prosecution being illegal.

Key Judgment

Lord Griffiths
'... the judiciary accept a responsibility for the maintenance of the rule of law that embraces a willingness to oversee executive action and to refuse to countenance behaviour that threatens either basic human rights or the rule of law.'

2.4.2 *A v Secretary of State for the Home Department* [2004] UKHL 56 (HL)

Key Facts

The power to detain foreign terrorism suspects under the Anti-Terrorism, Crime and Security Act 2001 was challenged under the Human Rights Act 1998.

Key Law

The law infringed the ECHR and could not be exercised in such a way as to detain indefinitely without charge or trial.

Key Judgment

Lord Nicholls
Imprisonment of such a nature would be 'anathema in any country which observes the rule of law'.

Key Comment

There has been much criticism of the policies and legislation adopted to deal with the 'war against terrorism'. Generally, executive assessment of what should be considered a 'time of emergency' will rarely, if ever, be successfully challenged in the courts. This case is significant in that it shows a clear example of the rule of law operating to check the executive and protect the individual, enhanced by the passing of the Human Rights Act 1998. Similarly, in *A v Secretary of State for the Home Department (No. 2)* [2005] UKHL 71 the House of Lords concluded that evidence that may have been obtained by torture in another country was not admissible.

2.8.2 *R v Secretary of State for the Home Department, ex parte Fire Brigades Union and Others* [1995] 2 WLR 1 (CA)

Key Facts

The Home Secretary decided not to implement a scheme for compensation under the Criminal Justice Act 1988 and wanted to set one up under prerogative powers that provided for lower levels of compensation.

Key Law

While in force, the prerogative cannot be used to frustrate the purposes of statute.

Key Judgment

Sir Thomas Bingham MR
'. . . what [the Home Secretary] could not do, so long as the 1988 provisions stood unrepealed . . . was to exercise prerogative powers to introduce a scheme radically different from what Parliament had approved.'

2.8.2 *Duport Steels Ltd v Sirs* [1980] 1 WLR 142 (HL)

Key Facts

Section 13(1) of the Trade Union and Labour Relations Act 1964 granted immunity to acts done 'in . . . furtherance of a trade dispute'. This had to be interpreted in respect of strike action aimed at third parties.

Key Law

The separation of powers underpins the constitution in that the judiciary only has the authority to interpret the law, as made by Parliament.

Key Judgment

Lord Diplock
'It cannot be too strongly emphasised that the British constitution . . . is firmly based upon the separation of powers; Parliament makes the laws, the judiciary interpret them.'

Key Comment

While there are numerous examples of fusion within the British constitution, this case provides recognition of adherence to the doctrine in the context of the legislature and judiciary.

Key Link

In *R v HM Treasury, ex parte Smedley* [1985] 1 All ER 589 Sir John Donaldson MR echoed the comments of Lord Diplock when he stated that 'it is a constitutional convention of the highest importance that the legislature and the judicature are separate and independent of one another'.

3 Parliamentary sovereignty

- Parliament is the supreme law-making authority
- Parliament is competent to legislate on any subject-matter
- No Parliament can be bound by a predecessor or bind a successor
- No other body has the ability to override or set aside an Act of Parliament

Traditional Scope of the Doctrine

Principles of Parliamentary Sovereignty

Limitations to Parliamentary Sovereignty

- Requirements of the correct 'manner and form' in creating a statute
- Territorial limitations on Parliamentary Sovereignty
- Implied repeal of statutes and limitations to scope/subject matter of statutes
- Practical limitation through non-conflict with EU law

3.1 A brief overview of parliamentary sovereignty, or 'parliamentary supremacy'

3.1.1 One of the key characteristics of the British constitution is the dominance of the legislature, Parliament. A result of the historical struggle between the Crown and Parliament (culminating in the Bill of Rights 1688), the doctrine is not laid down in statute but is a *fundamental rule of common law*. In other words, it is the judiciary that has created and maintained the doctrine as a basic principle of the constitution.

3.1.2 The classic definition of parliamentary supremacy is that offered by Dicey:

- Parliament is the supreme law-making authority;
- Parliament is competent to legislate on any subject matter;
- no Parliament can be bound by a predecessor or bind a successor; and
- no other body has the ability to override or set aside an Act of Parliament.

3.1.3 You should note that only an Act of Parliament is 'supreme'. Resolutions of either House do not have the force of law unless put on a statutory basis (*Stockdale v Hansard* (1839)); proclamations of the Crown issued under the prerogative do not have the force of law; and international treaties, also entered into under the prerogative, cannot have the force of law, unless incorporated by statute.

3.2 Potentially unlimited legislative power for Parliament?

3.2.1 Parliament theoretically has unlimited legislative power – that is, the potential ability to create any law.

3.2.2 This 'unlimited legislative power' principle means that Parliament traditionally has the authority to legislate on any subject matter. Examples include the following:

- Parliament can change the succession to the throne, for example, Act of Settlement 1700; HM Declaration of Abdication Act 1936.
- Parliament's enactments override the common law and can be retrospective, for example, *Burmah Oil Company v Lord Advocate* (1965).

- Parliament can change its own processes for the creation of statutes, for example, Parliament Acts 1911 and 1949.
- Parliament can grant independence to dependent States, for example, Nigeria Independence Act 1960; Zimbabwe Independence Act 1979.
- Parliament can legislate with retrospective effect, for example, War Damages Act 1965; War Crimes Act 1991.
- Parliament can legislate contrary to international law, for example, *Mortensen v Peters* (1906); *Cheney v Conn* (1968).

3.3 Exploring the details of legislative supremacy

3.3.1 It is often observed that **'No Parliament can be bound by a predecessor or bind a successor'**. This means that each and every Parliament must be supreme in its own right.

3.3.2 Consequently, no Parliament can be bound by a preceding Parliament, or bind a future one. The mechanism for securing this principle is known as the **doctrine of implied repeal**.

3.3.3 Parliament may expressly repeal any previous law. The courts must then give effect to the later statute. However, Parliament may not expressly repeal earlier legislation leaving two or more conflicting statutes. The doctrine of implied repeal then applies, in that the courts are required to apply the latest statute, considering earlier law to be impliedly repealed – see *Vauxhall Estates Ltd v Liverpool Corporation* (1932) and *Ellen Street Estates Ltd v Minister of Health* (1934).

3.3.4 The consequence of the application of implied repeal is that no legislation can be entrenched, in other words protected from future changes in the law that Parliament may wish to make.

3.3.5 It is also often claimed that **'No other body has the ability to override or set aside an Act of Parliament'.**

3.3.6 Before the Bill of Rights 1688, it was not uncommon for the courts to declare an Act of Parliament invalid because it did not conform to a higher, divine law or the law of nature (*Dr Bonham's Case* (1610) and *Day v Savadge* (1615)).

3.3.7 The courts no longer assert this authority and instead apply the principle that once an Act is passed, it is the law. This is known as the enrolled Act rule. Consequently, the enforcement of the procedural rules for creating an Act is in the hands of Parliament and the courts will refuse to consider whether there have been any procedural defects – see *Edinburgh and Dalkeith Railway v Wauchope* (1842), *Lee v Bude and Torrington Junction Railway Co* (1871) and *Pickin v British Railways Board* (1974). All a court can do therefore is to construe and apply Acts of Parliament.

3.3.8 In order for an Act to exist, it must comply with the requirements of common law on the creation of statute law. A Bill becomes an Act if it has been approved by both Houses of Parliament (unless the Parliament Acts 1911 and 1949 are invoked) and has received the Royal Assent.

3.3.9 Other requirements, such as standing orders, conventions and practices govern the passage of a Bill through the Houses and the enforcement of these rules is a matter entirely for Parliament.

3.4 Limitations to parliamentary supremacy

3.4.1 There are said to be limitations to parliamentary supremacy relating to what is known as the 'manner and form' of legislation, and the way that legislation is created. Typically controversy arises in this context if the House of Commons attempts to legislate in a manner that precludes the approval of new legislation by the House of Lords, also part of the Westminster Parliament; something that is possible under the Parliament Acts.

3.4.2 An example of this can be seen in the Colonial Laws Validity Act 1865 and its interpretation in *Attorney-General for New South Wales v Trethowan* (1932). In this case the New South Wales legislature was bound in the way in which it abolished its Upper House.

3.4.3 However, this precedent is a weak one when applied to the question of whether the British Parliament can limit itself as to the manner and form of subsequent legislation; the New South Wales legislature was different from the British Parliament in that it was a subordinate legislature, consequently bound to follow the law prescribed by Westminster.

3.4.4 In *R (Jackson) v Attorney-General* (2005) it was argued that the Parliament Act 1949 was invalid and that consequently the Hunting Act 2004 passed under it was also invalid, because the parliamentary House of Lords was bypassed in the creation of the 2004 Act using the mechanism allowed for in the 1949 Act. The judicial House of Lords held that the 1949 Act was valid. Consequently it appears that the Parliament Acts could technically be used to achieve constitutional change without the consent of the House of Lords.

3.4.5 However, this was expressly doubted by Lord Steyn, who implied that the courts would continue to have a role in ascertaining whether the use of the Acts was constitutionally proper or correct. Using the Acts in a way that was unchecked and increasingly common would probably also raise considerable political criticism.

Territorial limitations

3.4.6 Whilst Parliament may technically have the authority to legislate for anywhere in the world (extra-territorial jurisdiction), there are geographical limitations to the ability to enforce that law. Hence, the practical consequences render the law unenforceable and therefore redundant.

3.4.7 For example, in 1965 Parliament attempted to assert control over what was then Southern Rhodesia by passing the Southern Rhodesia Act. This invalidated any legislation passed in the country. Parliament's competence to pass such an Act was affirmed in *Madzimbamuto v Lardner-Burke* (1969). However, the practical effectiveness of the Act was limited by the fact that it could not be enforced. Hence, *de jure* power may have rested in the Westminster Parliament, but *de facto* power was in the hands of the Rhodesian Government.

3.4.8 We can see this recognised by the courts:

- In *Blackburn v Attorney-General* (1971) Lord Denning acknowledged that legal theory (parliamentary supremacy) had to sometimes give way to 'practical politics'. An example would be Parliament trying to reverse grants of independence.
- Similarly, in *Manuel and Others v Attorney-General* (1983) Megarry VC noted that 'legal validity is one thing, enforceability is another'.

Limitations as to scope and subject matter

3.4.9 In *Thoburn v Sunderland City Council* (2002) a hierarchy of statutes was recognised. **Constitutional statutes** were (somewhat controversially) considered as not subject to implied repeal because they protect the special status of constitutional rights. Hence such Acts are to some extent entrenched and limit Parliament's supremacy in the context of what it may legislate on.

3.4.10 Examples of such statutes include:
- Bill of Rights 1688
- Acts of Union
- European Communities Act 1972;
- Human Rights Act 1998; and
- Acts providing for devolution.

3.4.11 However, it should be noted that all of the limitations described below, which all stem from some particular statute, could be argued to be self-imposed; no other body can place such obligations on Parliament except itself. In theory at least, therefore, Parliament may repeal such legislation, although it would have to do so expressly.

A group of the most significant of the more recent 'constitutional statutes' that can be said to affect Parliamentary supremacy are described briefly below.

European Communities Act 1972

3.4.12 The European Communities Act 1972 section 2(4) requires that all past and future legislation be compatible with EU law. This has become a significant limitation on parliamentary supremacy and is discussed in detail in Chapter 3.

Human Rights Act 1998

3.4.13 In the context of this Act, implied repeal is effectively removed because if Parliament wishes to legislate contrary to the provisions of the ECHR it can only do so expressly. This is the effect of the duty of interpretation imposed on the courts under section 3 of the Act. Clarification of Parliament's intentions in terms of complying with human rights can be seen in any statements of compatibility issued under section 19.

Devolution acts

3.4.14 In *Thoburn* (above) the Acts providing for devolution were specifically cited as examples of constitutional statutes not subject to implied repeal. For more details on devolution issues, and the possible independence of countries currently within the United Kingdom, see Chapter 8.

3.5 Limitations on parliamentary sovereignty from a European dimension?

3.5.1 The scope of what is seen by some as a legislative interference from the European Union into parliamentary sovereignty in the United Kingdom is the constant source of debate about the ongoing UK membership of the European Union itself. The core issue, from a legal perspective, is that the body of European law-making institutions described in Chapter 6 of this book produce a large amount of the law which ultimately regulates the work of the UK Government and the operation of UK businesses.

3.5.2 The response a few years ago from the Coalition Government was to enact the European Union Act 2011.

3.5.3 The 2011 Act is notable for its declaration in section 18 that:

> 'Directly applicable or directly effective EU law (that is, the rights, powers, liabilities, obligations, restrictions, remedies and procedures referred to in section 2(1) of the European Communities Act 1972) falls to be recognised and available in law in the United Kingdom only by virtue of that Act or where it is required to be recognised and available in law by virtue of any other Act.'

3.5.4 This is in essence a reassertion of parliamentary sovereignty: the European Communities Act 1972 is not 'entrenched', and can be *expressly* repealed by another, future Act of Parliament.

3.5.5. Part 1 of the European Union Act 2011 also requires that there be a national referendum on any further transfer of law-making powers to the European Union in areas of governance, under any new Treaty of the European Union, beyond what are already considered to be areas of EU competence.

3.5.6 This question of national legal sovereignty, and legislative competence, will likely lead to a referendum on EU membership as a whole in 2016 or 2017, as promised by the Conservative Party in its manifesto prior to the General Election in May 2015.

3.6 Lord Hoffmann's version of the 'principle of legality'

3.6.1 As will be discussed in later chapters, since the United Kingdom is a signatory to the European Convention on Human Rights (ECHR), and as a Member State of the Council of Europe must adhere to and implement judgments of the European Court of Human Rights at Strasbourg, there are also concerns over the extent to which transposing the ECHR into UK law, through the Human Rights Act 1998, has undermined parliamentary sovereignty here in the United Kingdom.

3.6.2 At the time of writing in the summer of 2015, the Conservative majority in the House of Commons won at the General Election in May 2015 entails that plans to repeal the Human Rights Act 1998 and replace it with a British Bill of Rights will be moving ahead. This issue is discussed in later chapters of the book.

3.6.3 The notion that UK courts can declare UK legislation incompatible with the ECHR using provisions of the Human Rights Act 1998, and that UK judges are readily applying case law from the European Court of Human Rights in UK courts themselves, is troubling to some.

3.6.4 But, as Lord Hoffmann identified in *R v Secretary of State for the Home Department, ex parte Simms* (1999), parliamentary sovereignty strictly speaking remains untouched by the Human Rights Act 1998 (which can be repealed, after all, and is thus not 'entrenched' constitutionally).

3.6.5 The chief effect of the Human Rights Act 1998 is greatly to increase political pressure on the Westminster Parliament to legislate in a way that is respectful for the values of human rights. The chief issue for some is quite simply that these values of human rights in practice are determined by the European Court of Human Rights, and that these values strengthen and develop over time.

3.6.6 You might think that our courts would be tolerant of a body of law that develops over time, and which is made by judges in deciding cases – given that the UK courts have for hundreds of years developed the common law itself. But the European Court of Human Rights is not a UK court – and this might be where the chief problem lies for some UK politicians in the last two elected Westminster Governments. This is because the most controversial legislation created by a particular UK Government might be ultimately brought down because of political pressure following from cases determined by the European Court of Human Rights.

3.6.7 Lord Hoffmann described this constitutional and political position very eloquently in two particular paragraphs in the *Simms* decision, as follows:

- '*Parliamentary sovereignty means that Parliament can, if it chooses, legislate contrary to fundamental principles of human rights. The Human Rights Act 1998 will not detract from this power. The constraints upon its exercise by Parliament are ultimately political, not legal. But the principle of legality means that Parliament must squarely confront what it is doing and accept the political cost. Fundamental rights cannot be overridden by general or ambiguous words. This is because there is too great a risk that the full implications of their unqualified meaning may have passed unnoticed in the democratic process.*'

- [In this last point about the flaw in the UK democratic process, Lord Hoffmann is suggesting that Parliament may enact legislation which is capable of distortion in actual implementation by Government bodies or agencies, and that a constitutional role of the judiciary, as discussed in the last chapter, is to hold the Government (the executive) to account for the way they implement and use the law.]

- '*In the absence of express language or necessary implication to the contrary, the courts therefore presume that even the most general words [in an Act of Parliament] were intended to be subject to the basic rights of the individual. In this way the courts of the United Kingdom, though acknowledging the sovereignty of Parliament, apply principles of constitutionality little different from those which exist in countries where the power of the legislature is expressly limited by a constitutional document.*'

3.6.8 So the United Kingdom does not have a written or codified constitution to outline the exact nature of parliamentary sovereignty, but Lord Hoffmann seems to think that the current unwritten constitutional arrangements in the United Kingdom still provide a sound and sensible principle of constitutionality, whereby the courts can effectively monitor the work of Parliament and the Government and protect the rights of citizens.

Key Cases Checklist

Using key cases to explore Parliamentary Sovereignty

Burmah Oil Company v Lord Advocate (1965): Parliament's enactments override the common law and can be retrospective (see 1.7.2)

Cheney v Conn (1968): Parliament can theoretically legislate contrary to international law

Edinburgh and Dalkeith Railway v Wauchope (1842): all a court can do is construe and apply Acts of Parliament

Vauxhall Estates Ltd v Liverpool Corporation (1932): the courts are required to apply the latest statute, considering earlier conflicting law to be impliedly repealed (see 3.3)

R (Jackson) v Attorney-General (2005): the Parliament Acts can be used to achieve constitutional change without the consent of the House of Lords

R v Secretary of State for the Home Department, ex parte Simms (1999): Lord Hoffmann noted that 'Fundamental rights cannot be overridden by general or ambiguous words'

3.2.2 *Cheney v Conn* [1968] 1 All ER 779   (HC)

Key Facts

A taxpayer challenged his income tax assessment made under the Finance Act 1964 on the basis that some of the money would be used to finance the manufacture of nuclear weapons contrary to the Geneva Convention.

Key Law

International law cannot place any limitations on Parliament's power.

Key Judgment

Ungoed-Thomas J
'What the statute itself enacts cannot be unlawful, because what the statute says and provides is itself the law, and the highest form of law that is known to this country.'

3.3.7 *Edinburgh and Dalkeith Railway v Wauchope* (1842) 8 Cl & F 710 (HL)

Key Facts

Wauchope challenged an Act on the basis that he had not been notified of the Bill's introduction as required by standing orders of the House of Commons. The court rejected the challenge.

Key Judgment

Lord Campbell
'All that a court of justice can do is to look to the Parliament roll; if from that it should appear that a Bill has passed both Houses and received the Royal Assent, no court of justice can inquire into the mode in which it was introduced into Parliament, or into what was done previous to its introduction, or what passed in Parliament during its progress in its various stages through both Houses.'

Key Comment

With the development of the doctrine of parliamentary supremacy, the courts no longer have any jurisdiction to question the validity of legislation, hence the function of the court is only to construe and apply Acts of Parliament.

Key Link

In *Lee v Bude and Torrington Junction Railway Company* (1871) LR 6 CP 576 it was stated that 'if an Act of Parliament has been obtained improperly, it is for the legislature to correct it by repealing it; but so long as it exists as law, the courts are bound to apply it'. Similarly, in *Ex parte Canon Selwyn* (1872) 36 JP 54 on the validity of the Irish Church Act 1869, Cockburn CJ stated that there was no body that could question the validity of an Act on the basis that legislation 'is superior in authority to any court of law'. This principle is known as the **enrolled act rule**.

3.4.4 *R (Jackson) v Attorney-General* [2005] 4 All ER 1253 (HL)

Key Facts

The Hunting Act 2004 had been passed under the Parliament Acts 1911 and 1949. It was argued that the 1949 Act was invalid on the basis that since it was passed under the 1911 Act it was delegated legislation and as such could not extend the powers of the Commons and that the 1911 Act implied that its procedure could not be used to further reduce the power of the Lords.

Key Law

The 1949 Act was lawful since Acts passed under the 1911 Act's procedure were not delegated legislation and there was nothing within its terms that prevented it from being used to reduce the powers of the Lords. Since the 1949 Act was valid, the Hunting Act 2004 was too.

Key Comment

It appears therefore that the Parliament Acts could technically be used to achieve major constitutional change without the consent of the House of Lords. Whether this includes abolishing the Lords itself did not arise for decision. On extending the life of Parliament, expressly stated within the 1911 Act to require the consent of the House of Lords, a majority of nine held in *obiter* that the Parliament Act procedure could not be used to remove it. However, invoking the 1949 Act to make major constitutional changes was expressly doubted by Lord Steyn, implying that the courts have a role in ascertaining whether its use is constitutionally 'proper'. In addition, using the Act in such a way would probably raise considerable political criticism.

3.6.4 R v Secretary of State for the Home Department, ex parte Simms [1999] 3 WLR 328

(HL)

Key Facts

In this case a blanket policy adopted by the Home Secretary preventing professionals (e.g. journalists) visiting prisoners was held to be unlawful.

Key Law

Parliamentary sovereignty strictly speaking remains untouched by the Human Rights Act 1998 (which can be repealed, after all, and is thus not 'entrenched' constitutionally). The chief effect of the Human Rights Act 1998 is greatly to increase political pressure on the Westminster Parliament to legislate in a way that is respectful of the values of human rights.

Key Judgment

Lord Hoffmann
'Parliamentary sovereignty means that Parliament can, if it chooses, legislate contrary to fundamental principles of human rights. The Human Rights Act 1998 will not detract from this power. The constraints upon its exercise by Parliament are ultimately political, not legal. But the principle of legality means that Parliament must squarely confront what it is doing and accept the political cost. Fundamental rights cannot be overridden by general or ambiguous words. This is because there is too great a risk that the full implications of their unqualified meaning may have passed unnoticed in the democratic process.'

4 Constitutional conventions

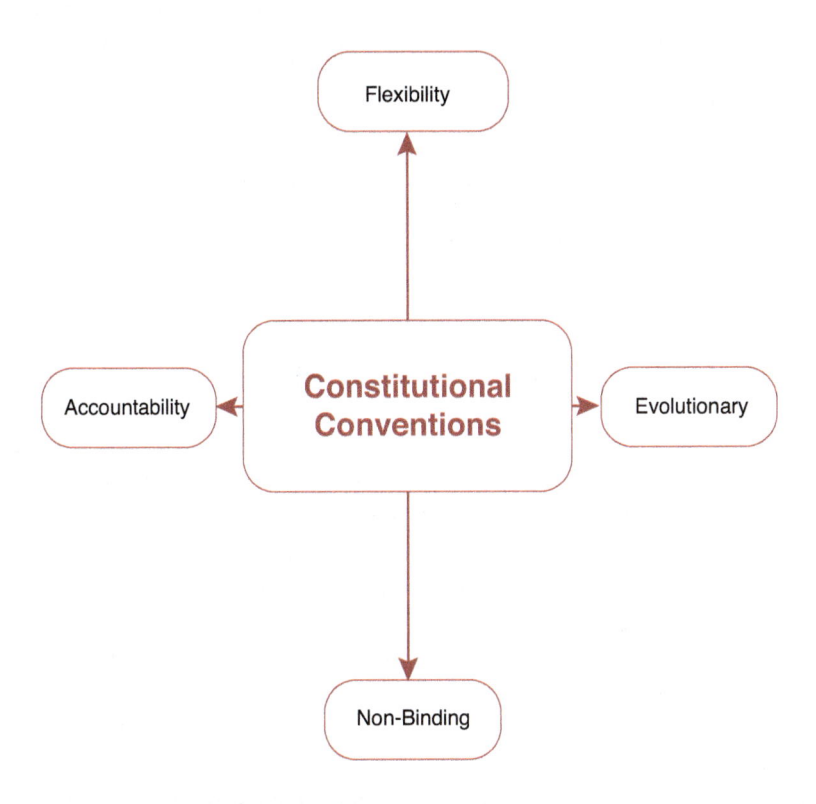

```
                    Flexibility
                        ↑
                        |
Accountability ← Constitutional → Evolutionary
                  Conventions
                        |
                        ↓
                   Non-Binding
```

▶ 4.1 Definitions of constitutional conventions

4.1.1　A significant number of important constitutional principles are not found in either statute or common law and are unwritten. They are called **conventions**.

4.1.2　Many definitions of conventions can be found including, for example:
- Austin – the 'positive morality' of the constitution;
- Mill – the 'unwritten maxims' of the constitution;

- Freeman – the 'whole system of political morality'; and
- Jennings – a source that 'fleshes out the dry bones of the law'.

4.1.3 Perhaps the most readily useable definition of a constitutional convention is that provided by Makintosh – that such conventions are 'generally accepted descriptive statements of constitutional and political practice'.

4.1.4 According to Jennings, the existence of a convention may be determined by asking whether there is precedent for the rule; whether those operating under the convention believe themselves obligated to do so; and whether there is a reason for the convention.

4.1.5 Conventions therefore are often **evolutionary** and develop through usage. There is no prescribed time or duration required to establish the existence of a convention. This, combined with their unwritten nature, means that it can be very difficult to identify whether a particular convention exists.

4.2 Examples of constitutional conventions

4.2.1 Two prominent examples of a constitutional convention are about the power exercised by the Monarch:

- the Monarch has the legal right to grant/refuse the Royal Assent; under convention exercises that right on the advice of Ministers; and
- the Monarch holds the legal right to appoint the Prime Minister, who under convention is the leader of the Party that holds the majority at a General Election and commands the confidence of the Commons.

4.2.2 Two of the most important constitutional conventions, designed to secure **executive accountability**, are individual and collective ministerial responsibility (see Chapter 10 for details).

4.2.3 Some conventions can be deliberately created, rather than emerging from practice. One example would be the 'Sewel Convention', created in 1999, which prevents Parliament from legislating in matters that have been devolved to the Scottish Parliament without obtaining its consent (for detail on devolution see Chapter 8).

4.2.4 Conventions offer the constitution **flexibility**. The principles provided in the form of conventions often develop because of a desire to avoid formal change through the production of legislation. Hence conventions can be helpful in easing constitutional change in an informal way, for example:

- from **monarchy to parliamentary supremacy** – the role of the Monarch in government has effectively disappeared since the 18th century, not as a result of statute, but of conventions. In this way the Prime Minister has also acquired significant Government powers;
- from **Empire to Commonwealth** – the recognition of the right to self-rule for the colonies of the Empire was originally reflected in the use of convention, requiring Westminster to seek the approval of such colonies before it could legislate for them.

4.3 Are constitutional conventions legally binding?

4.3.1 The most significant characteristic of constitutional conventions is that they are **not** legally binding.

4.3.2 Dicey stated that conventions may regulate conduct but 'are not in reality laws at all since they are not enforced by the courts';

4.3.3 Marshall and Moodie describe conventions as 'rules of constitutional behaviour which are considered to be binding by and upon those who operate the constitution but which are not enforced by the law courts'.

4.3.4 However, the courts may recognise the existence of a convention when coming to judgment. For example:

- *Attorney-General v Jonathan Cape Ltd* (1976) – where the court recognised the existence of convention, in this case the convention of collective ministerial responsibility, but would not enforce it *per se* since it was a non-legal rule;
- *Madzimbamuto v Lardner-Burke* (1969) – where it was held that no court could declare an Act of Parliament invalid purely because it breached a convention, in this case the convention that Westminster seek the approval of colonies before legislating for them;
- *Manuel v Attorney-General* (1983) – where it was confirmed that conventions are non-legal rules and are unable to limit parliamentary supremacy. Consequently any Act of Parliament that breaches convention will nevertheless be upheld by the courts.

4.3.5　Convention cannot crystallise into law: *Reference Re the Amendment of the Constitution of Canada* (1982). Therefore the only way a convention can become legally binding is if it is put into statutory form. Examples of statutes incorporating former conventions include the Statute of Westminster 1931 and the Parliament Act 1911.

4.3.6　The breach of a convention may result in a number of consequences, depending on the importance of the convention itself. Indeed, Dicey stated that the breach of some conventions could result in legal consequences. However, it is rarely the case that breach of a convention will have legal consequences: breaching a convention will most often result in political, not legal, consequences.

4.3.7　Therefore, conventions are generally followed not because of legal consequences but because of political difficulties that may arise otherwise, if they were not followed.

4.4 Should constitutional conventions themselves be codified?

4.4.1　There has been debate on the issue of codifying conventions. This debate centres on their perceived disadvantages and the controversy of relying on them as a source of constitutional law.

4.4.2　Criticisms of conventions include the fact that they are not clearly defined; that they are non-legally binding; and that they do not act as a rigorous check on the executive.

4.4.3　Academic criticism of convention includes the following:

- Hennessy – convention permits the Government of the day to control the constitution and therefore it is not subject to external limits;
- Bogdanor – because of the reliance on convention, 'the government of the day decides what the constitution is'; and
- Horwitz – conventions are essentially undemocratic.

4.4.4　Hence some of the advantages of codifying conventions could be, for example:

- they would be formally recognised and 'declared' (as, e.g., in respect of the Australian constitution);
- they would thus be easier to identify and 'enforce'; and
- they would be less malleable to change by the Government of the day.

Constitutional conventions

4.4.5 However, it should be recognised that conventions do bring advantages, such as flexibility so that the constitution may be continually modernised. Codifying conventions could remove this flexibility.

4.4.6 In addition, experience with codified constitutions reveals that conventions can often develop regardless, primarily as a means of adapting the constitution to change.

Key Cases Checklist

Reference Re the Amendment of the Constitution of Canada (1982) – convention cannot crystallise into law – therefore the only way a convention can become legally binding is if it is put into statutory form

Attorney-General v Jonathan Cape Ltd (1976) – the court recognised the existence of convention, in this case the convention of collective ministerial responsibility, but would not enforce it *per se* since it was a non-legal rule

Defining the role and effect of Constitutional Conventions

Madzimbamuto v Lardner-Burke (1969) – where it was held that no court could declare an Act of Parliament invalid purely since it breached a convention

Manuel v Attorney-General (1983) – where it was confirmed that conventions are non-legal rules and are unable to limit parliamentary supremacy

4.3.5 Reference Re the Amendment of the Constitution of Canada (1982) 125 DLR (3rd) 1

SCC

Key Facts

As a means of achieving full patriation of the Canadian constitution from residual British control, the Canadian Federal Government made proposals altering the distribution of powers between the provincial legislatures. A number of the Provincial Governments objected, claiming that the proposals would breach the convention that they had to both request and consent to such changes.

Key Law

The majority of the Supreme Court of Canada found that consent was required under convention but that the convention itself could not be enforced by the court. In addition, convention could not crystallise into law unless put in statutory form.

Key Judgments

Martland J and others

'The conventional rules of the Constitution present one striking peculiarity. In contradiction to the laws of the Constitution, they are not enforced by the Courts.'

'This conflict between convention and law which prevents the Courts from enforcing conventions also prevents conventions from crystallizing into laws, unless it be by statutory adoption.'

Key Comment

Examples of where conventions have been incorporated into statute are the Statute of Westminster 1931 and the Parliament Act 1911.

4.3.4 Attorney-General v Jonathan Cape Ltd [1976] QB 752

HC

Key Facts

The executors of the estate of Richard Crossman (a former Cabinet Minister) wished to publish his diaries. The diaries included Cabinet discussions. Under the convention of collective ministerial responsibility, such matters are confidential and may not be revealed except when required under law or with the authority of the Cabinet Secretary. The Government sought an injunction on the basis that publication would be a breach of confidentiality.

Key Law

The court recognised the existence of the convention but since it was a non-legal rule the court could not enforce it *per se*.

Key Comment

While the court concluded that publication of such information could be a breach of confidentiality, on the facts it concluded that the information was over 10 years old and therefore no longer confidential.

4.3.4 *Madzimbamuto v Lardner-Burke* [1969] 1 AC 645

Key Facts

It was argued that the Southern Rhodesia Act 1965 had been passed in breach of the convention that the consent of the colony first be obtained.

Key Law

The supremacy of Parliament was paramount and no court could declare an Act of Parliament to be invalid because it might breach a convention.

Key Judgment

Lord Reid
'It is often said that it would be unconstitutional for the United Kingdom Parliament to do certain things . . . But that does not mean that it is beyond the power of Parliament to do such things.'

Key Link

In *R v Secretary of State for the Home Department, ex parte Hosenball* [1977] 1 WLR 766; [1977] 3 All ER 452 a US citizen was to be deported on the basis that he was a threat to national security. The court used the existence of the convention to influence its decision. The court relaxed the usual rules of the law of natural justice justifying its decision by relying on the convention that the Minister would have to be responsible to Parliament for his actions.

4.3.4 *Manuel v Attorney-General* [1983] 1 Ch 77 (CA)

Key Facts

The facts are based on the same background as *Reference Re the Amendment of the Constitution of Canada* (1982). Aboriginal chiefs argued that the convention had crystallised into law so that actual consent had to be established. They had not provided their consent to the Canada Act 1982, although it had been agreed to by a large majority of the provinces. Section 4 of the Statute of Westminster 1931 was relied on, which did not enact the convention but incorporated it in a modified form.

Key Law

Conventions are non-legal rules and cannot limit parliamentary supremacy. Hence, any Act of Parliament in breach of convention would nevertheless be upheld by the courts. In addition, section 4 of the Statute of Westminster 1931 did not require actual consent to be given, only that any Act passed expressly declared that consent had been given, which the Canada Act did.

5 The role of international law

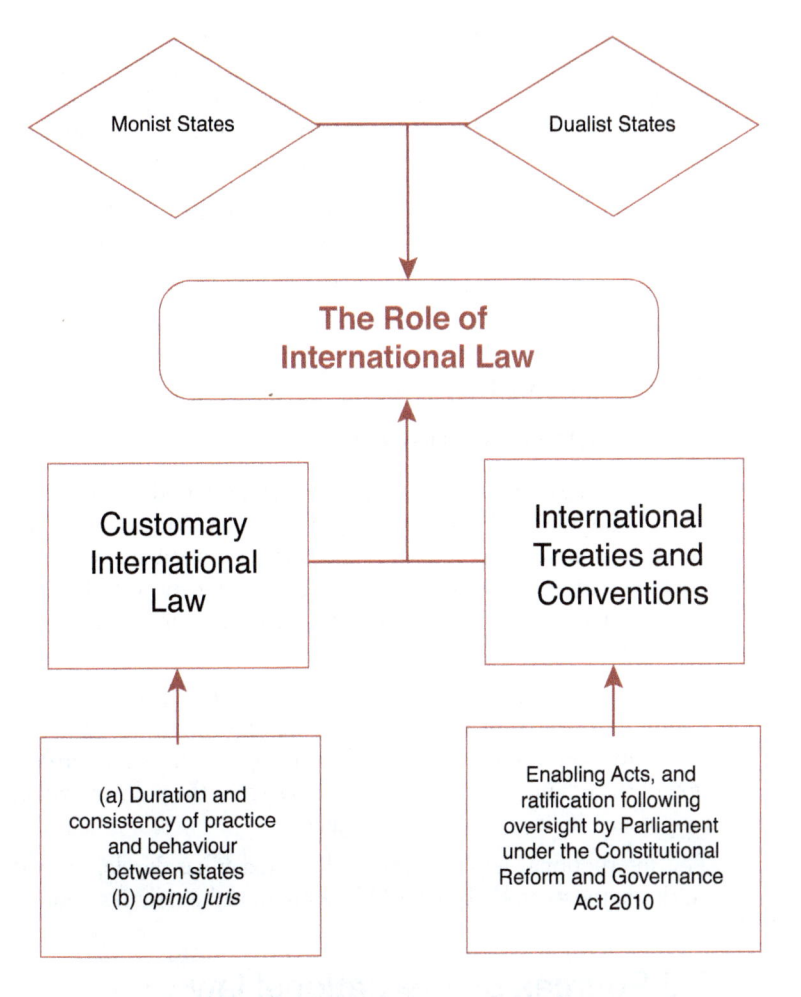

```
         Monist States ─────┐         ┌───── Dualist States
                            ↓         ↓
                    ┌─────────────────────┐
                    │   The Role of       │
                    │   International Law │
                    └─────────────────────┘
                              ↑
          ┌───────────────────┴───────────────────┐
    ┌──────────────┐                      ┌──────────────────┐
    │  Customary   │                      │  International   │
    │ International│                      │  Treaties and    │
    │     Law      │                      │  Conventions     │
    └──────────────┘                      └──────────────────┘
           ↑                                       ↑
    ┌──────────────┐                      ┌──────────────────┐
    │ (a) Duration │                      │ Enabling Acts, and│
    │ and consistency│                    │ ratification following│
    │ of practice  │                      │ oversight by Parliament│
    │ and behaviour│                      │ under the Constitutional│
    │ between states│                     │ Reform and Governance│
    │ (b) opinio juris│                   │ Act 2010          │
    └──────────────┘                      └──────────────────┘
```

> ## 5.1 What is international law?

5.1.1 Wallace and Martin-Ortega have written a most useful definition that contemporary international law 'refers to those rules and norms that regulate the conduct of States and other entities . . .'.

5.1.2 Such 'other entities' include supranational organisations such as the European Union, for example, and the Council of Europe – addressed across the next two chapters of this book (see Chapter 6 and Chapter 7).

5.1.3 International law as a whole comprises public international law (which is the focus of this chapter) and private international law, often known as the 'conflict of laws'.

5.1.4 Public international law is concerned with agreements between two or more different jurisdictions, in the form of a treaty, for example, or at a supranational level. This international agreement may then be binding on the State institutions in the two (or more) jurisdictions or States concerned. Often these agreements will concern matters of public law, or particularly human rights law, in the UK context.

5.1.5 Private international law, or the 'conflict of laws' is the body of international law which concerns the resolution of legal disputes between two private bodies across two or more jurisdictions, in a context, for example, of commercial law.

5.2 The development of international law

5.2.1 Wallace and Martin-Ortega have noted that the traditional definition of 'international law' as a body of rules regulating the conduct of States at times of peace, and indeed war, between themselves is now too narrow, particularly with the growth of considerable international trade law, and much international human rights law, as well as international criminal law.

5.2.2 Public international law as a body of rules aiming at promoting international justice (including, e.g., the prevention of crime and discrimination, the promotion of human rights values and protection of the environment) is only as successful as the political will to recognise it in any given State jurisdiction.

5.2.3 The international legal system we have today has developed most quickly in the second half of the 20th century and the early 21st century.

5.3 Sources of international law

5.3.1 Sources of international law can be described as either formal (articulating what the law is) or material (identifying where the law is to be found).

5.3.2   As there is no international legislature creating law for each and every State in the world, the creation of international sources of law is based on consensus between States. But the United Nations, established under an international Charter in 1945 at the end of the Second World War, does create a great amount of international law that is binding on member States within the United Nations itself, on the basis of common political consensus. Likewise, there is no single, literal international court which has jurisdiction over the entire globe, on all legal matters, but there is an International Court of Justice which a group of States (that is, 192 member States of the United Nations) have founded under the Statute on the International Court of Justice, again from 1945.

5.3.3   The international legal system possesses no 'written' or codified constitution as a single document – something it has in common as a legal system with the constitution of the United Kingdom. So the development of the recognition of sources of international law is not, and cannot be, entirely uniform.

5.3.4   But in Article 38 of the UN Statute on the International Court of Justice, categories of different sources of international law are set out, which are very useful examples for the purposes of this short introduction to international law.

5.3.5   In accordance with Article 38, for example, the International Court of Justice decides cases brought by UN member States against other UN member States specifically in **international conventions** (including international treaties) and **international custom**.

5.4 Custom in international law

5.4.1   Just as convention in the UK constitution is important to a fuller understanding of the constitution itself, so too the notion of custom as a source of international law is important in gaining an understanding of the international legal system as a whole.

5.4.2   Custom in international law is a body of rules or norms with which States comply because they feel they ought to, legally, or have complied with consistently.

5.4.3   Whether a particular behaviour by a State over a period of time, at an international level, can be considered customary international law, is defined by several factors, including:

- the duration of the practice of that behaviour between States; and
- the consistency and uniformity of that practice between States.

5.4.4 Sometimes customary international law can on the face of it be readily confused with international voluntary behaviour by States. States will regularly assist one another in times of need, and in humanitarian emergencies, for example. But this morally laudable behaviour does not lead to binding legal positions between States.

5.4.5 Key to a determination in the International Court of Justice as to whether some particular State behaviour is actually **'crystallised' into international law** as *customary international law* is the notion of *opinio juris sive necessitatis*: 'an opinion of law or necessity'. ***Opinio juris***, as it is often more simply known, is the **subjective belief** by a State itself that it is bound in customary international law to follow a particular course of action.

5.4.6 If a particular practice by a State with regard to other States is both (a) largely consistent and uniform over a period of time, and (b) believed by that State to be a legal obligation (fulfilling the criterion of *opinio juris*) then the practice can be determined to be part of **customary international law**.

5.5 Treaties

5.5.1 We can largely consider the term 'treaties' to be equivalent to the 'conventions' described in Article 38 of the UN Statute on the International Court of Justice.

5.5.2 Treaties are commonly designed to be binding only on the States which agree to be bound by those treaties. This is rather different to the notion of domestic statutes or other legislation, such as Acts of Parliament in the United Kingdom – as well as the common law in England and Wales, for example – since no individual can 'opt out' of the application to them of the criminal law, for example.

5.5.3 While treaties and customary international law are both equally valid and binding on States, if there is a clash between an express provision in a treaty and a matter in customary international law then it is accepted as a principle of international law that the treaty provision takes precedence over the item of customary international law.

5.5.4 A key issue with treaties as objects of international law, and with customary international law for that matter, is how a particular State's domestic jurisdiction gives effect to that treaty, convention or custom as a particular item of international law. The important questions arise of whether it is operative in that jurisdiction (the question of whether it has municipal recognition) and, if so, what weight is given to that item of international law.

5.6 International law and national law

5.6.1 How an item of international law takes effect in a State jurisdiction or domestic legal system (known as the 'municipal' law or legal system) depends very much on whether that State has a **monist** or a **dualist** approach to international law.

Monist approaches to international law

5.6.2 The monist approach to the question of integrating international law into municipal law is to see them as two halves of the same whole – with the proviso that international law takes precedence over municipal in the event of any clashes on any issue addressed by national, municipal law.

Dualist approaches to international law

5.6.3 The dualist approach to international law is that it is not integrated automatically into municipal, nation-level law, and that the two form distinct and separate legal systems. Sometimes, in dualist States, international law and municipal law are seen as having very different spheres or areas of competence.

5.6.4 Dualist States in effect are characterised by their attempts to harmonise their domestic law with a system of international law.

5.6.5 In the domestic courts of the United Kingdom, in the words of Lord Diplock in *Salomon v Commissioners of Customs and Excise* (1967), there is a presumption that:

> 'Parliament does not intend to act in breach of international law, including therein specific treaty obligations; and if one of the meanings which reasonably be ascribed to the legislation is consonant with the treaty obligation and another or others are not, the meaning which is consonant is to be preferred.'

5.6.6 At this point, it is prudent to turn to the manner in which international law takes effect in the UK constitution.

5.7 The effect of international law in the UK constitution

5.7.1 As the constitution of the United Kingdom is unwritten, that is, not codified, there is no single source of authority to dictate how bodies of international law take effect in the United Kingdom. However, some practices and rules have developed which shape how this process takes place.

Customary international law taking effect in the United Kingdom

5.7.2 In the United Kingdom, courts will readily apply customary international law in their reasoning in relation to a case if they can be assured of the belief by the UK Government that the international customary practice is a legal obligation (fulfilling the criterion of *opinio juris*, as described above).

5.7.3 Lord Alverstone explained in *West Rand Central Gold Mining Co* (1905) that customary international law:

> '...will be acknowledged and applied by municipal [courts] when legitimate occasion arises for those [courts] to decide questions to which doctrines of international law may be relevant. But any doctrine so invoked must be one really accepted as binding between nations, and the international law sought to be applied must, like anything else, be proved by satisfactory evidence...'

The effect of customary international law on the common law doctrine of precedent

5.7.4 A development in customary international law that takes place during the time that has passed since the last consideration of that particular point of law by a UK court means that a UK court may be able to break with the doctrine of precedent, and move away from a previously decided case in the United Kingdom on the basis that the relevant customary international law has developed in that time, rendering the precedent concerned obsolete: *Trendtex Trading Corporation v Central Bank of Nigeria* (1977).

The power of an Act of Parliament over any customary international law

5.7.5 As an important aspect of the doctrine of parliamentary sovereignty, or supremacy, where there is a conflict between an Act of Parliament in the United Kingdom and some rule from customary international law the rule from the Act of Parliament takes precedence over the rule from customary international law.

Acts of Parliament and treaties in international law

5.7.6 International treaties and conventions, as sources of international law, do not take effect in UK 'municipal' or domestic law automatically upon their creation by two or more States (which would naturally include the United Kingdom).

5.7.7 An Act of Parliament, often described as the Enabling Act with regard to that international treaty or convention between those States, must be passed by the UK Parliament in Westminster to put that particular international legal instrument into effect in the UK legal system.

5.7.8 Two particular examples are the European Communities Act 1972, which enables the body of EU treaty law to apply directly in the United Kingdom (see Chapter 6), and the Human Rights Act 1998, which was designed to give greater direct effect in the UK legal system to principles of human rights law found in the European Convention on Human Rights (ECHR) and its Protocols (see Chapter 7).

5.7.9 However, the ECHR was a guide to statutory interpretation by UK judges for decades between its ratification by the UK Government and its direct transposition into the UK constitutional framework by the Human Rights Act 1998.

5.7.10 Traditionally, in the United Kingdom, treaty-making with other States has been an exercise of the royal prerogative by Government Ministers representing the Crown.

5.7.11 Because Parliament does not take part in this function of the Government (the executive in the UK constitution), the constitutional convention that an Enabling Act is passed before the treaty concerned takes effect in UK law is something of a constitutional safeguard against abuse of that self-same royal prerogative power by the Government Ministers concerned.

5.7.12 Normally an Enabling Act will be passed after a treaty or convention has been finalised as co-written by the UK Government (where is it 'signed'), but before that treaty or convention has been **ratified** (that is, formally acknowledged as binding in effect on the UK

Government and other Governments party to it), allowing domestic UK law more precisely to keep pace with the international law articulated in that treaty or convention.

5.7.13 The convention known as the 'Ponsonby Rule' required treaties to be laid before Parliament for 21 days to allow for challenge and discussion before their **ratification**.

5.7.14 Part 2 of the Constitutional Reform and Governance Act 2010 has placed this constitutional convention with regard to the exercise of royal prerogative, and the laying of treaties before Parliament for 21 days, on a statutory, binding footing, for Government Ministers to observe as a strict requirement, lest they act unlawfully in adopting an international treaty or convention.

5.7.15 In the recent Supreme Court case of *R (SG) v Secretary of State for Work and Pensions* (2015) it was confirmed that for an international legal instrument to have effect in the United Kingdom, in this case the UN Convention on the Rights of the Child (UNCRC), the instrument concerned must have been given effect by Parliament in an Enabling Act.

5.7.16 The UNCRC had been a ground of challenge to a set of regulations which the Secretary of State had put in place to reduce the overall welfare and benefits costs to the UK Government arising from housing benefits, which SG objected to as damaging to the interests of children who would need to be relocated with their families when they could no longer afford to live in the same home, with less housing benefit to rely on as a result of the new regulations.

5.7.17 It was argued in the SG case that the relevant UK regulations, created under the Welfare Reform Act 2012, had not taken into account a need for compliance with the UNCRC – but the UK Supreme Court held that the rule that the UK courts could not criticise the interpretation by the UK Government of an unincorporated treaty or convention was a strict one.

5.7.18 The next two chapters of this book turn to what can be described as different aspects of not just international law, but European 'supranational law', which take effect in the United Kingdom: the law of the European Union (outlined in Chapter 6) and European human rights law (described in Chapter 7).

Key Cases Checklist

Salomon v Commissioners of Customs and Excise (1967): Interpretations of statute law that are consistent with international law are preferred to promote consistency with international law (see 5.6.5)

Trendtex Trading Corporation v Central Bank of Nigeria (1977): Developing customary international law can have an effect on the use of precedent in UK courts (see 5.7.4)

Cases highlighting the role of International Law in the UK Constitution

An example of the non-effect of international law in a UK case: *R (SG) v Secretary of State for Work and Pensions* (2015): For an international legal instrument to have effect in the UK the instrument concerned must have been given effect by Parliament in an Enabling Act (see 5.7.11)

An example of the effect of an Enabling Act: EU Law is given effect in the United Kingdom through the European Communities Act 1972

6 European Union law

```
┌─────────────────────┐     ┌─────────────────────┐
│  Treaty on European │     │      Treaty on the  │
│    Union (TEU)      │     │   Functioning of the│
│                     │     │    European Union   │
│                     │     │        (TFEU)       │
└─────────────────────┘     └─────────────────────┘

        ┌─────────────────────────┐
        │   Source of European    │
        │        Union Law        │
        └─────────────────────────┘

            ┌─────────────────┐
            │  EU Regulations │
            └─────────────────┘

            ┌─────────────────┐
            │   EU Directives │
            └─────────────────┘

            ┌─────────────────────┐
            │ Case law of the Court of │
            │    Justice of the EU    │
            └─────────────────────┘
```

▶ 6.1 The origins and development of EU law

6.1.1 The European Economic Community came into being with the Treaty of Rome (1957), which established the foundations for a new level of European co-operation on issues of economic and social development. Initially there were six Member States. **The UK joined in 1973** and at present there are **28 Member States**.

6.1.2 As the European Union itself has noted, the 'EU was not always as big as it is today. When European countries started to cooperate economically in 1951, only Belgium, Germany, France, Italy, Luxembourg and The Netherlands participated ... The union reached its current size of **28 member countries** with the accession of Croatia on 1 July 2013.'

6.2 EU Treaties

6.2.1 The Single European Act, the Treaty on European Union (Maastricht Treaty, TEU), the Treaty of Amsterdam and the Treaty of Nice provided for further integration in relation to economic, monetary and social policy.

6.2.2 The Treaty Establishing a Constitution for Europe was signed in Rome in 2004. However, to come into effect, each Treaty requires ratification in each of the Member States under their constitutional requirements. In some States this requires a positive vote in a national referendum – the French and Dutch 'No' votes in 2005 suspended this treaty.

6.2.3 The revised Treaty of Lisbon (ToL) was signed in December 2007. The Treaty was due to be ratified by the summer of 2008 but a 'No' vote in the Irish referendum delayed this. In Ireland the referendum was held again in 2009 – a compromise reached between the Council and the Irish Government, part of which was agreement not to reduce the size of the Commission. The result was a 'Yes' vote.

6.2.4 The Treaty of Lisbon came into force on 1 December 2009. It established a single European Union. The EC Treaty was renamed the **Treaty on the Functioning of the European Union** (TFEU).

6.2.5 The primary changes introduced by the coming into force of the ToL were designed to:

- create a more democratic and transparent system, with an increased role for the European Parliament (see below);
- improve efficiency with increased use of qualified majority voting and creation of the post of President of the European Council (see below);
- enhance the protection of human rights, with introduction of the Charter of Fundamental Rights; and

- enhance the European Union on the global stage, with a new High Representative for the Union in Foreign Affairs and Security Policy and European External Action Service.

6.2.6 The objectives of the European Union include (Article 3 TEU):
- to promote peace, its values and the well-being of its people;
- to offer an area of freedom, security and justice without internal frontiers in which the free movement of persons is ensured;
- to establish an internal market working for the sustainable development of Europe, combating social exclusion and discrimination, promoting social justice, equality and solidarity;
- to establish an economic and monetary union; and
- to uphold and promote its values globally with emphasis on peace, sustainable development, mutual respect, free and fair trade, eradication of poverty and the protection of human rights.

6.3 Institutions within the European Union

The European Council

6.3.1 The European Council was created in 1974 with the intention of establishing an informal forum for discussion between Heads of State or Government. It rapidly developed into the body which fixed goals for the Union and set the course for achieving them, in all fields of EU activity, for example, introduction of the euro.

6.3.2 The European Council acquired some formal status in the 1992 TEU, which defined its function as providing the impetus and general political guidelines for the Union's development. On 1 December 2009, with the entry into force of the ToL, it became a formally recognised institution of the European Union.

6.3.3 It consists of the Heads of State or Government of the Member States, together with its President (a new post created by the ToL that is elected for a two-and-a-half-year term) and the President of the Commission.

The Council of the European Union

6.3.4 The Council is attended by a Government representative of each Member State, who must be 'at ministerial level' and authorised to commit the Government of that Member State (Article 263 TFEU).

6.3.5 The Council is the principal decision-making body of the Union, where on most matters a decision is made by qualified majority voting on a weighted basis. Each State has a set number of votes based on its population size.

The Commission

6.3.6 Commissioners are appointed for a five-year term. The Commission represents the interests of the Union and must act in its best interests. Consequently, the Commissioners must act independently of their national Government (Article 245 TFEU).

6.3.7 The Commission is the driving force behind Union policy and proposes policies and presents drafts of legislation to the Council.

6.3.8 The Commission is also the 'guardian' or 'watchdog' of the Treaties and ensures that the law is enforced and measures are implemented by the Member States. To this end it has the ability to enforce the law against a Member State in the European Court of Justice under Article 258 TFEU.

The European Parliament

6.3.9 Members of the European Parliament (MEPs) are elected by the citizens of the Member States every five years. The Parliament is therefore the only directly elected institution within the European Union.

6.3.10 Over the years, the Parliament has seen a greater role in the decision-making process, with the introduction of new methods of creating legislation, such as co-decision and co-operation.

6.3.11 The Parliament also has the authority to dismiss the Commission; has some control over the EU's budget; and appoints an Ombudsman to receive complaints of maladministration by Union institutions (this does not extend to national institutions).

6.4 The Court of Justice of the European Union

6.4.1 The function of the Court (often referred to as the European Court of Justice, or ECJ, as well as the 'CJEU') is to ensure that in the interpretation and application of the Treaty the law is observed.

6.4.2 It hears cases brought by the institutions, Member States and individuals through the preliminary reference procedure under Article 267 TFEU.

6.4.3 Article 267 provides that domestic courts must refer questions of EU law to the Court where the national court is the final court of appeal in the case at hand. A lower court may refer such a question for a preliminary ruling/reference.

6.4.4 A preliminary ruling should be sought where the court cannot otherwise reach a decision on the issue, which itself must be central to the case (*Bulmer v Bollinger* (1974));

6.4.5 The purpose of Article 267 is to ensure uniform interpretation of EU law across all Member States (*CILFIT S & I v Ministro della Sanita* (1982)), a necessary prerequisite for the supremacy of EU law over national law.

6.4.6 The Court is assisted by the General Court, created by the Single European Act 1986 (and previously known as the Court of First Instance). It currently has limited jurisdiction and hence does not hear preliminary references.

6.5 Different EU law instruments: Treaties, Regulations and Directives

Treaties

6.5.1 Treaties form the primary source of EU law. The Treaties are directly applicable in that they are automatically incorporated into national law. In the United Kingdom this is achieved under section 2(1) of the European Communities Act 1972, which states that all Treaties are 'without further enactment to be given legal effect or used in the United Kingdom'.

6.5.2 In addition, the Treaties may have **direct effect**. This means that they are capable of creating rights that an individual may enforce in their own national courts.

6.5.3 In order to have direct effect, a provision must be clear and precise, unconditional and non-dependent, according to the case of *Van Gend en Loos* (1963).

6.5.4 Direct effect can be of two types:

- **vertical** direct effect provides that the provision may be enforceable against the 'State'; whereas

- **horizontal** direct effect provides that the provision may be enforced against another private or legal person. Treaty articles are capable of both types of direct effect.

Regulations

6.5.5 Regulations are a form of secondary legislation. They are also binding without further enactment, known as **direct applicability**, which gives Regulations the effect of being 'binding in every respect' and automatically part of the legal system of every Member State (Article 288 TFEU). Member States must therefore enforce Regulations (*Commission v UK: Re Tachographs* (1979)).

6.5.6 Regulations, by their very nature, are capable of having both vertical and horizontal direct effect (*Leonesio v Ministero dell'Agricoltura* (1972)).

Directives

6.5.7 Directives are binding as to the result to be achieved by the implementing Member State. However, they require the State to choose the 'form and means' by which they will be implemented: Article 288 TFEU.

6.5.8 Directives are issued to Member States with a time limit for such implementation to occur.

6.5.9 If the Directive has not been implemented by the deadline, as long as it is clear and unconditional, it may acquire vertical direct effect, according to the case of *Marshall v Southampton and South West Hampshire Area Health Authority* (1986).

6.5.10 However, unimplemented Directives are not capable of having horizontal direct effect, which means that they cannot be relied on against a private body or an individual (*Marshall and Dori v Recreb Srl* (1994)). This is unless the unimplemented Directive, and the specific provision at issue, is tantamount to some manifestation of a general principle of EU law, stemming from an EU Treaty, Regulation etc. See *Mangold v Helm* (2005).

6.5.11 Where a Directive has not been implemented by its deadline, an individual who can satisfy the following multi-part test may be able to sue the State for damages suffered as a result of the non-implementation:

- the Directive provides rights for individuals;
- those rights are clearly defined in the Directive; and
- there is a direct causal link between the failure to implement and the damage suffered (*Francovich and Bonifaci v Italian Republic* (1991) and *Dillenkofer and Others v Federal Republic of Germany* (1996)).

6.5.12 If damage is caused by a Directive that has been incorrectly implemented, the breach must be 'manifest and serious' (*R v HM Treasury, ex parte BT plc* (1996)). This latter principle applies to all other breaches of Community law (*Brasserie du Pêcheur v Federal Republic of Germany*; joined with *R v Secretary of State for Transport, ex parte Factortame* (1996)).

6.6 Supremacy of EU law and the European Communities Act 1972

6.6.1 EU law was created as a supranational legal system, which will prevail in the event of a conflict with a Member State's national law. This principle, along with that of direct effect (see above), was created by the ECJ through its use of **teleological** or purposive interpretation.

6.6.2 In *Van Gend en Loos* (1963) the ECJ stated that the 'Member States have limited their sovereign rights ... and have created a body of law which binds both their nationals and themselves'.

6.6.3 In *Costa v ENEL* (1964) there was conflict between a number of Treaty provisions and a later Italian law, which, under Italian constitutional law, would take priority. The ECJ held that it was impossible for a Member State to 'give preference to a unilateral and subsequent measure' and that precedence therefore had to be given to EU law.

6.6.4 In *Internationale Handelsgesellschaft* (1970) the ECJ held that an EU Regulation took priority over the codified principles of the German constitution.

6.6.5 In *Simmenthal SpA (No. 2)* (1979) the Court stated that national courts are under a duty to give full effect to the provisions of EU law and, if necessary, should refuse to apply national laws that conflict with it.

6.6.6 By enactment of the European Communities Act 1972 (ECA 1972), the United Kingdom incorporated the legal system of the European Union into English law:

Section	Content	Explanation
s 2(1)	Rights, liberties, obligations, restrictions, remedies, procedures . . . under the Treaties are without further enactment to be used, followed, enforced . . . in the UK	Treaty provisions shall be directly applied in English law
s 2(2)	Her Majesty may by Order in Council, and designated Ministers or Departments may by regulations, make provisions for the purpose of implementing Community obligations or enabling any rights to be enjoyed	The Government has power to implement provisions to give effect to EU law
s 2(4)	. . . any enactment passed or to be passed . . . shall be construed and have effect subject to the foregoing provisions . . .	The principle is retrospective; Acts passed before the ECA 1972 must be read as intending to conform to EU obligations. The **prospective** effect of this provision has caused considerable legal debate (see below)
s 3(1)	. . . any question as to the meaning and effect . . . of the Treaties or other Community instrument . . . shall be treated as a question of law . . .	The interpretation of rights and obligations is to be decided under EU law, by the ECJ or according to its principles or decisions

6.6.7 The effect of the ECA 1972 on the principle of parliamentary supremacy has been the focus of considerable legal and political debate. The main difficulty stems from section 2(4) of the Act, which provides that **future** legislation will also have to be compatible with EU law.

6.6.8 The difficulty in achieving this derives from the fundamental constitutional principle of **implied repeal**, discussed in detail in Chapter 3. In brief, implied repeal is the mechanism protecting the principle that no one Parliament can bind a successor Parliament.

Consequently, no legislation can be entrenched and protected from future repeal, either expressly or by implication.

6.6.9 Reconciling the doctrine of parliamentary supremacy with that of EU law supremacy was therefore difficult. This is particularly so because the choice of national measure to bring effect to EU law was to introduce an ordinary statute – under the traditional doctrine of parliamentary supremacy, such an Act would itself be subject to implied repeal by any later legislation.

6.6.10 **A vital factor in the application of EU law in the United Kingdom is judicial interpretation of section 2(4) of the ECA 1972, and what is known as the 'rule of construction'.**

6.6.11 The courts have taken two approaches to interpreting the obligation under section 2(4) of the Act.

6.6.12 In *Macarthys v Smith* (1979) the Court of Appeal concluded that the effect of the ECA 1972 was to require the court to undertake a process of **interpretation**. Thus, the national court will interpret the national law in the light of EU law to ensure that it complies.

6.6.13 In *Garland v BREL* (1982) the House of Lords accepted this approach. Lord Diplock stated that English courts were well used to the concept of interpreting national law so that it conformed with Treaty obligations.

6.6.14 In *Webb v EMO Air Cargo (UK) Ltd* (1992) the House of Lords confirmed that the courts are obligated to construe a statute so it complies with EU law (in this case a Directive), regardless of whether the statute is passed before or after the EU law.

6.6.15 Examples of the use of this process of interpretation include:

- In *Litster v Forth Dry Dock Ltd* (1990) the House of Lords interpreted a UK regulation, contrary to its clear meaning, in order to ensure its compatibility with an EU Directive.
- In *Pickstone v Freemans plc* (1989) the House of Lords departed from a literal interpretation of a statute so it could ensure compatibility with EU law.

6.6.16 This approach is sometimes referred to as the **'rule of construction'** and it acknowledges the supremacy of EU law, albeit through a 'back door' route. Indeed, the ECJ has concluded that all national courts are under an obligation to interpret national law in the light of the wording and purpose of EU law: *Von Colson and Kamann* (1984) and *Marleasing* (1990).

6.6.17 The rule of construction approach, however, is not sufficient to secure the full supremacy of EU law. What is required is the ability of a court to set aside statutes that conflict with EU law. However, the traditional concept of parliamentary supremacy would make this impossible, because of implied repeal and the enrolled Act rule, which provides that no other body can question the authority of an Act of Parliament.

6.7 *Factortame* and the impact on parliamentary sovereignty

6.7.1 The most significant development on the issue of compatibility came about in the *Factortame* litigation, arising from the conditions placed on the registration of Spanish vessels to fish within UK waters via the Merchant Shipping Act 1988.

(a) The ECJ ruled in 1989 (Case 213/89) that the Merchant Shipping Act 1988 should be suspended since it was incompatible with a number of principles of EU law enshrined in the Treaty, such as the freedom of establishment and the prohibition of discrimination based on nationality. This was, however, ignored by the British Government.

(b) In *R v Secretary of State for Transport, ex parte Factortame (No. 2)* (1989) the House of Lords granted interim relief to the applicants and disapplied the offending provisions of the Merchant Shipping Act. This only occurred after the ECJ provided a preliminary reference. The reference focused on whether a constitutional principle had to be set aside to secure an individual's EU rights. The Court, following the judgment it had given in earlier cases (see above), stated that all principles of national law, regardless of status within the national system, had to be set aside in such circumstances. Lord Bridge concluded that 'it was the duty of a United Kingdom court, when delivering final judgment, to override any rule of national law to be found in conflict with any directly enforceable rule of Community law'.

(c) In *R v Secretary of State for Transport, ex parte Factortame (No. 5)* (1999) the House of Lords ruled that the United Kingdom was sufficiently in breach of the applicant's rights for the applicant to be awarded substantial damages. (See also *R v Secretary of State for Employment, ex parte EOC* (1995).)

6.7.2 In understanding UK constitutional and administrative law, it is vital to consider the impact of EU law compliance on the doctrine of parliamentary supremacy.

6.7.3 As a result of judicial interpretation of the obligation stemming from section 2(4) of the ECA 1972 (either by the rule of construction or by simply granting EU law primacy as in the *Factortame* litigation) we can conclude that there have been changes to the traditional doctrine of parliamentary supremacy.

6.7.4 In particular, the constitutional principle of implied repeal has been **suspended** in relation to both the ECA 1972 itself, meaning that it is to some extent **entrenched** from change, thus binding a successive Parliament, and to any legislation passed post 1972. In other words, all legislation passed since 1972 and in the future has to conform to EU law because of the obligation stemming from section 2(4). If a statute fails to conform to EU law, the doctrine of implied repeal will not apply and the Act will be overridden by the EU legal principle.

6.7.5 This is now recognised by the courts, witnessed particularly in the judgment of *Thoburn v Sunderland City Council* (2002), by referring to the ECA 1972 as one of a range of '**constitutional statutes**'. According to the Court of Appeal in this case such statutes cannot be subject to implied repeal.

6.7.6 However, it should be noted that this limitation on Parliament is one that it has placed on itself by virtue of passing the ECA 1972. Consequently, the courts have concluded that should Parliament ever **expressly** state that the provisions of a statute are to stand, regardless of their compatibility with EU law, the courts will be bound to apply such a statute. This was the conclusion reached by both the Court of Appeal and the House of Lords in the cases of *Macarthys* and *Garland* (above).

6.7.7 To date, the above scenario has not occurred. It could be suggested that the political consequences of doing so would render the likelihood of such an event happening extremely unlikely.

6.8 The EU Charter on Fundamental Rights and overlaps with European human rights law

6.8.1 The EU Charter on Fundamental Rights (CFREU) has recently been acknowledged by the Ministry of Justice, in 2014, as taking effect in domestic UK litigation. This means that the rights outlined in the CFREU, which are similar (but not identical) in their drafting to the articled rights in the European Convention on Human Rights (ECHR), can also now strengthen the basis of legal claims before UK courts: but only where there is a matter of EU law in question. In *Benkharbouche v Embassy of Sudan* (2015) the Court of Appeal noted that claims before the UK courts drawing on the Charter:

> '... must be claims which fall "within the scope of" EU law. As to this, Article 51 EU Charter confirms that the EU Charter is addressed to the EU institutions and like bodies and that it does not extend the field of application of the EU Treaties. Article 52(5) of the EU Charter states that the EU Charter only applies to these entities when they are implementing Union law, in the exercise of their respective powers. The EU Charter does not, therefore, apply to claims based [solely] on national law.'

6.8.2 To date, there have only been a handful of prominent UK cases which have been determined using the CFREU in this manner.

6.8.3 In *AB v Secretary of State for the Home Department* (2013), where the claimant (unsuccessfully) drew on the CFREU, Mostyn J noted that the ECJ in *NS v Secretary of State for the Home Department* (2011) had determined that Article 1 of the Seventh Protocol to the Lisbon Treaty did not exempt domestic UK courts from a duty to apply the broad rights found in the Charter itself. As such, this decision of the ECJ makes the rights in the CFREU justiciable in the UK courts, in addition to those in the ECHR (through the Human Rights Act 1998), despite what (as Mostyn J admitted) was commonly and previously thought by the UK Government, which had tried to negotiate the opt-out in the Seventh Protocol.

6.8.4 In *Vidal-Hall v Google Inc.* (2015), the Court of Appeal determined that Google had breached EU data protection law, under the EU Data Protection Directive from 1995, which is adopted in UK law as the Data Protection Act 1998. However, section 13 of the Data Protection Act 1998 contained provisions which stipulated that damages could not normally be awarded as a remedy for breach of UK data protection law, unless the breach fell under certain headings. Those headings did not include the kind of breach caused by Google (which had been the unlawful and secret use of internet search data that identified the browsing habits of Apple Safari browser software users). Articles 7 and 8 of the CFREU together protect the personal data and the right to a private life of individuals. However, the CFREU, in Article 47, also stipulates that should any right in the CFREU or rule of EU law be breached, then domestic courts must afford successful claimants an effective remedy. In this case, that effective remedy was pecuniary (that is, monetary) damages in compensation. So the Court of Appeal held, as a principle of EU law, under the framework of both the ECA 1972 and now the CFREU, that the limiting provisions of the Data Protection Act 1998 should be disapplied.

6.8.5 In *Benkharbouche v Embassy of Sudan* (2015) the Court of Appeal again determined that provisions of an Act of Parliament should be disapplied. In this case, employees working at the Libyan and Sudanese embassies in the United Kingdom claimed that they were treated in breach of employment law over their hours of work. Their employers asserted that they could not make a claim under UK employment law, because of the effects of the State Immunity Act 1978. But the relevant provisions of this statute which prevented the claimants seeking an effective remedy in UK employment law clashed with relevant EU law, and could again be deemed to a breach of the right to an effective remedy found in Article 47 CFREU.

6.8.6 It is important to note, further, that while the rights protected by the CFREU do not, in essence, greatly extend beyond those rights protected by the ECHR, and they are only invoked as a means of ensuring compliance with applicable EU law, the manner in which the courts are empowered to treat Acts of Parliament through the framework of the ECA 1972 is very different to the way that the Human Rights Act 1998 allows the courts of the UK to operate.

6.8.7 While the UK courts may make a declaration of incompatibility in relation to the provisions of an Act of Parliament if that Act is not in compliance with the ECHR (under section 4 of the Human Rights Act 1998), they cannot disapply the effect of the statutory provisions themselves (see Chapter 7). Parliament can choose to keep the offending provisions in place, and may even do so after the European Court of Human Rights has ruled the statute in breach of the ECHR.

6.8.8 But an Act of Parliament which is not in compliance with an aspect of EU law (including because of a breach of an Article of the CFREU) can be disapplied in full or in part if its language cannot be interpreted to give effect to that principle of EU law concerned – with EU law taking precedence under the ECA 1972, the chief lesson of the *Factortame* case (see above).

6.9 An ongoing relationship between the United Kingdom and the European Union?

6.9.1 In his 2015 Queen's Speech announcements to Parliament, following a success for the Conservative Party in the May 2015 General Election, Prime Minister David Cameron pledged to put an EU Referendum Bill before the House of Commons as soon as possible.

6.9.2 This EU Referendum Bill (2015) would, if enacted, allow for an EU membership referendum in 2016, as is expected at the time of writing in late May.

6.9.3 This referendum could see enormous constitutional upheaval follow as a matter of course, if the outcome were a majority of the eligible UK electorate in the referendum indicating they would rather the United Kingdom withdraw from the European Union. Such a result would give political weight to any draft legislation which would be placed before Parliament – leading, potentially, to repeal or drastic reform of the ECA 1972 and significantly if not completely changing the way that EU law has an effect on the UK legal system and constitution.

6.9.4 It is the current position of the Conservative Government in the summer of the 2015 that before this legislative programme of reform was entered into, and before a referendum took place in 2016, there would be efforts at reforming the way that the European Union is shaped along particular policy lines.

6.9.5 Two contentious areas that the Conservative Government will be seeking to renegotiate with the institutions of the European Union have been reported in late May 2015.

6.9.6 Firstly, the Conservative Government has in mind reforms to the aims of the European Union to develop a 'single currency' for the European Union – meaning that the United Kingdom would aim for explicit recognition that the pound (UK sterling) is a permanent and distinct currency within the European Union.

6.9.7 Secondly, that the fundamental right to freedom of movement across the European Union be redefined in such a way as to allow the United Kingdom to control immigration rates from other EU Member States, with regard to the settlement of their citizens in the United Kingdom.

Key Cases Checklist

Van Gend en Loos (1963): Treaties may have direct effect – capable of creating rights that an individual may enforce in their own national courts, though a provision must be clear and precise, unconditional and non-dependent.

Commission v UK: Re Tachographs (1979): Member States must enforce the provisions of Regulations due to their 'direct applicability'. The exact effect of Directives depends on the status of their implementation.

(see 6.5.5)

Van Gend en Loos (1963): the ECJ stated that the 'Member States have limited their sovereign rights . . . and have created a body of law which binds both their nationals and themselves'.

The Operation of EU Law

Cases outlining the operation of EU Law (in the UK)

Costa v ENEL (1964): the ECJ held that it was impossible for a Member State to 'give preference to a unilateral and subsequent measure' and that precedence therefore had to be given to EU law.

EU Law in the UK

Marleasing (1990): the ECJ concluded that all national courts are under an obligation to interpret national law in the light of the wording and purpose of EU law.

Simmenthal SpA (No. 2) (1979): the Court stated that national courts are under a duty to give full effect to the provisions of EU law and, if necessary, should refuse to apply national laws that conflict with it.

R v Secretary of State for Transport, ex parte Factortame (No. 2) (1989): the House of Lords concluded that 'it was the duty of a United Kingdom court, when delivering final judgment, to override any rule of national law to be found in conflict with any directly enforceable rule of Community law'. As such we can conclude that there have been changes to the traditional doctrine of parliamentary supremacy.

6.5.3 and 6.6.2

Van Gend en Loos v Nederlandse Tariefcommissie (Case 26/62) [1963] ECR 1

(ECJ)

Key Facts

Van Gend en Loos imported products from Germany into the Netherlands and was charged an increased customs duty contrary to Article 12 of the EEC Treaty (now Article 25 EC).

Key Law

The European Economic Community (now the European Union) was a *sui generis* (unique) legal order and Member States had limited their sovereign rights when joining, hence EU law takes precedence over national law.

Key Judgments

ECJ preliminary reference

'. . . the Community constitutes a new legal order . . . for the benefit of which the states have limited their sovereign rights.'

'Community law . . . not only imposes obligations on individuals but is also intended to confer on them rights which become part of their legal heritage.'

Key Comment

The court used teleological (or purposive) interpretation to come to the conclusion that while the Treaty did not expressly state that EC law had supremacy, it was required in order for the Treaty to meet its objectives and purpose.

Also, there are two types of direct effect: vertical and horizontal. Vertical direct effect means that the measure is capable of being enforced against the State; horizontal direct effect means that the measure can be enforced against another natural or legal person. This case is an example of a Treaty provision having vertical direct effect.

6.6.3 Costa v ENEL (Case 6/64) [1964] ECR 1125 [ECJ]

Key Facts

Costa contended that Italian law breached the Treaty.

Key Law

The Member States had limited their sovereign rights, were bound by Community law and Community law took precedence over conflicting national law.

Key Judgment

ECJ preliminary reference
'. . . the law stemming from the Treaty . . . could not, because of its special and original nature, be overridden by domestic legal provisions . . . without being deprived of its character as Community law and without the legal basis of the Community itself being called into question.'

Key Link

In *Amministrazione delle Finanze dello Stato v Simmenthal SpA* (Case 106/77) [1978] ECR 629 the Court of Justice stated that national courts are bound to apply Community law in its entirety and set aside any conflicting provision of national law regardless of whether it is prior or subsequent to Community law.

6.6.16 Marleasing SA v La Commercial Internacional de Alimentacion SA (Case 106/89) [1992] 1 CMLR 305 [ECJ]

Key Law

In *Marleasing*, the ECJ ruled that national courts must, as far as possible, interpret national law so that it is compatible with any relevant Directive, regardless of whether the national provisions were adopted prior to or after the Directive.

7 European human rights law and the Human Rights Act 1998

European Court of Human Rights upholds the ECHR

Derogation from some Articles permissible

Engaging rights subject to the **proportionality** test

Rights articulated by **Articles of the ECHR**

European Convention on Human Rights (1950)

States afforded a **margin of appreciation**

European Human Rights Law and the Human Rights Act 1998

S.2 HRA 1998 sees UK courts take ECtHR case law into account

S.3 HRA 1998 sees UK courts give effect to Convention rights

S.4 HRA 1998 permits the UK court to make declarations of incompatibility

S.6 HRA 1998 requires public bodies to uphold Convention rights

S.7 HRA 1998 requires protection of 'victims' of rights infringements

S.8 HRA 1998 requires remedies for rights infringements

7.1 The European Convention on Human Rights and Fundamental Freedoms

7.1.1 The Council of Europe was founded in 1949 with the goal of post-war harmonisation across Europe. The Council accepted the UN Declaration of Human Rights 1948 as a model for a European charter and the European Convention on Human Rights and Fundamental Freedoms (ECHR) came into force on 3 December 1953.

7.1.2 The Convention established a European Court of Human Rights (ECtHR), which sits at Strasbourg. It may convene as a committee of three judges, as a chamber of seven, or in Grand Chamber of all 17 judges.

7.2 Particular rights from the ECHR and its Protocols

7.2.1 Applications to the Court may be brought by States, an individual, groups of individuals and non-governmental organisations. The applicant must be personally affected by the issue.

7.2.2 Under Article 35 of the Convention, an applicant cannot proceed to the ECtHR until all domestic remedies available are first exhausted. An application must be made within six months of the final decision of the highest court having jurisdiction.

Article	Right
2	**Right to life** Allowable exceptions excuse unintentional death as result of violent situations, e.g. to quell riots, acting in self-defence but force used must be 'no more than absolutely necessary'
3	**Freedom from torture, inhuman and degrading treatment**
4	**Freedom from slavery and forced labour** Does not include compulsory labour as part of lawful detention
5	**Right to liberty and security of person** Applies except in accordance with lawful arrest or detention

6	**Right to a fair trial before an independent and impartial tribunal** Protects the presumption of innocence Provides for minimum rights to receive information and prepare defence Special circumstances can be justified where publicity would prejudice national security or the interests of justice, e.g. protection of juveniles
7	**Prohibition of retrospective criminal law**
8	**Respect for private and family life** Interference with this right by the State is permitted only if necessary in a democratic society including in the interests of: National security; Public safety; Economic well-being of the State; Prevention of disorder and crime; Protection of health and morals; and Protection of the rights and freedoms of others
9	**Freedom of thought, conscience and religion** Interference with this right by the State is permitted only if necessary in a democratic society including in the interests of: Public safety; Public health and morals; and Protection of the rights and freedoms of others The protection of the right to privacy is limited
10	**Freedom of expression** Interference with this right by the State is permitted only if necessary in a democratic society including in the interests of: National security; Territorial integrity; Public safety; Prevention of disorder and crime; Protection of health and morals; Protection of the reputation or rights of others; and Prevention of the disclosure of information received in confidence or to maintain the authority and impartiality of the judiciary
11	**Freedom of assembly and association** Interference with this right by the State is permitted only if necessary in a democratic society including in the interests of: National security; Public safety; Prevention of disorder and crime; Protection of health and morals; and Protection of the rights and freedoms of others
12	**Freedom to marry and found a family** Rights must be exercised according to the State's laws on marriage
13	**Right to an effective remedy**

7.2.3 Article 14 does not provide a substantive right but that the rights and freedoms of the Convention are to be enjoyed by all, regardless of race, age, sex, language or other classification. A case cannot be founded purely upon Article 14; discrimination on the application of a substantive right must be shown.

7.2.4 In addition to the Convention rights, there are **Protocols** that:
- alter the machinery of the Convention; and
- add rights to the Convention, which are optional and only come into force between ratifying States.

Protocol	Coverage
First	Article 1 – right to peaceful enjoyment of possessions Article 2 – education Article 3 – holding of regular and free elections
Fourth	Article 1 – prohibits imprisonment for breach of contract Article 2 – right to freely move Article 3 – prohibits expulsion of nationals and provides for right to enter the country of nationality Article 4 – prohibits collective expulsion of non-nationals UK signed but has not ratified this Protocol
Sixth	Requires parties to restrict the application of the death penalty to times of war or 'imminent threat of war'
Seventh	Article 1 – right to fair procedures for lawfully resident foreigners facing expulsion Article 2 – right to appeal in criminal matters Article 3 – compensation for victims of miscarriages of justice Article 4 – prohibits the re-trial of anyone who has already been finally acquitted or convicted of a particular offence Article 5 – equality between spouses UK has not signed this Protocol
Twelfth	Applies the indefinite grounds of prohibited discrimination to the exercise of any legal right and to the actions and obligations of public authorities UK has not signed this Protocol
Thirteenth	Total abolition of the death penalty
Fourteenth	Permits the filtering of cases that have less chance of succeeding along with those that are similar to cases brought previously against the same State Case will not be considered admissible where an applicant has not suffered a 'significant disadvantage' Came into force on 1 June 2010

7.2.5 Some illustrative examples of ECtHR decisions on the scope of the substantive rights under the Convention in the context of the United Kingdom include:

Article 2

Case	Decision
Paton v UK (1980)	Right to life begins at birth
McCann v UK (1996)	Inappropriate control and organisation over a covert military operation resulted in the 'more than was absolutely necessary' deaths of suspected terrorists
Pretty v UK (2001)	There is no right to assisted suicide
Evans v UK (2007)	The right to refuse an ex-partner the ability to use embryos does not violate Article 2 (or Article 8, see below)

Article 3

Case	Decision
East African Asians v UK (1983)	Immigration controls based on racial discrimination amount to degrading treatment
D v UK (1997)	Deportation of an individual to a country lacking suitable health care that could result in their death violates the Article
Chahal v UK (1996)	A person cannot be forcibly returned to their country of origin when they are likely to face torture, inhuman or degrading treatment
A v Secretary of State for the Home Department (No. 2) (2005)	Evidence obtained by torture in another country cannot be used in the courts

Article 5

Case	Decision
Johnson v UK (1996)	Failure to release a mentally ill patient because of lack of suitable accommodation breaches the Article
T and V v UK (1999)	Setting sentence periods without an opportunity for the lawfulness of the continued detention to be judicially reviewed breaches the Article
Murray v UK (1994)	The State must have 'reasonable suspicion' of an offence to justify detention
Caballero v UK (2000)	Automatic denial of bail for some offences breaches the Article
O'Hara v UK (2001)	Arrested persons must be brought before a judge in a prompt and timely manner

Article 6

Case	Decision
Osman v UK (1998)	Striking out a negligence claim against the police on the grounds of public policy breached the Article
T and V v UK (1999)	Trying juveniles in an adult court violates the Article
Steel and Morris v UK (2005)	Denial of legal aid to defend a libel action brought by McDonald's breached the Article

Article 8

Case	Decision
Dudgeon v UK (1982)	Prohibition under statute of homosexual acts between male adults in Northern Ireland amounted to a breach of the Article
Malone v UK (1984)	Tapping of a private telephone without a warrant breached the Article
McMichael v UK (1995)	If interference with family life is justified in the interests of a child, the family member's rights must still be protected
Lustig-Prean and Beckett v UK (2000)	Banning homosexuals in the armed forces breached the Article
Gillan and Quinton v UK (2010)	Section 44 of the Terrorism Act 2000 was not in accordance with the law because the power to stop and search dispensed with the condition of reasonable suspicion

Article 10

Case	Decision
Sunday Times v UK (1979)	The common law on contempt of court was too imprecise and unsatisfactory to justify the granting of an injunction and this was a breach of the Article. The UK changed the law by passing the Contempt of Court Act 1981
The Observer and The Guardian v UK (1991)	The continuation of injunctions against the publication of *Spycatcher* had breached the Article because they were no longer justifiable since the information was no longer confidential
Goodwin v UK (1996)	A court order under the Contempt of Court Act 1981 to disclose a journalist's sources violated the Article

7.3 Derogation

7.3.1 Derogation by a State is not permitted in respect of all Convention rights. Only in specific circumstances (e.g. a state of emergency) can a State inform the Council of Europe that it will take steps that do not conform to its obligations. For example, in 2002 the United Kingdom entered a new derogation in respect of Article 5 in order to legitimise detention of non-nationals pending determination of their asylum status.

7.3.2 Reservations may be entered only before ratification. Under a reservation, the State will accept the obligations of a particular Convention right, subject to the application of its domestic legislation then in force.

7.4 The proportionality principle

7.4.1 The Convention itself makes reference to the need to uphold rights whilst ensuring that the community, the State and individuals are not thereby damaged.

7.4.2 The exercise of a right must therefore be proportionate to the effects of such exercise on others. Similarly, the response of the State to an administrative or legislative necessity must be proportionate to the desired outcome.

7.4.3 The application of the proportionality principle as a ground of judicial review is addressed in more detail in Chapter 16, Human rights grounds for judicial review, along with other considerations of the different steps in making human rights-based claims for judicial review.

7.5 The margin of appreciation

7.5.1 While a State has positive obligations under the Convention, the Council and the Court recognise that there should be a degree of discretion permitted, on the basis that each State is uniquely placed to gauge the necessity for limitations on Convention rights within its territory. This degree of discretion over engaging rights is known as the 'margin of appreciation' each State is afforded when the Court considers potential violations of the Convention by that State.

7.5.2   If such measures are challenged, the Court will require the State to justify its actions and demonstrate their reasonableness.

7.6 The UK constitution and the impact of the Human Rights Act 1998

7.6.1   The United Kingdom was an early signatory to the Convention and accepted the right to individual petition in 1965, but the UK courts were not bound to apply the Convention directly until incorporated into UK law by statute.

7.6.2   However, where there were two interpretations of national law, one in conformity with the Convention and one not, the courts would presume it was Parliament's intention to legislate in conformity: *R v Secretary of State for the Home Department, ex parte Brind* (1991).

7.6.3   The duty to interpret national law in light of the obligations under the Convention related to both legislation (*Waddington v Miah* (1974)) and the common law (*Derbyshire County Council v Times Newspapers Ltd* (1993)).

7.7 Section 2 of the Human Rights Act 1998: UK courts drawing on the case law of the ECtHR

7.7.1   The Human Rights Act 1998 came into effect on 2 October 2000.

7.7.2   The Act incorporates the ECHR into domestic law, making it directly enforceable in the UK courts. The Act gives 'further effect' to the Convention rights, which appear in Schedule 1. The Act does not give effect to Article 13 of the Convention (the right to an effective remedy).

7.7.3   Section 1 provides that Convention rights are to have effect subject to any reservation or derogation in force.

7.7.4   Importantly, Section 2 of the Human Rights Act 1998 requires UK courts to 'take into account' the case law of the ECtHR when making their own judgments as to alleged breaches of the ECHR by UK public bodies. For discussion of the scope of this issue, see Chapters 11, 12, and 16.

7.7.5   Using some of the rights provided for by the ECHR, the following are illustrative cases heard in UK courts under the Human Rights Act 1998.

Article 2 – right to life

Case	Decision
R (Pretty) v DPP (2001)	Article 2 does not extend to the right to die
NHS Trust A v M (2001)	The lawful withdrawal of treatment of a patient in a permanent vegetative state does not breach Article 2
R (Gentle) v PM (2008)	Article 2 does not impose on the UK Government an obligation to ensure the legality of its action prior to sending troops (or to carry out a public inquiry into their deaths)

Article 3 – freedom from torture, inhuman and degrading treatment and punishment

Case	Decision
R (Limbuela) v Secretary of State for the Home Department (2005)	Article 3 may be breached if the State fails to provide the barest life necessities for asylum seekers
R (Ullah) v Special Adjudicator (2004)	Article 3 would be breached by a decision to expel an individual to a country where they would be likely to face torture, inhuman or degrading treatment
R (N) v Secretary of State for the Home Department (2005)	Expelling a seriously ill immigrant to their country of origin, where her life expectancy could potentially be reduced, was not a violation of Article 3

Article 5 – right to liberty

Case	Decision
R (H) v Mental Health Review Tribunal (2001)	Section 72 of the Mental Health Act 1983 reversing the burden of proof on a detained applicant to prove they were no longer suffering from a mental disorder was a breach of Article 5. A declaration of incompatibility was issued
Pennington v Parole Board (2009)	Delay on setting a parole hearing breached Article 5(4)

Article 6 – right to a fair trial	
Case	Decision
R (Anderson) v Secretary of State for the Home Department (2002)	The Home Secretary was not independent under Article 6 in terms of reviewing the detention of prisoners serving life sentences. A declaration of incompatibility was issued
R (KB) v Mental Health Tribunal (2003)	Patients' hearings had not been sufficiently speedy and they were therefore entitled to damages

Article 8 – right to respect for private and family life	
Case	Decision
R (Daly) v Secretary of State for the Home Department (2001)	Home Office policy of requiring prisoners to leave their cells while officers conducted searches, including legal correspondence, was a breach of Article 8
Douglas v Hello! Ltd (2001)	Article 8 extended to the prevention of publication of materials in breach of confidence, although there was no duty of confidentiality in the case at hand
Campbell v Mirror Group Newspapers (2004)	The right to privacy had been intruded upon by a newspaper, exacerbated by the publication of photographs, and damages were awarded
Mosley v News Group Newspapers (2008)	Mosley was awarded damages after it was held that a newspaper exposé of his involvement in a sado-masochistic sex act was not in the public interest and therefore a breach of Article 8

Article 9 – freedom of religion and conscience	
Case	Decision
R (Begum) v Denbigh High School (2006)	School policy on permissible uniforms prohibiting the jilbab did not violate Article 9

7.7.6 A number of more recent cases involving the application of ECHR rights in litigation in the domestic (UK) courts are discussed in Chapter 16, which deals with human rights-based grounds of judicial review.

7.8 Section 3 of the Human Rights Act 1998: interpreting statute in the light of the ECHR

7.8.1 Section 3 states that 'so far as it is possible to do so primary legislation and subordinate legislation must be read and given effect in a way which is compatible with the Convention rights'.

7.8.2 The courts have held that this requires **more** than ordinary statutory interpretation. If considered necessary the courts will read words into a statute to ensure compliance with the Convention: *R v A (Complainant's Sexual History)* (2002).

7.8.3 In *Ghaidan v Godin-Mendoza* (2004) the House of Lords held that even if the ordinary meaning of a statute is clear, a court may distort its language or read in additional words in order to achieve a meaning that is compatible with the Convention.

7.8.4 The courts are therefore required to take a **purposive** approach to the interpretation of legislation.

7.8.5 However, there should, because of the doctrine of parliamentary supremacy, be a distinction between legitimate interpretation and effectively undertaking the redrafting of legislation. This has been recognised by the courts:

- in *W and B (Children: Care Plan)* (2002) the House of Lords concluded that the Court of Appeal's interpretation of the Children Act 1989 could not be upheld; and
- in *R v DPP, ex parte Kebeline and Others* (1999) Lord Hope referred to areas where the judiciary must defer to the 'considered opinion of the elected body' (see also *R v Lambert, Ali and Jordan* (2001)).

7.9 Sections 4 and 10 of the Human Rights Act 1998: Declarations of Incompatibility and fast-track statutory reform

7.9.1 The Human Rights Act 1998, however, respects the doctrine of the supremacy of Parliament in that if there is a breach of the Convention the courts are not able to declare the Act invalid.

7.9.2 Instead the High Court and superior courts may make a '**declaration of incompatibility**' under section 4.

7.9.3 However, the power to issue a declaration of incompatibility only exists if there is a duty of interpretation under section 3 and that process has first been attempted.

7.9.4 A declaration of incompatibility cannot therefore be issued when the facts of a case took place before the Human Rights Act 1998 came into force: *Wilson v First County Trust (No. 2)* (2003). The Act consequently has no retrospective effect.

7.9.5 Section 4(6) provides that a declaration of incompatibility is not binding on the parties and does not affect the validity of legislation. The Government therefore has to decide whether it wishes to present to Parliament amendment or repeal of the offending legislation.

7.9.6 For example, in *R (Anderson) v Secretary of State for the Home Department* (2002) the House of Lords made a declaration of incompatibility in relation to the ability of the Home Secretary to decide the minimum period of incarceration for a murderer. It was concluded that this was a breach of Article 6 of the Convention – it did not provide for a fair trial because such a decision was not being made by an independent and impartial tribunal but by a politician. The law was changed by the introduction of the Criminal Justice Act 2003.

7.9.7 A higher court may overturn a declaration of incompatibility made by a lower court on the grounds that there has in fact been no breach of the Convention. This occurred in, for example, *R (Alconbury Developments Ltd) v Secretary of State for the Environment, Transport and the Regions* (2001) and *Wilson v First County Trust (No. 2)* (2003).

7.9.8 Where a declaration of incompatibility has been made, or a violation found, section 10 of the Human Rights Act 1998 provides for a fast-track procedure to amend legislation.

7.9.9 Amendment will be made by way of statutory instrument – the relevant Minister may lay before Parliament either a draft or final order to remove the incompatibility where there are, in the Minister's opinion, compelling reasons for so doing.

7.9.10 Declarations of incompatibility have not been common and even when made it has not been unusual for a higher court to overturn them.

7.9.11 Originally it appeared that the courts were prepared to create what Lord Steyn called a 'new legal landscape'. In *R v Lambert* (2001) Lord Slynn commented that the Human Rights Act 1998 had to be given its 'full import' and that 'long entrenched ideas may have to be put aside'.

7.9.12 The reasoning for such an approach can be seen in *R v DPP, ex parte Kebeline* (1999) where Lord Hope concluded that in certain areas the judiciary should defer 'on democratic grounds, to the considered opinion of the elected body or person whose act or decision is said to be incompatible with the Convention'. A similar approach can be seen in the decision of the House of Lords in *Bellinger v Bellinger* (2003).

7.9.13 The courts appear to prefer to exercise the interpretative power under section 3 of the Act rather than the power to issue a declaration of incompatibility under section 4. In *Ghaidan v Godin-Mendoza* (2004) Lord Steyn referred to section 3 as the 'lynch-pin' and section 4 as a 'measure of last resort'.

7.9.14 This is a reflection of the unwillingness of the courts to come into direct conflict with the executive.

7.10 Section 6 of the Human Rights Act 1998: duties to be upheld by public bodies under the ECHR

7.10.1 Section 6 of the Act states that it is unlawful for **public authorities/bodies** to act in a way that is incompatible with Convention rights (sometimes described as **vertical effect**). The following should be noted:

- Section 6(3)(b) states that a public authority includes any other person 'whose functions are functions of a public nature'. It does not extend to Parliament acting in its legislative capacity.

- Section 6(1) defines courts and tribunals as being public authorities/bodies, meaning their judgments must comply with human rights. Therefore judges have a duty to act in compatibility with the ECHR, even in private actions, and consequently the Act can also be described as having **horizontal effect**. (See e.g. the cases on freedom of expression and privacy such as *Venables v News Group Newspapers* (2001), *Douglas v Hello! Ltd* (2001), *Campbell v Mirror Group Newspapers* (2002), and *Mosley v News Group Newspapers* (2008).)

7.10.2 To determine whether a body is a public authority, reference can be made to the following factors (*Aston Cantlow and Wilmcote with Billesley Parochial Church Council v Wallbank* (2003)):

- whether the body is publicly funded;
- whether the body is exercising statutory powers;

- whether the body is taking the place of central Government or local authorities; and
- whether the body is providing a public service.

7.10.3 Examples of cases examining whether a body is a public authority include the following:
- In *Aston Cantlow* (above) the Church Council was held not to be a public authority.
- In *Poplar Housing and Regeneration Community Association Ltd v Donoghue* (2001) a housing association was held to be a public authority because it was exercising functions similar to a local authority.
- In *YL v Birmingham City Council and Others* (2007) the House of Lords decided that when providing accommodation and care under a local authority contract, independent sector care providers were not carrying out a public function and were therefore not public authorities for the purposes of the Human Rights Act 1998.

7.10.4 The position in *YL* was altered with the passing of the Health and Social Care Act 2008, section 145 of which ensures that the Human Rights Act does now apply to people receiving publicly arranged care in an independent sector care home.

7.11 Section 7 of the Human Rights Act 1998: cases brought by the 'victims' of rights infringements under the ECHR

7.11.1 Section 7 provides that an individual may make an application only if they are the 'victim' of the alleged violation or, if not the immediate victim, are still affected.

7.11.2 Interest groups do not have standing to make an application unless they can establish that their members are or will be potential victims. However, interest groups that have expertise in the matter may be permitted by the court to make submissions.

7.11.3 The time limit for applications is one year from the alleged violation (section 7(5)) or within such period as the court considers equitable in the circumstances.

7.12 Section 8 of the Human Rights Act 1998: remedies for the unlawful interference with rights under the ECHR

7.12.1 Section 8 provides for the court to award a remedy or 'make such order within its jurisdiction as it considers just and appropriate'.

7.12.2 Damages are not awarded unless the court is satisfied they are necessary. In *Anufrijeva v London Borough of Southwark* (2003) the Court of Appeal concluded that damages should be considered a last resort under the Act. The scale of damages for any maladministration has to be modest.

7.12.3 Section 12(4) provides that in the case of an injunction application, the court is to have particular regard to the right of freedom of expression.

7.13 Possible reform of the UK human rights framework

7.13.1 The summer of 2015 promised much potential upheaval for the system of human rights law in the United Kingdom.

7.13.2 The UK Supreme Court has recently begun to take the opportunity to comment, where relevant, on the extent that principles of judicial review previously thought to be dependent on the deployment of EU law or European human rights law, such as the proportionality principle, should actually be seen as fundamental principles of the common law instead. (See Chapters 11 and 14 for more details, including discussion of relevant cases such as *Kennedy v Charity Commission* (2014) and *R (Pham) v Secretary of State for the Home Department* (2015).)

7.13.3 This is thought by some legal scholars to be because of the ambitions of a Conservative majority Government, which have now been realised, following the General Election of May 2015.

7.13.4 Under the Coalition Government of 2010–2015, a Commission on a Bill of Rights had been split over the extent to which it was possible that UK human rights law may require reform; in the particular manner in which it incorporates the ECHR into domestic UK law through the distinct mechanisms of the Human Rights Act 1998. The cross-Party experts that made up the Commission on a Bill of Rights also disagreed, across a series of contradictory reports, on the manner in which human rights law reform might be carried out, and how this might have an impact on the UK constitution.

7.13.5 The main claims by (mainly) Conservative opponents of the Human Rights Act 1998 framework is that the Act needs to be reformed because it:
- allows for, and even demands, the steady growth of influence of the case law of the ECtHR over the common law, that is, the case law decided by the UK courts themselves;
- waters down the sovereignty of Parliament since it allows UK judges adapt the statutory language of an Act of Parliament better to give effect to ECHR rights, distorting and undermining Government policy, or so it is claimed; and
- it further allows UK judges to make declarations that an Act of Parliament is incompatible with the ECHR, again threatening parliamentary sovereignty, and placing undue pressure on the Government of the day to reform issues in a way that might not reflect overall public opinion

7.13.6 This public opinion might be, overall, particularly offended by the idea of non-UK judges having the 'last word' on a particular matter if an issue is deemed, in the ECtHR, to fall outside of the particular margin of appreciation on that issue afforded to the Government of a Council of Europe member.

7.13.7 Cases involving prisoners in the United Kingdom challenging the prohibition of them voting in any elections, such as *Hirst v UK (No. 2)* (2005) and more recent ones (see Chapter 16), have become a particular exemplary case in this manner.

7.13.8 Some writers such as Richard Cornes have noted that opponents of possible reforms, that is, those who would like the Human Rights Act framework to remain as it is, have linked the issue of human rights law reform to that of the UK relationship to the law and institutions of the European Union.

7.13.9 But it should be noted, as Cornes has observed, that Conservative proposals for a 'British Bill of Rights' of some sort, aimed at reforming the concerns outlined above, would not go so far as to sever the formal link between the United Kingdom and the Council of Europe, nor would it preclude the ECtHR from hearing cases brought by those challenging UK law and Government policy.

7.13.10 However, there remain real concerns over the extent to which a move to a more 'municipal', that is, distinctly 'British', concept of 'fundamental rights', rather than universal human rights, might leave some of the most vulnerable people in society (prisoners, or immigrants) less well protected by the newer system of UK law seeking compliance with the ECHR.

7.13.11 The beauty of the current framework is that through section 6 of the Human Rights Act 1998, the burden of upholding the rights of individuals under the ECHR falls on UK public bodies, regardless of their role or actions, whether in the United Kingdom or overseas, and whether the individual whose rights must be protected is a UK citizen or a citizen of another State.

7.13.12 Sadly, as Alice Donald has written, already 'public authorities do not always understand or act upon their positive obligation to take proactive steps to secure human rights and not merely to restrict their interference with them'. So at the current time, more is needed, it could be argued, to make UK public bodes understand the scope of their positive obligations to promote and secure ECHR rights, not just refrain from unlawfully interfering with them. The practical and possible reach of the Human Rights Act 1998 is indeed considerable – and the concept of a British Bill of Rights might put this sense of universal fairness at considerable risk.

7.13.13 Though at the time of writing a draft British Bill of Rights is not forthcoming from the new Conservative Government, one will be on its way following the Queen's Speech made to Parliament by David Cameron in late May 2015.

7.13.14 Mark Elliott, in analysing the Conservative proposals on reform of the Human Rights Act framework, from their document *Protecting Human Rights in the UK* (published in October 2014, when the Conservatives were in Coalition Government with the Liberal Democrats), has argued that the proposed reform of the Human Rights Act would constitute a 'glossing' of the ECHR in UK law.

7.13.15 By the term 'the glossing of rights', Elliott means that the specific definitions of rights currently linked in the Human Rights Act directly and literally to the ECHR, but then placed within a British Bill of Rights, introduced via a distinct Act of Parliament in the future, could be given a specific meaning which is less protective of particular rights, in particular contexts, than as currently provided by the Human Rights Act–ECHR link. Elliott has given the example of Article 3 ECHR, which is addressed in the Conservative proposals from 2014 in the following way:

> 'Some terms used in the Convention rights would benefit from a more precise definition, such as "degrading treatment or punishment", which has arguably been given an excessively broad meaning by the ECtHR in some rulings.'

7.13.16 What is certain is that the parliamentary process required to enact legislative change to the Human Rights Act–ECHR framework is sure to be decisive and very heated. The (possible) end result of a British Bill of Rights is also guaranteed to introduce a layer of initial uncertainty amongst UK judges then dealing with an entirely new system of the law on fundamental rights in the United Kingdom.

Key Cases Checklist

Cases demonstrating the operation of the ECHR through the Human Rights Act 1998

R v A (Complainant's Sexual History) (2002): if considered necessary the courts will read words into a statute to ensure compliance with the Convention

Ghaidan v Godin-Mendoza (2004): even if the ordinary meaning of a statute is clear, a court may distort its language or read in additional words in order to achieve a meaning that is compatible with the Convention

R v Secretary of State for the Home Department, ex parte Brind (1991): where there are two interpretations of national law, one in conformity with the Convention and one not, the courts would presume it was Parliament's intention to legislate in conformity

R v DPP, ex parte Kebeline (1999): in certain areas the judiciary should defer 'on democratic grounds, to the considered opinion of the elected body or person whose act or decision is said to be incompatible with the Convention'

Anufrijeva v London Borough of Southwark (2003): the Court of Appeal concluded that damages should be considered a last resort under the Act – other remedies such as injunctions are more meaningful (see 7.12.2)

Wilson v First County Trust (No. 2) (2003): a higher court may overturn a declaration of incompatibility made by a lower court on the grounds that there has in fact been no breach of the Convention

7.8.2

R v A (Complainant's Sexual History) [2001] UKHL 25 [HL]

Key Facts

It was contended that statutory restrictions under the Criminal Evidence Act 1999 on the admissibility of evidence of a complainant's sexual history prejudiced the right to a fair trial for the defendant.

Key Law

A court is obligated under section 3 to find an interpretation compatible with the ECHR. The court could therefore construe the Act so as to permit the necessary evidence to ensure a fair trial since this was the general purpose of the statute.

Key Judgment

Lord Steyn
Section 3 'went further than requiring the court to take the Convention into account: the court had a duty to strive to find a possible interpretation compatible with Convention rights'.

Key Comment

Thus, the courts may, as Lord Steyn noted, have to 'adopt an interpretation which may appear linguistically strained'. However, there must be a distinction between legitimate interpretation and stepping into the realm of redrafting legislation.

7.8.3 and 7.9.13

Ghaidan v Godin-Mendoza [2004] UKHL 30 [HL]

Key Facts

The Rent Act 1977 provided that on the death of a protected tenant their spouse, if then living in the house, became a tenant by succession. In a previous case the House of Lords had ruled that this did not extend to same-sex relationships. That was challenged in this case.

Key Law

The House of Lords used section 3 to reinterpret the statute so that it was compatible with the Convention, extending the rights to same-sex relationships, rather than issue a section 4 declaration of incompatibility.

Key Judgment

Lord Steyn
'. . . interpretation under section 3(1) is the prime remedial remedy and . . . resort to section 4 [and a declaration of incompatibility, under the Human Rights Act] must always be an exceptional course.'

Key Link

In *Wilson v First County Trust (No. 2)* [2003] 3 WLR 568 the House of Lords concluded that there is no power to grant a declaration on incompatibility under section 4 (see below) unless the interpretative duty under section 3 had first been attempted.

7.6.2 *R v Secretary of State for the Home Department, ex parte Brind* [1991] 1 AC 696 (HL)

Key Facts

The Secretary of State was empowered under statute to issue Directives. One Directive prohibited the broadcasting of statements by representatives of proscribed organisations. The applicants were journalists seeking judicial review of the issuing of the Directive, on the basis that the Secretary of State's powers should be exercised in accordance with Article 10 of the ECHR.

Key Law

The UK courts were not bound to apply the ECHR directly until incorporated into UK law by the passing of statute (which they were with the coming into force of the Human Rights Act 1998). However, *where there could be two interpretations of national law, one in conformity with the Convention and one not, the courts would presume that it was Parliament's intention to legislate in conformity*.

Key Judgment

Lord Bridge
'. . . like any other treaty obligations which have not been embodied in the law by statute, the Convention is not part of the domestic law . . . the courts accordingly have no power to enforce Convention rights directly and . . . if domestic legislation conflicts with the Convention, the courts must nevertheless enforce it.'

Key Comment

Because of the dualist nature of the constitution, international legal obligations, such as those stemming from treaties signed by the United Kingdom, do not have the force of law until incorporated by an Act of Parliament (see Chapter 5). (See Chapter 6 for explanation of this in the context of the EC Treaty.) The incorporation of the ECHR did not occur until the passing of the Human Rights Act 1998.

7.8.5 and 7.9.12

R v DPP, ex parte Kebeline and Others [1999] 3 WLR 175   (HL)

Key Law

A constitutional boundary has to be maintained between the legislative supremacy of Parliament in drafting and amending statute and the role played by the courts in interpreting statute. There is therefore a notion of **judicial deference**.

Key Judgment

In *Kebeline*, Lord Hope stated that in certain circumstances it would be appropriate for the courts 'to recognise that there is an area of judgment within which the judiciary defer, on democratic grounds, to the considered opinion of the elected body'.

Key Comment

Similarly, in *R v Lambert, Ali and Jordan* [2001] 1 All ER 1014 Lord Woolf stated that 'legislation is passed by a democratically elected Parliament and therefore the courts . . . are entitled to and should, as a matter of constitutional principle, pay a degree of deference to the view of Parliament . . .'.

7.9.4 and 7.9.7

Wilson v First County Trust (No. 2) [2003] 3 WLR 568

(HL)

Key Law

In *Wilson*, it was held that the power to issue a declaration of incompatibility only exists where the duty of interpretation is applicable and this cannot be the case when the facts of the case took place before the Human Rights Act 1998 came into force.

Key Comment

Some declarations of incompatibility have been upheld and promoted legislative reform. However, as in this case, whilst the High Court has been prepared to issue them, a number have been overturned on appeal.

8 Devolution and independence

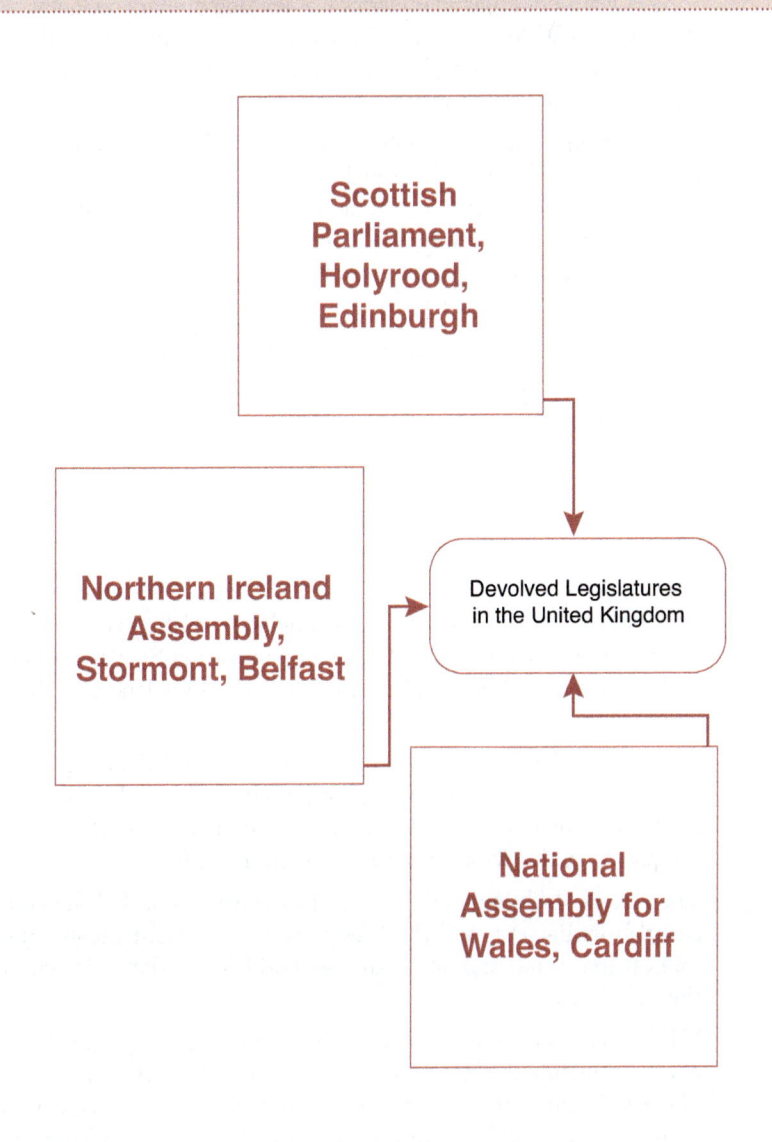

- Scottish Parliament, Holyrood, Edinburgh
- Northern Ireland Assembly, Stormont, Belfast
- National Assembly for Wales, Cardiff

→ Devolved Legislatures in the United Kingdom

8.1 Historical overview of the formation of the United Kingdom

Wales

8.1.1 King Edward I of England undertook a defining military conquest of large parts of Wales between 1277 and 1283. Since then, the Prince of Wales has always owed allegiance (and has most often been a member of) the English monarchy.

8.1.2 The Laws in Wales Act 1536 ensured that Welsh subjects of the English Monarch had rights equal to those in England and Ireland (Scotland had its own Government and Monarch at that time). Welsh representatives were also empowered to attend the House of Commons in Westminster as a result of the 1536 Act.

8.1.3 Courts administering English laws were created in each county of Wales, following further legislation from Westminster in 1543.

8.1.4 The common law of England and Wales has developed in tandem ever since.

Scotland

8.1.5 England never militarily overpowered Scotland in a way that resembled English domination of Wales. England and Scotland united their respective Crowns in 1603, when James VI of Scotland inherited the throne of England, becoming James I of England and VI of Scotland.

8.1.6 England and Scotland, however, retained separate Parliaments until 1707, when the Scottish Parliament passed an Act of Union with England, to reciprocate with the Act of Union with Scotland that was passed by the Westminster Parliament in 1706.

8.1.7 These **Acts of Union**, as they are collectively known, abolished the Scottish Parliament, and the Westminster Parliament became the sole (at that time) and dominant (as it still is) legislative forum in the British Isles.

8.1.8 While there were Scottish representatives as Members of the House of Commons and the House of Lords from that point onwards, as part of the political settlement that went along with the Acts of Union themselves, as Neil Parpworth notes, those 'laws in either kingdom which were contrary to or inconsistent with the articles of the Union were thereby abolished'.

8.1.9 The substance of Scottish private law, and the structures of the Scottish civil and criminal courts have remained distinct and unique – many would say markedly different – from the Anglo-Welsh common law and court system ever since, as the Acts of Union preserved the Scottish judicial and doctrinal preferences in place at the time.

Northern Ireland

8.1.10 Historically, Ireland as a whole had been subject to English and other influences since the 12th century, and effective government by Britain (comprising England, Wales and Scotland) following the Acts of Union from 1706/7 onwards.

8.1.11 As Neil Parpworth has observed, for example, in 1720 'the British Parliament passed the Declaratory Act in which it was declared that it had the power to legislate for Ireland'. Later in the 18th century, Henry Grattan led an Irish Parliament which had had legislative powers restored to it in 1782, but this was abolished under the Union with Ireland Act of 1800, passed by the British Parliament. The trigger for this was an uprising by a group called the United Irishmen in 1798. After this point, and on 1 January 1801, as enacted in Article 1 of the Union with Ireland Act 1800, the United Kingdom of Great Britain and Ireland was established. Some Irish MPs represented the country in the Westminster Parliament.

8.1.12 The story of the relationship between Ireland and the rest of the United Kingdom in the 19th century is the story of a move to increasing demands for 'Home Rule' – the term then given to Irish independence. This movement was principally led in the later 19th century by the Irish National League leader Charles Stewart Parnell, but 'Home Rule' was essentially frustrated.

8.1.13 After the end of the First World War, British politicians could, however, no longer ignore Irish demands for self-governance. There were though some who would not support an entirely independent Ireland – with Ulster Unionists chief amongst them. Edward Carson, a staunch supporter of the United Kingdom, secured a compromise with those senior British politicians who were in favour of a fully independent Ireland under Home Rule.

8.1.14 Unfortunately for the course of British and Irish history, the divide between Home Rule and Ulster Unionism was motivated by rampant sectarianism – that is, extremist views against either Christian Catholicism or Christian Protestantism. The historical roots of this cultural and religious divide ran very deep – based on remembered bloodshed perpetrated in Ireland in the name of religious difference over centuries. Ulster Unionism for the majority of the 20th century was characterised by anti-Catholic sectarianism – but in 1920, it was a sufficiently powerful political force that Edward Carson and his allies could secure 'Partition' in Ireland under the Government of Ireland Act. A devolved legislature for Southern Ireland never actually sat, after an Anglo-Irish Treaty in 1922, which created the Irish Free State (all of Ireland bar the six of nine Ulster counties that now constitute Northern Ireland), was brought about by a Civil War in Ireland. The Irish Free State became Eire in 1937, through the creation of a new written constitution, and so rejecting UK dominion status (and as a by-product, ensuring Eire neutrality in the Second World War); and in 1949 Eire became the Republic of Ireland.

8.1.15 Northern Ireland (the six Protestant-dominated of nine counties in the historical Irish province of Ulster) had its own Parliament with legislative powers, until these were removed by the Westminster Parliament in 1972 (see below).

8.2 Key developments in the late 20th century

Wales

8.2.1 In 1973, a Royal Commission on the Constitution recommended that there be some degree of devolution in Wales.

8.2.2 The Wales Act 1978 was put on the statute book to create a Welsh executive to govern more locally in Wales, with directly elected officials to administer laws created in Westminster in a Welsh setting. But this plan did not come to fruition, despite the 1978 Act being passed; because a key referendum, the outcome of which the proposals rested upon, was heavily in favour of the *status quo* in maintain a single central executive.

8.2.3 It was the New Labour Government of 1997 that had included more legislative devolution for Wales in its manifesto, prior to its landslide General Election success. As such, the Government of Wales Act received Royal Assent in July 1998. The effects are discussed below.

Scotland

8.2.4 Much as in Wales, while momentum toward Scottish devolution grew in the late 20th century, and again, while there was a Scotland Act of 1978 in place to deliver some real devolved legislative powers to a Scottish Government, it too was dependent on the favourable outcome of a referendum, though the referendum itself needed a turnout of at least 40% of voters to be binding.

8.2.5 Whilst a majority of those eligible to vote did vote in favour of the move towards devolution that would have in place under the 1978 Act, fewer than 40% of the eligible electorate actually voted in the referendum, so the plans for Scottish devolution at that point again, as in the same period in Wales, never came to fruition.

8.2.6 Again, in a parallel fashion to that in Wales, the election of a Labour Government in May 1997 led to the creation of the Scotland Act 1998, which is also described below.

Northern Ireland

8.2.7 Legislative powers of the Northern Ireland Parliament were revoked by the Westminster Parliament in 1972. Sectarian divisions had created a situation in Northern Ireland whereby the terrorist group known as the Irish Republic Army (IRA) and their allies, seeking a United Ireland entirely free from British influence, had perpetrated atrocities in 'the Troubles' of the 1960s and early 1970s. Radical Protestant Ulster Unionist-allied groups also perpetrated atrocities of their own devising against the Catholic population in Northern Ireland. Sadly this mutual bloodshed lasted until the late-1990s, despite political and diplomatic efforts by the Governments of both the United Kingdom and the Republic of Ireland.

8.2.8 In 1997 the IRA and Unionist terrorist organisations entered into a ceasefire that has been observed ever since, at least by the majority of the groups that had been engaged in sectarian violence; and this ceasefire allowed ongoing peace talks to include the Irish nationalist political party, Sinn Féin.

8.2.9 These peace talks led to the Good Friday Agreement of 1998, known formally as the Belfast Agreement. In turn this led to the Northern Ireland Act 1998 (see below), and the creation of a devolved legislature in the form of the Northern Ireland Assembly, at Stormont.

8.3 Key legislation – an overview

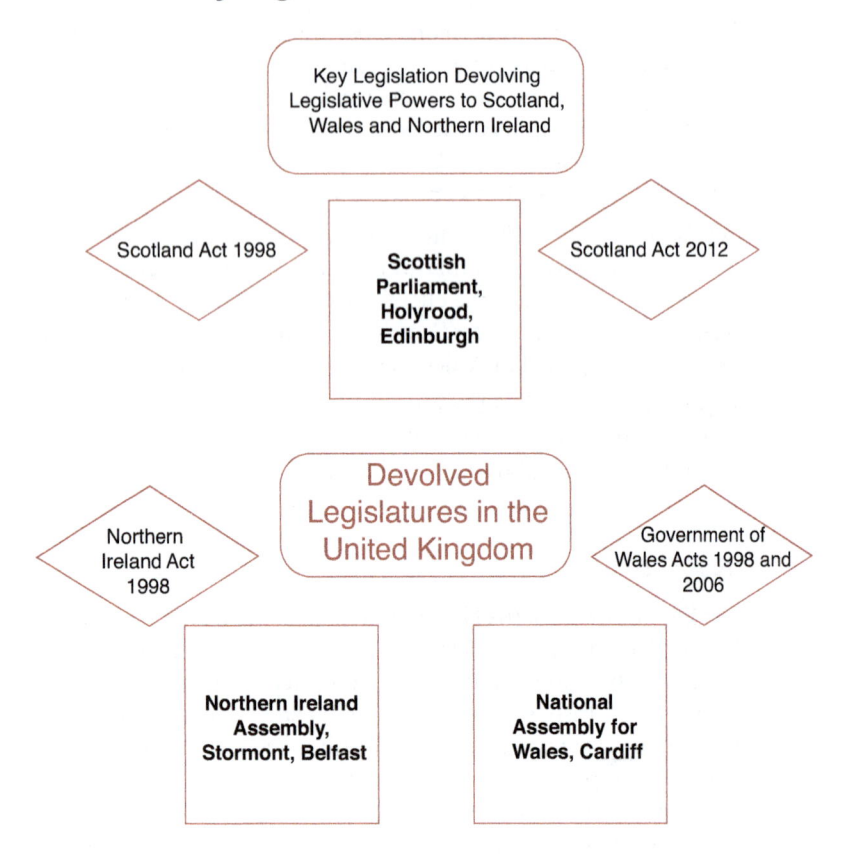

Key Legislation Devolving Legislative Powers to Scotland, Wales and Northern Ireland

- Scotland Act 1998
- Scotland Act 2012
- Scottish Parliament, Holyrood, Edinburgh

Devolved Legislatures in the United Kingdom

- Northern Ireland Act 1998
- Government of Wales Acts 1998 and 2006
- Northern Ireland Assembly, Stormont, Belfast
- National Assembly for Wales, Cardiff

Wales

8.3.1 The Government of Wales Act 1998 devolved powers to a directly elected National Assembly for Wales, commonly known as the Welsh Assembly, which assumed responsibilities formerly exercised by the Secretary of State for Wales.

8.3.2 Under the Act the Assembly had law-making powers that were restricted to secondary legislation.

8.3.3 The Government of Wales Act 2006 conferred additional legislative power. It identifies matters on which the Assembly may legislate; legislation on matters outside of this competence is not considered law.

8.3.4 The 2006 Act also preserves the right of the Westminster Parliament to legislate for Wales: section 93.

8.3.5 Assembly Measures can be passed on a range of 20 different competencies. They cannot be used to amend various Acts including the European Communities Act 1972 and the Human Rights Act 1998.

8.3.6 Assembly Acts can be passed only if a referendum is held and the outcome approves the passing of the Act: Government of Wales Act 2006, section 105.

Scotland

8.3.7 The Scotland Act 1998 established a Scottish Parliament, which has the power to make statutes within the sphere of competence laid down in the Act. Section 29 provides that any Act made outside of this legislative competence will not be considered as law.

8.3.8 The legislative competence of the Scottish Parliament does not affect the power of the Westminster Parliament to still make laws for Scotland, which is a reflection of its continued supremacy: section 28.

8.3.9 In addition, certain matters are reserved to the Westminster Parliament. These are:

- the constitution;
- the registration of political parties;
- foreign affairs;
- the Civil Service; and
- defence and treason.

8.3.10 There are additional, 'reserved' matters with particular exceptions, which mean that in such areas the Westminster Parliament can retain some degree of uniformity across the United Kingdom, whilst devolving power to the Scottish Parliament to deal with the matter as it thinks fit, in areas the Westminster Parliament felt appropriate for the Scottish Parliament to do so. These were expanded to include greater taxation and financial borrowing powers for the Scottish Parliament, under the Scotland Act 2012. Reserved matters with exceptions are found in Part 2 of Schedule V to the Scotland Act 1998, addressing 'Specific reservations'; and they include, *inter alia*, elements of the regulation of:

- financial and economic matters;
- home affairs;
- trade and industry;

- energy;
- transport, social security, regulation of the professions;
- employment;
- health and medicines; and
- media and culture.

Northern Ireland

8.3.11 The Northern Ireland Act 1998 provides for a (unicameral) Northern Ireland Assembly, which is based on the principle of a creating a 'power-sharing' executive. This aims to ensure that both of Northern Ireland's largest political communities participate in governing the region.

8.3.12 However, the Assembly was suspended on a number of occasions; the longest suspension being between 2002 and 2007. During suspensions the powers of the Assembly were held by the Northern Ireland Office, that is, part of the UK Government in Westminster.

8.3.13 In 2006 the St Andrews Agreement was reached, providing for a Transitional Assembly, with elections to the suspended Assembly being held in 2007. Full power was handed back to the devolved institutions in May 2007.

8.3.14 The Assembly may legislate in competences referred to as 'transferred matters', which are not specifically identified in the Northern Ireland Act 1998, and which are therefore any competence not explicitly retained by the Westminster Parliament.

8.3.15 Those powers retained by Westminster can be either 'excepted matters' or 'reserved matters'.

- Excepted matters are retained by the Westminster Parliament indefinitely, examples being international relations; defence and the armed forces; and nationality, immigration and asylum.

- Reserved matters may be transferred should the Westminster Parliament wish to do so. For example, in April 2010 powers in respect of policing and justice were devolved. Examples of current reserved matters include international trade and financial markets; navigations and civil aviation; and intellectual property.

8.4 Recent moves toward greater devolution or independence

Wales

8.4.1 The Government of Wales Act 2006 created a new executive body for Wales, now known as the Welsh Government after the Wales Act 2014. This Government can now make Welsh laws known as 'Measures', under delegated powers from 'Acts of the Welsh Assembly'.

8.4.2 According to the decision of the UK Supreme Court in *Attorney-General v National Assembly for Wales Commission* (2012) it is acceptable for the Attorney General to refer a draft Bill under deliberation by the Welsh Assembly to the Supreme Court, under section 112 of the Government of Wales Act. This pre-legislative scrutiny is appropriate, just as it is appropriate for the Supreme Court to scrutinise the eventual Act of the Welsh Assembly after it has been passed in Cardiff, under section 149 of the 2006 Act. The purpose of this scrutiny is to determine whether the effect of the Welsh legislation is in compliance with the boundaries of devolved powers in Wales, that is, in areas of legislative competency for the Welsh Assembly.

8.4.3 In 2013, the Government in control of the Welsh Assembly argued for greater devolution in Wales under what would be a new Government of Wales Act.

8.4.4 This would mean the Westminster Parliament, retaining legislative functions in relation to more sovereign matters such as foreign affairs, defence, national security and immigration controls – with greater autonomy for future Welsh Governments in legislative areas such as taxation, health and welfare.

8.4.5 In early 2015, the Coalition Government responded to a final report by the Silk Commission in 2014 with proposals for greater devolution of legislative competences to the Welsh Assembly in key areas such as energy, transport, taxation, borrowing and the environment.

8.4.6 At the time of writing in May 2015, it remains to be seen how the new Conservative majority Government will give effect through legislation in Westminster to these legislative ambitions of the Welsh Assembly in Cardiff. The Prime Minister David Cameron has promised that a new 'Wales Bill' would feature as a new legislative move in the first 100 days of his new, solo, Conservative Government.

Scotland

8.4.7 The Calman Commission recommended in 2009 that greater fiscal powers relating to borrowing and taxation should be devolved, and afforded to the Scottish Parliament. This has occurred under the Scotland Act 2012, passed by the Westminster – but only after the Scottish Nationalist Party (SNP) was convinced that its views on the scope and purposes of the Bill were taken into account.

8.4.8 This latter element was vital because the 'Sewell Convention' means that Westminster will not ordinarily legislate in such as a way as to affect the powers of the devolved legislature in the form of the Scottish Parliament without a consenting resolution from the Scottish Parliament itself.

8.4.9 As SNP Members of the Scottish Parliament (MSPs) were in overall political control of Holyrood, the home of the Scottish Parliament, such a resolution of MSPs was required before the Bill that became the Scotland Act 2012 could progress through the House of Commons at Westminster.

Northern Ireland

8.4.10 In Northern Ireland, at the time of writing, political momentum is not necessarily in favour of greater devolution of powers.

8.4.11 Between 2010 and 2015, the Westminster Coalition Government set into motion a chain of welfare reforms across the whole of the United Kingdom which have proven deeply divisive. The Coalition did this in such a way as to try and reduce central Government expenditure on welfare, such as housing benefit etc. This culture of so-called 'austerity' in government, controversial across the political divide, has proven just as divisive in the Northern Ireland Assembly, and its executive body in government, the Northern Ireland Executive.

8.4.12 In May 2015, it was reported that following the election of a Conservative majority Government in the Westminster Parliament, the Government in Northern Ireland would be required to implement welfare reforms that had up until that point been delayed because of opposition from Sinn Féin members of the Northern Ireland Government to the Coalition welfare reforms, which were more broadly supported by their chief political opponents, the Democratic Unionist Party.

8.4.13 At the time of writing, in May 2015, the First Minister of the Northern Ireland Executive, Democratic Unionist leader Peter Robinson, had concerns that while fines imposed on the Northern Ireland Executive by Westminster mounted up at the rate of £2 million per week, with the welfare reforms unimplemented due to reluctance from Sinn Féin partners in Government. There is also the possibility that central Government in the United Kingdom might hand back legislative competence over welfare in Northern Ireland to the Westminster Parliament – apparently running the risk that the Assembly would need to be suspended once more over Party political intransigence.

8.5 Looking ahead

The Sewel Convention, human rights and the devolved legislatures

8.5.1 Described above, the 'Sewel Convention' is still highly relevant, since at the time of writing in May 2015, the SNP has greatly increased its number of MPs in the Westminster Parliament (to 56 in 2015, from just 6 in 2010), following a disastrous General Election campaign for the Labour Party in Scotland.

8.5.2 The Conservative majority Government has announced plans in the summer of 2015 to repeal the Human Rights Act 1998, and replace it with a 'British Bill of Rights' (see 7.13) – and yet the Human Rights Act is enshrined in the Scotland Act 1998 as a basis of Scottish devolution, and there is no popular mandate to see the Human Rights Act repealed in Scotland itself.

8.5.3 So the Sewel Convention – the requirement of legislative consent from the Scottish Parliament, or the practical difficulty in obtaining that consent – might preclude the Conservative Government from being able to repeal the Human Rights Act, without pressing ahead in a way that is not respectful of that constitutional convention.

8.5.4 Ultimately, the Sewel Convention is not law, and is not binding as a mere convention, and so political pragmatics will dictate its usefulness to those who would seek to preserve the Human Rights Act.

8.5.5 In the context of only a slender Conservative majority in the House of Commons, SNP MPs in Westminster would be likely to oppose any legislation to replace the Human Rights Act with a British Bill of Rights if a resolution in favour of such plans had not been obtained in advance from their SNP MSP counterparts in control of the Scottish Parliament – and such consent is currently highly unlikely.

8.5.6 SNP opponents, added to opposition from Labour and Liberal Democrat MPs in England, as well as an array of other Northern Irish, Scottish and Welsh MPs from several different Parties, and crucially, Conservative 'rebel' MPs who might oppose the repeal of the Human Rights Act themselves, a British Bills of Rights might not pass through the House of Commons in the three votes required.

8.5.7 The Sewel Convention will thus be likely to prove a fundamental constitutional principle with regard to both securing the fundamental role of the Human Rights Act in founding each of the devolved legislatures, as well as any further Scottish devolution or, indeed, independence.

The prospect of Scottish independence

8.5.8 Complete Scottish independence from the rest of the United Kingdom is very much live discussion in the United Kingdom today, at the time of writing in May 2015. A 2014 referendum in Scotland on full independence led to a narrow victory for the 'No' campaign – with a slight majority of Scottish voters happier to see Scotland remain part of the United Kingdom at the time of the referendum in September 2014.

8.5.9 But the greatly increased number of SNP MPs in Westminster will be pressing for the greater package of devolution powers, including perhaps the full fiscal autonomy that has been labelled as *de facto* independence, which was encompassed in the recommendations in the Smith Commission set up after the narrow referendum result in late 2014. Conservative Prime Minister David Cameron has promised a new devolution settlement for Scotland, based on more legislation to be created by the Westminster Parliament, and drawing on the conclusions and recommendations of the Smith Commission. This would likely entail:

- greater powers for the Scottish Parliament over matters of taxation, including setting rates of income tax;
- an attempt at entrenching the constitutional existence of the Scottish Parliament and the Scottish Government – see below;
- greater control by the Scottish Government over welfare law and the benefits system in Scotland;
- the ability of the Scottish Parliament to extend the vote to 16- and 17-year-olds when electing Members of the Scottish Parliament; and
- greater control by the Scottish Government over the oil and gas industry in Scotland

8.5.10 Again, at the time of writing, another independence referendum for Scotland is not something that is explicitly planned by the Conservative majority Government in Westminster, and there is a constitutional convention that with regard to a referendum that an Act of the Westminster Parliament is required to legitimise a popular vote as a politically binding referendum.

8.5.11 Nicola Sturgeon, at the time of writing the current leader of the SNP, is publicly somewhat antagonistic over the way in which she might press ahead with a popular vote in Scotland, however, since while the SNP has overall control of the Scottish Parliament, there still exists this constitutional convention with regard to referenda.

8.5.12 In late 2014, the **Smith Commission recommended not only greater fiscal powers** for a devolved legislature in Holyrood, but also **a permanent status for the Scottish Parliament in law** (something that would be in conflict with the notion of the sovereignty of the Westminster Parliament, that is to say, the UK Parliament, since the Westminster Parliament is traditionally regarded as being able to repeal any Act of Parliament with the creation of another Act to undertake the exercise expressly).

8.5.13 This doctrine of parliamentary sovereignty entails that no Act of Parliament is 'entrenched', and not even, in this context, the Scotland Act 1998 (as amended) – which currently empowers the Scottish Parliament.

8.5.14 The issue of a greatly increased number of SNP MPs in the House of Commons at Westminster has ratcheted up the already-considerable political interest in the notion of 'English votes for English laws'.

8.5.15 This phrase outlines a response to the so-called 'West Lothian question': why are Members of Parliament in the House of Commons, who are representing Scottish constituencies, able to help create legislation which affects issues in England; which are issues that MPs representing English constituencies in the Commons, cannot legislate upon in relation to Scotland, since the issues concerned are dealt with legislatively in Scotland by MSPs at Holyrood?

8.5.16 'English votes for English laws', also known in shorthand as the 'EVEL' proposal, would see a sub-set of MPs in the Commons representing only English constituencies form, in effect, a devolved English sub-Parliament, legislating on the same issues and to the same extent as something like one of Holyrood in Scotland, Stormont in Northern Ireland or the Welsh Assembly in Cardiff.

Part 2
Public law in practice

9   The contemporary role and possible reform of Parliament

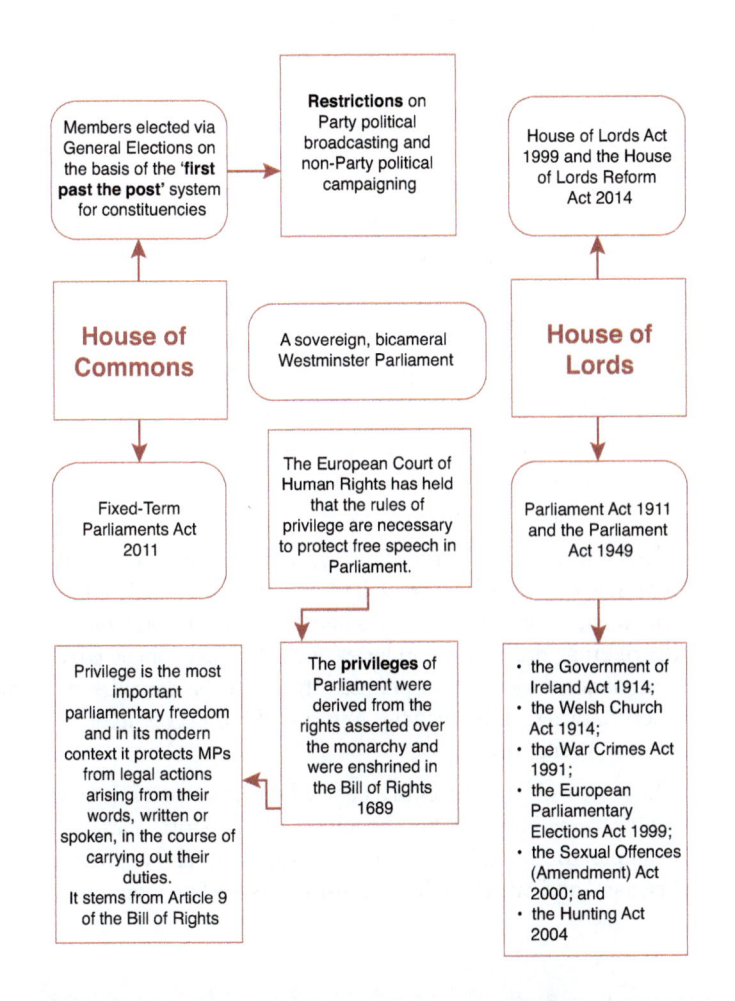

```
┌──────────────────────┐      ┌──────────────────────┐      ┌──────────────────────┐
│ Members elected via  │      │ **Restrictions** on  │      │ House of Lords Act   │
│ General Elections on │ ───▶ │ Party political      │      │ 1999 and the House   │
│ the basis of the     │      │ broadcasting and     │      │ of Lords Reform      │
│ 'first past the post'│      │ non-Party political  │      │ Act 2014             │
│ system for           │      │ campaigning          │      │                      │
│ constituencies       │      │                      │      │                      │
└──────────────────────┘      └──────────────────────┘      └──────────────────────┘
           ▲                                                            ▲
           │                                                            │
┌──────────────────────┐      ┌──────────────────────┐      ┌──────────────────────┐
│   **House of         │      │ A sovereign,         │      │   **House of         │
│     Commons**        │      │ bicameral            │      │     Lords**          │
│                      │      │ Westminster          │      │                      │
│                      │      │ Parliament           │      │                      │
└──────────────────────┘      └──────────────────────┘      └──────────────────────┘
           │                                                            │
           ▼                                                            ▼
┌──────────────────────┐      ┌──────────────────────┐      ┌──────────────────────┐
│  Fixed-Term          │      │ The European Court of│      │ Parliament Act 1911  │
│  Parliaments Act     │      │ Human Rights has held│      │ and the Parliament   │
│  2011                │      │ that the rules of    │      │ Act 1949             │
│                      │      │ privilege are        │      │                      │
│                      │      │ necessary to protect │      │                      │
│                      │      │ free speech in       │      │                      │
│                      │      │ Parliament.          │      │                      │
└──────────────────────┘      └──────────────────────┘      └──────────────────────┘
                                         │                              │
                                         ▼                              ▼
┌──────────────────────┐      ┌──────────────────────┐      ┌──────────────────────┐
│ Privilege is the most│      │ The **privileges** of│      │ • the Government of  │
│ important            │      │ Parliament were      │      │   Ireland Act 1914;  │
│ parliamentary freedom│      │ derived from the     │      │ • the Welsh Church   │
│ and in its modern    │      │ rights asserted over │      │   Act 1914;          │
│ context it protects  │      │ the monarchy and     │      │ • the War Crimes Act │
│ MPs from legal       │ ◀─── │ were enshrined in    │      │   1991;              │
│ actions arising from │      │ the Bill of Rights   │      │ • the European       │
│ their words, written │      │ 1689                 │      │   Parliamentary      │
│ or spoken, in the    │      │                      │      │   Elections Act 1999;│
│ course of carrying   │      │                      │      │ • the Sexual Offences│
│ out their duties.    │      │                      │      │   (Amendment) Act    │
│ It stems from Article│      │                      │      │   2000; and          │
│ 9 of the Bill of     │      │                      │      │ • the Hunting Act    │
│ Rights               │      │                      │      │   2004               │
└──────────────────────┘      └──────────────────────┘      └──────────────────────┘
```

▶ 9.1 A bicameral Parliament

9.1.1 Parliament is the main legislative body in the UK's constitution. It is a **bicameral** body, meaning that it is comprised of two chambers, the House of Commons and the House of Lords.

9.1.2 The main functions of Parliament are:

- to sustain the executive by authorising the raising and spending of funds;
- to hold the executive to account; and
- to scrutinise, approve or amend legislation.

9.1.3 Perhaps the most significant of these roles is to secure **executive accountability** and Parliament attempts to do this using a range of methods.

9.1.4 Parliament's ability to hold the executive accountable is weakened by the fact that the executive has become dominant. The primary reason for this is the strong Party system that has developed since the early 20th century. The first past the post electoral system supports the creation of a strong, two-Party system and makes it difficult for smaller Parties to win seats.

9.1.5 The ability of Parliament to hold the executive accountable can be impacted on by the Party system in the following ways:

- the electoral system can result in the Party holding executive power having a large majority;
- control of parliamentary business and the timetable in the House of Commons rest largely in the hands of the executive; and
- Parliament exercises its will by voting but each Party has a 'whip' system, which is designed to enforce Party discipline and persuade members to vote in a certain way.

9.1.6 The United Kingdom is divided into 659 constituencies, each represented by one Member of Parliament (MP). Each constituency should be approximately the same in terms of voter numbers and distribution and the boundaries should respect local government boundaries. However, in practice there can be considerable differences between constituencies in terms of both geographical size and voting population.

9.1.7 The review of boundaries in a particular part of the United Kingdom is now the responsibility of the relevant Boundary Commissions – for example, the Boundary Commission for England. Northern Ireland, Scotland and Wales each have distinct Boundary Commissions.

9.1.8 The criteria for review of boundaries allow discretion in their exercise (*R v Boundary Commission for England, ex parte Foot* (1983), *R v Home Secretary, ex parte McWhirter* (1969) and *Harper v Secretary of State for the Home Department* (1955)).

9.2 The electoral system relevant to the 'Westminster Parliament'

9.2.1 The principle of universal adult suffrage was not fully realised in the United Kingdom until the 1920s, and is based upon one equal vote per voter. The rules for eligibility of voters are contained in the Representation of the People Act 1983. A voter must be an adult, a citizen of the United Kingdom (or an EU citizen for local elections), and registered on the electoral roll of a local authority.

9.2.2 The following are disqualified from voting:

- minors;
- persons subject to a Mental Health Act incapacity;
- persons serving a prison sentence following conviction (still the case despite the ruling in *Hirst v UK (No. 2)* (2005));
- peers of the realm;
- persons convicted of an electoral offence; and
- persons who are aliens.

9.2.3 Eligibility for standing as a candidate in a parliamentary General Election is governed by the House of Commons Disqualification Act 1975. The following categories are disqualified:

- holders of judicial office;
- civil servants;
- police officers and members of the armed forces; and
- Crown appointees.

9.2.4 There are also restrictions upon individual eligibility to stand as a candidate in a General Election:

- the minimum age is 18;
- no one may stand who has a mental incapacity;
- peers may not stand unless they renounce their title;
- clergymen may not stand while they remain in office;
- bankrupts may not stand until discharged;

- persons convicted of treason may not stand until rehabilitated; and
- persons convicted of electoral offences are banned for a period of five years.

9.2.5 The voting system in the United Kingdom was traditionally a simple majority system known as **'first past the post'** or 'plurality' system. In such a system a winning candidate need achieve only one more vote than the next candidate in a constituency in order to take a seat as a Member of Parliament (MP).

9.2.6 Criticisms of the first past the post system include the fact that it is defective in securing democratic representation since it ignores all votes except for the winning candidate. Hence the smaller political parties and minorities often have little or no representation. For example:

- in 1951 Labour won more votes than the Conservatives but lost the election;
- in 1974 the Conservatives won more votes than Labour but lost the election;
- in 1983 the Liberal Party gained 25% of the votes but won only 3.5% of the seats; and
- in 2001 Labour won only 40.7% of votes but secured 62.6% of seats in the House of Commons.

9.2.7 In 2005 the General Election results were as follows:

2005 General Election (first past the post)			
Party	% votes cast	% of seats	No. of seats
Labour	35.2	54.9	355
Conservative	32.4	30.7	198
Lib Dem	22.0	9.6	62
Other	10.4	4.8	31

In 2010 the General Election results were as follows:

2010 General Election (first past the post)			
Party	% votes cast	% of seats	No. of seats
Labour	28.99	39.7	258
Conservative	36.48	47.2	307
Lib Dem	23.03	8.08	57
Other	11.5	4.5	28

9.2.8 In May 2015 the General Election results were as follows (for 650 seats in the House of Commons):

2015 General Election (first past the post)			
Party	% votes cast	% of seats	No. of seats
Conservative	36.9	50.9	331
Labour	30.4	35.7	232
SNP	4.7	8.6	56
Other	28	4.8	31

9.2.9 It is notable that in 'Loyal Opposition' to the Conservative majority Government elected in May 2015, as well as 232 Labour MPs, there sits a group of 56 Scottish Nationalist Party (SNP) MPs, who between them received only 4.7% of the votes cast in the United Kingdom as a whole, but occupy 8.6% of the seats.

9.2.10 Contrast this with the United Kingdom Independence Party (UKIP), whose 12.6% share of the national voting won them a single seat in the Commons.

9.2.11 Outright 'proportional representation', with a share of the vote transferred to a straightforward share of 650 seats in the Commons, as opposed to the 'first past the post' system currently used, would have secured UKIP more than 50 seats.

At this point we can now address other electoral system formats used in the United Kingdom today.

9.3 Other electoral systems used in the United Kingdom

9.3.1 Recent changes have introduced forms of proportional representation to elect certain representatives and moved the United Kingdom to a position where there is a '**mixed**' electoral system (see table below). The first past the post system is, however, still currently used to elect Members of Parliament.

Types of proportional representation system	Used to elect
Party List System	**Members of the European Parliament** (MEP)
Additional Member System	**Members of the Scottish Parliament** (Scotland Act 1998)

(*Continued*)

	Members of the Welsh Assembly (Wales Act 1998) Members of the London Assembly (Greater London Authority Act 1999)
Single Transferable Vote (Northern Ireland Act 1998)	**Members of the Northern Ireland Assembly**

9.3.2   The major political parties considered **reform of the electoral system** as part of their manifestos for the 2010 General Election with:

- the Conservative Party advocating continuing with the first past the post system for Westminster;
- the Labour Party stating that it would hold a referendum by October 2011 on using the Alternative Vote system;
- the Liberal Democrats stating they would introduce the Single Transferable Vote system and multi-member constituencies and reduce the number of MPs to 500.

9.3.3   The Conservative-Liberal Democrat Coalition Agreement 2010 led to a national referendum in 2011 on the introduction of the Alternative Vote system of electing Members of Parliament to the House of Commons, which was rejected.

9.4 The Electoral Commission and controls on lobbying and campaigning

9.4.1   The Electoral Commission is an independent body that monitors and regulates elections of different kinds, including General Elections, across the United Kingdom.

9.4.2   The Law Commission of England and Wales, the Scottish Law Commission and the Northern Ireland Law Commission jointly consulted over the body of electoral law in the United Kingdom, with a view to possible reforms after the summer of 2015. With this in mind the Law Commission produced an overview of electoral law as part of a consultation paper from late 2014, and which informs this section of this chapter.

9.4.3   The Electoral Commission itself also produces basic guides to electoral processes each time a significant election approaches, and the legal position in this section of this chapter is also based on this material, and is accurate at the time of writing in May 2015. See http://www.electoralcommission.org.uk/ for further details and updates.

9.4.4 The Political Parties, Elections and Referendums Act 2000 (PPERA 2000) introduced new controls on Party spending and campaign funding and established the Electoral Commission with wide responsibilities for the conduct of elections (discussed below). The Act also regulates the activities of a range of participants.

9.4.5 The Electoral Commission was established under the PPERA 2000 as a new independent body charged with responsibility for all aspects of elections, local and general or regional, in the United Kingdom. The body as a whole is accountable to Parliament.

9.4.6 The Electoral Commission's duties include:

- reporting on the administration of elections;
- reviewing law and practice;
- promoting awareness of issues and systems to the public; and
- compiling an annual report.

9.4.7 The Commission deals with issues relating to the transparency of political campaigns and parties, for example:

- registrations of donations received;
- monitoring of bans on foreign donations;
- control of campaign expenditure;
- maintenance of various registers; and
- monitoring of compliance with the PPERA 2000.

9.4.8 One important role is to regulate the funding of political parties. The PPERA 2000 defines permissible and impermissible donors and requires the disclosure and recording by the Commission of donations. Anonymous or unidentifiable donations are impermissible.

9.4.9 An impermissible donation should be returned to the donor; if it is from an unidentifiable source it should be returned to the Commission. The Commission may apply for a court order if an impermissible donation is accepted.

9.4.10 The Political Parties and Elections Act 2009 granted the Commission a variety of additional supervisory and investigatory powers; increased the transparency of donations to political Parties; and proposed a range of new civil sanctions that may be imposed on donees and political Parties.

9.4.11 The Electoral Commission is also responsible for monitoring compliance with the Transparency of Lobbying, Non Party Campaigning and Trade Union Administration Act 2014 ('the Lobbying Act'), which affected the responsibilities of 'non-party campaigners'.

9.4.12 The Lobbying Act requires, controversially, that non-Party campaigning groups, such as charities and trade unions, must register with the Electoral Commission if they expect to spend £20,000 or more in the run-up to a General Election in support of one or more political Parties. At a more national level, campaign spending for a non-Party campaigning group is then limited to:

- £319,800 in England;
- £55,400 in Scotland;
- £44,000 in Wales; and
- £30,800 in Northern Ireland.

9.4.13 Perhaps most importantly, non-Party campaigning groups can only spend a maximum of £9,750 per constituency in the build-up to an election – greatly limiting their ability to advocate in favour of a particular candidate in crucial constituencies for a particular political Party.

9.4.14 This new regulation of non-Party campaigning groups was introduced to increase transparency in the way that financial support is indirectly marshalled behind particular political Parties.

9.4.15 The Commission continues to review the future development of electoral systems and regulations and produces consultation documents on new ideas such as the expansion of electronic voting systems. In particular, the impact of the new Lobbying Act will be reviewed by Government in an inquiry led by Lord Hodgson, beginning in 2015. (Critics of the Lobbying Act 2014 have called the legislation the 'Gagging Act' because of the way that it limited spending on political awareness-raising by non-Party campaigning organisations, such as trade unions, which naturally support the Labour Party, in the run-up to the General Election 2015.)

9.5 Broadcasting

9.5.1 No political Party can make a broadcast unless it is first registered under the PPERA 2000.

9.5.2 Under the Broadcasting Act 1980, and the BBC's Charter, broadcasters have a requirement to be impartial, exercising some editorial control over the exact allocation of airtime to each Party. This is based upon the level of support at the last General Election. New parties will therefore not receive much, if any, airtime.

9.5.3 Legal challenges to the allocation of broadcast time have not generally been successful (e.g. *R v British Broadcasting Corporation, ex parte Referendum Party* (1997)).

9.5.4 In the *Referendum Party* case the court found it had not been irrational to include previous success with voters amongst the criteria used to determine the number of party political broadcasts allotted to any party. In *R v Broadcasting Complaints Commission, ex parte Owen* (1985), similarly, a wide element of discretion was found to apply to investigations of broadcasting complaints by political parties.

9.5.5 In *R (Pro-Life Alliance) v BBC* (2003) the House of Lords concluded that the BBC (and other broadcasters) had a legal duty not to broadcast material that offended against good taste and decency and that showing the Pro-Life Alliance broadcast would breach this duty.

9.5.6 In *Animal Defenders International v UK* (2013) the European Court of Human Rights found that the prohibition on political advertising in the Communications Act 2003 was within the UK's margin of appreciation (meaning it was a tolerable legal position in the light of the ECHR) despite interfering with a campaign group's right to freedom of expression.

9.6 The House of Commons

9.6.1 The House of Commons was established by the 13th century but was recognisable as the representative body we see today only in the 19th century, following a programme of reforms of electoral practices.

9.6.2 There are 650 elected MPs in total, allied to the Government, the Opposition Parties or an independent Party. Each Member represents a constituency in the House.

9.6.3 Under the Parliament Act 1949, the maximum length of a Parliament was five years but it was the prerogative of the Prime Minister to set the exact date for a General Election and to ask the Monarch to dissolve Parliament.

9.6.4 The Fixed-Term Parliaments Act 2011 amended this practice, and now, barring a particular kind of 'double vote' of 'no confidence' in the Government, a period of five years' duration passes between General Elections – making the default length of a Parliament five years.

9.6.5 In the House of Commons, the Prime Minister and the Cabinet sit on the front bench facing the Leader of the Opposition and the Shadow Cabinet. The rest of the Members sit on the benches behind and it is these backbenchers who are needed to vote in support of a Bill.

9.6.6 The main functions of the House are as follows:

- indirect choosing of the Government by virtue of the convention that the political Party that commands a majority in the House is entitled to form the Government;

- approval of taxation and expenditure;
- scrutiny and approval of legislation;
- supervising of the executive occurs in the House of Commons since by convention Ministers are accountable to Parliament. The House of Commons can in effect force a Government to resign by a vote of no confidence so long as it is also followed by another, in effect, less than two weeks later, under reforms in the Fixed-Term Parliaments Act 2011. Again, under the 2011 Act, the House of Commons can also bring down the Government of the day by another vote (with a two-thirds majority) to end the Parliament and bring on a General Election;
- the redress of grievances raised by an MP on behalf of their constituents; and
- debating matters of public concern, such as the Iraq War, although it should be noted that there are limited procedural opportunities for such debates.

9.6.7 Bills introduced in Parliament undergo the following procedure:

First Reading	A formal introduction without debate
Second Reading	Substantive debate
Committee Stage	Detailed scrutiny
Third Reading	Amendments approved or rejected
Division	House of Commons votes (legislation then proceeds to the House of Lords, unless it was introduced there, and then presented for the Royal Assent)

9.7 The House of Lords

9.7.1 The House of Lords is the oldest part of Parliament and derives from the circle of advisers to the Monarch who were rewarded with lands and titles.

9.7.2 A hereditary peerage passes from generation to generation, usually through the male line, and, until recently, entitled the holder to sit in the Lords as of right. Prior to the reforms listed below there were more than 750 hereditary peers in the Lords.

9.7.3 The Life Peerages Act 1958 gave non-hereditary peers the right to a seat in the Lords, usually after a period of service in the Commons, or as recognition of their contribution to society.

9.7.4 The main function of a second chamber in a bicameral legislative body is to act as a revising chamber to scrutinise legislation proposed by the first chamber, ensuring that there is a constitutional safeguard.

9.7.5 According to the Wakeham Commission 2000, the functions of the House of Lords included the following:

- to provide advice on public policy and a forum for general debate on matters of public concern without Party political pressures;
- to act as a revising chamber scrutinising the details of proposed legislation;
- to introduce relatively uncontroversial legislation or private bills as a means of reducing the workload of the House of Commons;
- to provide Ministers;
- to provide Committees to discuss general topics, for example, European Communities Committee;
- to permit persons other than politicians to participate in Government (Life Peerages Act 1958); and
- to act as a 'constitutional watchdog'.

9.7.6 However, the ability of the House of Lords to carry out these functions was always undermined by criticism of its unrepresentative and undemocratic composition.

9.7.7 With regard to the idea of the House of Lords as a 'constitutional watchdog': it was the House of Lords, led by notable legally qualified peers who had been judges or barristers, that softened the reforms that would have otherwise have been introduced to the permission stage of judicial review procedure by the eventual Criminal Justice and Courts Act 2015. These reforms, as they were originally shaped, would have meant, ultimately, less scrutiny of decisions and actions through the important mechanism of judicial review by the High Court. (See Chapters 12 and 13 for more details and some context for this example.)

9.7.8 Before 1999, in addition to hereditary and life peers, the Lords included the Lords Spiritual, namely the bishops and archbishops of the Church of England, and the Lords of Appeal in Ordinary.

9.7.9 The composition of the Lords attracted much comment and criticism, principally directed towards the undemocratic nature of the hereditary peers' right to sit in the House.

9.7.10 Throughout the 20th century, reforms and abolition proposals were made but none was implemented until the Labour Government of

1997 came to power with a specific reform agenda, which according to its manifesto, was to replace the House with an elected second chamber using proportional representation.

9.7.11 The House of Lords Act 1999 removed the parliamentary membership rights of hereditary peers and members of the Royal Family, although prior to the enactment of the Act a deal was struck between the Government and the Leader of the Lords concerned for the continuity of the House in the interim period before the reforms were completed. As a consequence, 92 peers were selected to continue to serve until the final shape of the House was established.

9.7.12 A Royal Commission was established to consider the process of further reform and to make recommendations. It produced a report in 2000 (the Wakeham Report) recommending a House of 550 members, with the majority being nominated and the rest being selected or elected to represent regional interests. There was no agreement on the number of selected or elected members or their method of selection, but three models were suggested:

- **Model A** = 65 members selected by dividing up the regional allocation of seats according to each Party's share of the vote in that region in the General Election and one-third of the regions selecting regional members at each General Election;
- **Model B** = 87 members elected directly using proportional representation at the same time as the European Parliament elections; and
- **Model C** = 195 regional members elected at the same time as the European Parliament elections. The Report also recommended that the system of granting honours should not result in membership of the House and that nominations for the House be by an independent commission.

9.7.13 In 2000 the House of Lords Appointments Commission was established. It makes recommendations for non-Party political peerages and vets all nominations from political Parties.

9.7.14 In 2001 the Government produced a White Paper on further reform of the House with the aim of reducing the number of members from 700 to 600 over ten years: 120 would be directly elected; 322 nominated by Party leaders; 120 chosen by the Appointments Commission; and the number of bishops reduced to 16 from 26. The remainder would have been active or retired Law Lords. In 2003 the House of Commons rejected all options for reform and the Lords voted for a fully appointed House.

9.7.15 In 2007 the Government produced a new White Paper proposing a membership of 540 with 20% non-Party and 30% appointed Party political representation. Elections would be by the 'partially open list system' at the same time as European Parliament elections; appointment would be by the Appointments Commission.

9.7.16 In 2007 a debate on the proposals was conducted in both Houses. The Commons voted in favour of a wholly elected chamber (337 to 224 votes) and for an 80% elected chamber (305 to 267 votes) and rejected all other options.

9.7.17 In response, a 2008 White Paper advocated a directly elected second chamber, smaller than the Commons, which would be either wholly elected or 80% elected and 20% nominated.

9.7.18 The Conservative–Liberal Democrat Coalition Agreement 2010 stated that a committee would be established to bring forward proposals for a wholly or mainly elected upper chamber on the basis of proportional representation.

9.7.19 The House of Lords Reform Act 2014 now allows for members to resign or retire, which was not previously possible, and makes it possible to exclude those members of the Lords who commit serious criminal offences or who do not participate at all in the business of the House of Lords for an entire Parliament.

9.8 The Parliament Acts

9.8.1 Prior to the Parliament Act 1911, the House of Lords had equal power with the House of Commons except for financial measures. According to convention, the Lords recognised the supremacy of the Commons in this respect.

9.8.2 This convention was breached in 1909. The resulting political conflict preceded the passing of the Parliament Act 1911, which left the Lords with the power to delay Money Bills for one month and non-Money Bills for two years. The power of the Lords to veto legislation was therefore removed since under the Act its assent is no longer required for the Bill to proceed for Royal Assent.

9.8.3 The Parliament Act 1949 reduced further the Lords' power of delay over non-Money Bills to one year.

9.8.4 In *R (Jackson) v Attorney-General* (2005) the Parliament Act 1949 was held to be valid and consequently any legislation passed under it (e.g. the Hunting Act 2004) is also valid.

9.8.5   The Parliament Acts have not been frequently used (primarily because of the Salisbury Convention, which means in effect that the Lords will not normally attempt to vote down a Government Bill which is mentioned in an election manifesto). The following are the only examples of use of the procedure:

- the Government of Ireland Act 1914;
- the Welsh Church Act 1914;
- the War Crimes Act 1991;
- the European Parliamentary Elections Act 1999;
- the Sexual Offences (Amendment) Act 2000; and
- the Hunting Act 2004.

9.9 Parliamentary privilege

9.9.1   Historically, the privileges of Parliament were derived from the rights asserted over the monarchy and were enshrined in the Bill of Rights 1688. These rights were a means to ensure that Parliament could go about its business without interference or undue influence.

9.9.2   At the opening of each parliamentary session, the Speaker announces and asserts these 'ancient and undoubted' rights and privileges. In a modern context, some privileges are of little importance, but the rules of parliamentary conduct remain significant. Because of the nature of these rules and the variance in application over time, it can be difficult to ascertain an exact definition of the rules, or to identify with certainty in what context they may be applied.

9.9.3   This is the most important freedom and in its modern context it protects MPs from legal actions arising from their words, written or spoken, in the course of carrying out their duties. It stems from Article 9 of the Bill of Rights. It can act as a shield to an action under the Official Secrets Acts, as in *Duncan Sandys Case* (1938), or block jurisdiction for judicial review.

9.9.4   More frequently, the right of freedom of speech is used as a defence to a potential action in defamation, for example, *Church of Scientology v Johnson-Smith* (1972). (It should be noted that prior to May 2015 the Defamation Act 1996 section 13 permitted an individual member to waive their privilege so that an action could be brought, but that this statutory right of an MP to waive their privilege was abolished under the Deregulation Act 2015.)

9.9.5   The case of *Stockdale v Hansard* (1839) demonstrated that the courts will preserve their jurisdiction to determine the extent of privilege and try to protect the rights of individuals. But the case of *The Sheriff of Middlesex* (1840) which followed showed that the courts could not interfere with the House's ruling that a breach of privilege had been committed, even though no reasons were given.

9.9.6 Parliamentary privilege is made up of two types. Absolute privilege extends to parliamentary proceedings and is a bar to all actions. Qualified privilege may extend to newspaper or media reports, so long as the report is fair and accurate and malice cannot be demonstrated (*Wason v Walter* (1868)). For example:

- a parliamentary sketch may be privileged (*Cook v Alexander* (1974)); and
- a letter from an MP to the Lord Chancellor and Law Society may have qualified privilege (*Beach v Freeson* (1972)).

9.9.7 The law on parliamentary proceedings also has a considerable constitutional role. Under Article 9 of the Bill of Rights, freedom of speech extends to words, both spoken and written, in the course of '**proceedings in Parliament**'. This term has never been statutorily defined, and is consequently unclear.

9.9.8 Attempts to provide some explanation have been undertaken by parliamentary committees where it has been defined as extending to all things done or written by a Member of Parliament as part of their duties or for the purpose of enabling them to do their duties. A 1999 committee defined it as all activities that are 'recognisably part of the formal collegiate activities of the Parliament'.

9.9.9 This lack of clarity has not been resolved by issues involving questions of whether a particular matter was a proceeding or not. For example:

- In the *Strauss Affair* in 1958, the question was whether a letter of complaint from a constituent to an MP was privileged because it was a proceeding in Parliament. The Committee on Privilege considered that it was, but the House of Commons rejected this finding. The threat of suit was subsequently withdrawn and no conclusion was reached.
- In the *Green Affair* in 2008, the police raided the office of a Conservative MP as part of an investigation into leaks. The resulting controversy included whether seized documents were privileged. The investigation was, however, later dropped.
- In February 2010 the Director of Public Prosecutions announced that four MPs would face criminal prosecution over expenses claims.
- In June 2010, Southwark Crown Court held that proceedings in Parliament did not extend to MPs' expenses and that there was

consequently no bar to their trial for charges brought under the Theft Act 1968.

9.9.10 In December 2010, the Supreme Court determined that it was indeed the case that proceedings in Parliament did not extend to MPs' expenses and that there was consequently no bar to their trial for charges brought under the Theft Act 1968: see *R v Chaytor* (2010).

9.9.11 In *A v UK* (2002) the applicant argued that the rules of privilege breached the Convention, in particular Article 6 (the right to a fair trial), Article 8 (respect for private life) and Article 13 (right to an effective remedy).

9.9.12 The European Court of Human Rights held that the rules of privilege were necessary to protect free speech in Parliament and there was no violation of the Convention. The Court also noted that the British rules were narrower in scope than in many other countries.

9.9.13 The House has the right to regulate its own composition and its own proceedings. Hence:

- where a vacancy arises, the House orders a by-election;
- Parliament determines if a Member is qualified to take their seat in the House (*Re Parliamentary Election for Bristol South East* (1964));
- Parliament may expel a Member it considers unfit (*Bradlaugh v Gossett* (1884)); and
- Parliament may suspend a Member for improper conduct, for example, in the case of a Member seizing the Mace in the course of a speech.

9.9.14 Freedom from arrest for attending Members is of little significance, since it does not prevent an arrest for a criminal charge and there are few arrestable civil offences.

9.9.15 Privilege is based upon the concept of Parliament being free to operate without fear or favour and this requires that its Members be above corruption and influence.

9.10 Parliamentary standards

9.10.1 It has long been accepted that bodies may sponsor MPs, such as trade unions, but there has been concern, with regard to both Labour and Conservative Governments, that certain contributions or gifts amounted to bribes.

9.10.2 The **Register of Members' Interests** is designed to be an open record of all MPs' consultancies and allegiances, as well as revealing any financial benefits and benefits in kind. Unfortunately, MPs have not always been scrupulous in keeping the Register up to date.

9.10.3 The **Committee on Standards in Public Life** (the Nolan Committee) was convened, following the cash for questions affair, to report on all aspects of MPs' financial interests. The Committee published its report in 1995, which concluded that interests outside Parliament should not be banned but that the Register should be kept more assiduously. It also concluded that the rules on required disclosures of financial and other interests be clarified.

9.10.4 In response to the Report, the House approved a **Code of Conduct**. The Code sets out general principles to guide standards of conduct and use of the Register (now the Register of Members' Financial Interests).

9.10.5 MPs must now:

- notify any contracts where they act in a parliamentary capacity on behalf of any organisation;
- disclose their annual remuneration;
- disclose any monetary benefits of any kind; and
- disclose, whenever they approach another Member or Minister, any financial interest they may have in the subject at hand.

9.10.6 Paid advocacy is banned in relation to:

- initiating parliamentary proceedings;
- presentation of petitions;
- asking parliamentary questions;
- tabling or moving motions; and
- moving amendments to Bills.

9.10.7 Following the controversial expenses scandal, the **Parliamentary Standards Act 2009** was passed. This created a new and independent statutory body called the Independent Parliamentary Standards Authority (IPSA). IPSA is charged with:

- deciding a new allowances system for MPs and administering the system once established;
- drawing up the Code of Conduct on financial interests; and
- establishing rules for investigations.

9.10.8 The **Parliamentary Standards Act 2009** also creates a new criminal offence of knowingly providing false or misleading information in a claim for an allowance, for which the maximum sanction is up to 12 months' custodial sentence or an unlimited fine.

Key Cases Checklist

Hirst v UK (No. 2) (2005): a person serving a prison sentence following conviction is disqualified from voting (see also Chapter 16)

R v Chaytor (2010): the Supreme Court determined that proceedings in Parliament did not extend to MPs' expenses and that those expenses were not protected by parliamentary privilege

R (Jackson) v Attorney-General (2005): the Parliament Act 1949 was held to be valid; consequently any legislation passed under it is also valid (see 3.4.4)

Parliament

Case law defining the rights and duties within the common law relating to Parliament and broadcasting

Broadcasting

R (Pro-Life Alliance) v BBC (2003): broadcasters had a duty not to broadcast material that offended against good taste and decency

Animal Defenders International v UK (2013): the European Court of Human Rights found that the prohibition on political advertising in the Communications Act 2003 was lawful

9.2.2 Hirst v UK (No. 2) [2005] BHRR 441 (ECtHR)

Key Facts

Under section 3 of the Representation of the People Act 1983, persons convicted of a criminal offence and detained in a penal institution in pursuance of a sentence are not eligible to vote.

Key Law

The blanket exclusion of prisoners violates the right to free elections (see Article 3 of the First Protocol to the ECHR); there was no legitimate policy reason for excluding all convicted prisoners.

Key Problem

The UK Government has yet to act on the decision in *Hirst v UK (No. 2)* – despite several more cases from the European Court of Human Rights confirming the unlawfulness of the blanket ban on prisoner voting under the 1983 Act. See the Key cases checklist? in Chapter 16 for more details on these more recent Strasbourg cases.

9.9.10 R v Chaytor [2010] UKSC 52 (SC)

Key Facts

Former MPs appealed against their convictions for fraud-type offences ('false accounting'), on the basis that the documents that evidenced their dishonest expenses claims could not be admitted as evidence against them in a criminal trial on the basis of the protection afforded under the doctrine of parliamentary privilege. Their appeal failed.

Key Law

The Supreme Court found that the scope of the protection of parliamentary privilege under Article 9 of the Bill of Rights 1689 did not preclude the prosecution of the MPs in the Crown Court for a criminal offence such as fraud.

9.5.5 R (on the application of Pro-Life Alliance) v BBC [2003] UKHL 23 [HL]

Key Facts

The BBC refused to transmit the Pro-Life Alliance Party's election broadcast, on the basis that it was offensive and indecent. The applicants contended that this amounted to censorship and breached Article 10 ECHR.

Key Law

The Court of Appeal held that it had to protect freedom of speech under the Human Rights Act 1998. The House of Lords disagreed, concluding that the BBC and other broadcasters had the right to refuse to show the broadcast on the basis that it would be offensive.

Key Comment

It is unlikely that a court will intervene with the broadcasting authority's decision, except in cases of bad faith or clear irrationality.

9.5.6 R (on the application of Animal Defenders International) v Secretary of State for Culture, Media and Sport [2008] 3 All ER 193 [HL]

Key Facts

The Broadcast Advertising Clearance Centre refused to permit the broadcast of a television advert produced by Animal Defenders International – which was deemed a politically motivated advert campaigning against the use of primates for entertainment purposes.

Key Law

Whilst it was acknowledged by the House of Lords in this case that a blanket ban on political advertising by the means of television and radio broadcasts under provisions of the Communications Act 2003, something that interfered with the applicants' rights to freedom of expression under Article 10 of the European Convention, the ban was justified as necessary in a democratic society, since those means of advertising could be used by powerful and wealthy groups to influence a disproportionate section of society in matters of political discourse. There were other media to which political advertisers had recourse.

Key Comment

In *Animal Defenders International v UK* (2013) the European Court of Human Rights found that the prohibition on political advertising in the Communications Act 2003 was within the UK's margin of appreciation (meaning it was a tolerable legal position in the light of the ECHR) despite interfering with the campaign group's right to freedom of expression.

10 The contemporary role, scope and powers of the executive

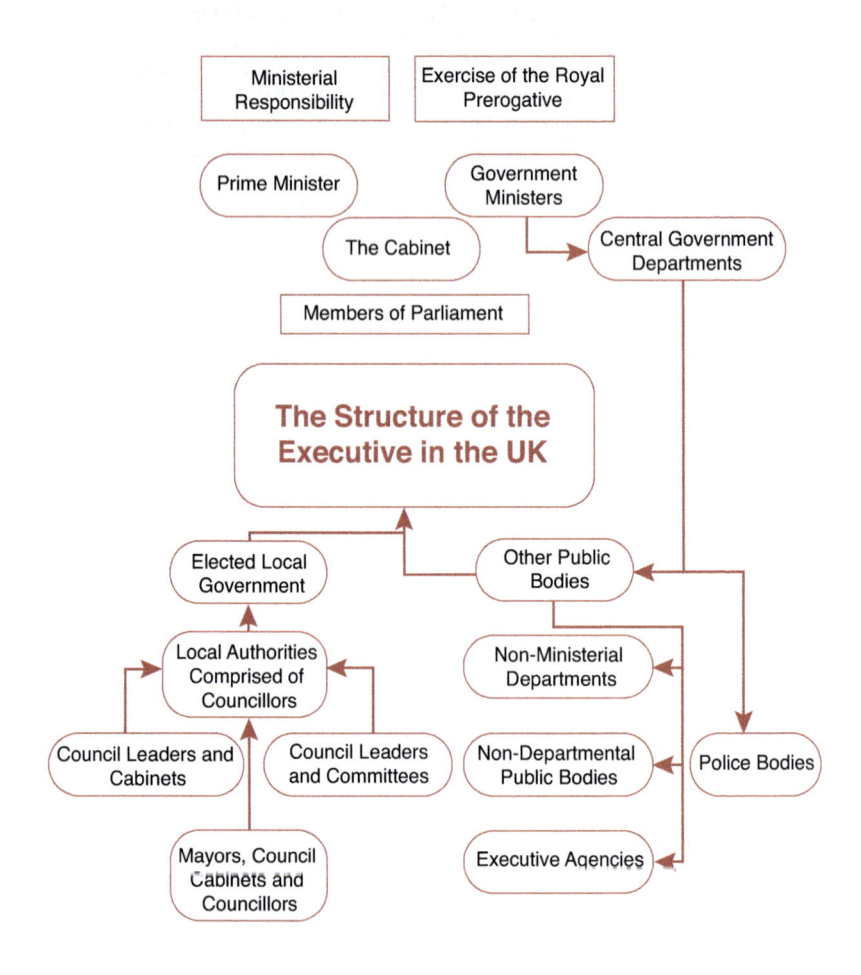

- Ministerial Responsibility
- Exercise of the Royal Prerogative
- Prime Minister
- Government Ministers
- The Cabinet
- Central Government Departments
- Members of Parliament

The Structure of the Executive in the UK

- Elected Local Government
- Other Public Bodies
- Local Authorities Comprised of Councillors
- Non-Ministerial Departments
- Council Leaders and Cabinets
- Council Leaders and Committees
- Non-Departmental Public Bodies
- Police Bodies
- Mayors, Council Cabinets and Councillors
- Executive Agencies

10.1 Defining the executive: Ministers, Government departments and public bodies

10.1.1 The huge scope of the executive in the United Kingdom today is a complex feature of the constitution, and the executive is the principal means of governance in the country – indeed, it is the entire system of government, in most senses of the term.

The Prime Minister and the Cabinet

10.1.2 The office of Prime Minister (PM) is a historical creation. The earliest statutory basis of the position was the provision of a salary (Ministerial and Other Salaries Act 1975). The first individual to occupy what we now regard as the post of PM was William Walpole.

10.1.3 By the 1830s a structure of ministerial government with departmental responsibilities, under the leadership of an elected Party leader, was established.

10.1.4 The PM today retains personal control of many key responsibilities of Government, which can be exercised under the prerogative:

- the right to nominate the Government;
- the control of the Cabinet agenda;
- election of the Lord Chancellor; and
- Chair of Cabinet Committees.

10.1.5 The question most commonly raised with regard to the PM is the extent to which such a concentration of power in the hands of one individual is appropriate in a democracy, and whether there are sufficient controls on the exercise of this power.

10.1.6 One recently created check on the conventional powers of the PM is the shift from the ability of the holder of that office to request the Monarch dissolve Parliament, thereby triggering a General Election, to a system of regularly elected Parliaments every five years, under the Fixed-Term Parliaments Act 2011. (Though there is still a system in place under the 2011 Act for triggering 'early' General Elections if the Government of the day loses the confidence of the House of Commons, by May 2015, at the time of writing, this had not been used during the period of the 2010–15 Coalition Government led by David Cameron of the Conservative Party.)

Government Ministers and their departments

10.1.7   The Cabinet of Government Ministers in its modern form is derived from the ancient circle of advisers to the Monarch. It was not until the 19th century that clear areas of ministerial responsibility at Cabinet level emerged.

10.1.8   The modern Cabinet is selected by the PM; typically, its membership numbers around 20. In addition to the Lord Chancellor, the Secretary of State for Justice and the Chancellor of the Exchequer, each post represents a Department of State designated as the PM determines.

10.1.9   The Cabinet functions as a policy forum and as a means of co-ordinating departmental strategies.

10.1.10 A key criticism of modern Cabinets is the extent to which they have become a 'rubber stamp' for policy-making by the PM rather than a collective decision-making body.

10.1.11 The Cabinet's timetable of meetings is determined by the PM. There is no requirement that a full Cabinet take key decisions. For example, Margaret Thatcher controversially took decisions in the Falklands War without summoning a full Cabinet.

10.1.12 There can be up to 33 attendees at the Cabinet, at the time of writing in May 2015, although the core Cabinet membership consists of:

- the Prime Minister,
- the Deputy Prime Minister (or the First Secretary of State, in the nomenclature used by the current Conservative Government of 2015);
- the Leader of the House of Commons,
- the Chancellor of the Exchequer;
- the Secretary of State for the Home Department (known as the Home Secretary);
- the Secretary of State for Foreign and Commonwealth Affairs (known as the Foreign Secretary);
- the Lord Chancellor;
- the Secretary of State for Justice;
- the Secretary of State for Defence;
- the Secretary of State for Business, Innovation and Skills;
- the Secretary of State for Work and Pensions;

- the Secretary of State for Health;
- the Secretary of State for Communities and Local Government;
- the Secretary of State for Education;
- the Secretary of State for International Development;
- the Secretary of State for Energy and Climate Change;
- the Secretary of State for Transport;
- the Secretary of State for the Environment, Food and Rural Affairs;
- Chief Secretary to the Treasury;
- the Secretary of State for Scotland;
- the Secretary of State for Northern Ireland; and
- the Secretary of State for Wales.

10.1.13 **The convention of ministerial responsibility** is an essential means of ensuring that Government is responsible for its actions. A responsible Government is one that is both accountable and responsive to Parliament and to the electorate.

10.1.14 Under the UK constitution this is not secured by formal or legal rules but by convention. The **convention of ministerial responsibility** comprises two aspects:
- individual ministerial responsibility; and
- collective ministerial responsibility.

10.1.15 However, at the same time it should be noted that the convention is difficult to define with any degree of certainty.

10.1.16 Whilst the Cabinet is at the core of government and has extensive powers, the doctrine of collective responsibility is a reminder that Parliament remains sovereign and that the Cabinet must answer to Parliament for its actions and inactions.

10.1.17 The classic definition of the convention of collective ministerial responsibility is that of Lord Salisbury in 1878: 'For all that passes in Cabinet every member of it who does not resign is absolutely and irretrievably responsible and has no right afterwards to say that he agreed in one case to a compromise, while in another he was persuaded by his colleagues.'

10.1.18 The convention is justified by the need for the Government to present a united front to maintain public confidence, hence the Government as a whole should resign if defeated in a vote of no confidence, for example.

10.1.19 There are two rules under the convention of collective ministerial responsibility:

- under the **unanimity rule**, once agreement is reached in the Cabinet, all members are bound to speak in support of the decision in public, regardless of whether they agreed or were present; and
- under the **confidentiality rule**, all formal records of Cabinet meetings are protected from immediate disclosure and are released after a normally lengthy period of time (previously 30 years), which will be 20 years when the reforms provided by the Constitutional Reform and Governance Act 2010 are fully in effect.

10.1.20 Non-official accounts, such as memoirs, are subject to the principle set out in *Attorney-General v Jonathan Cape Ltd* (1976), which tells us that the publication of confidential information from Cabinet meetings in ministerial memoirs is subject, upon challenge, to the application of a public interest test under the law of confidentiality.

10.1.21 Resignations on the basis of a breakdown in the ability of the Cabinet to maintain a united front can result in considerable embarrassment for the Government. For example, the resignation of Geoffrey Howe was considered extremely influential in ending Margaret Thatcher's Prime Ministership. Geoffrey Howe resigned over the Government's policy on the issue of European Community (now European Union) membership.

10.1.22 In practice, the above rules should operate to protect a Minister under attack for a policy, decision etc. because their colleagues should help defend them. However, this may not be effective if the media is determined to pursue the matter and/or the Minister loses the support of the PM, which could force his or her resignation.

10.1.23 The convention is flexible and can be relaxed by the PM where in extreme circumstances agreement cannot be reached. For example, in 1975 the PM, Harold Wilson, waived the convention in respect of the UK's continued membership of the then European Economic Community prior to a referendum.

10.1.24 This convention places Ministers in a position of having to answer for the work of their departments. The doctrine is identified with the *Carltona* principle (*Carltona Ltd v Works Commissioners* (1943)), which provides that a decision taken by a junior/subordinate official is regarded as being the decision of the Minister in charge of the department and he or she must answer for it in Parliament.

10.1.25 Ministers are also responsible for the actions of civil servants, specifically the principle that the Minister is responsible if the civil servant is following direct instruction and/or policy.

10.2 Ministerial responsibility and accountability, and a Ministerial Code

10.2.1 The modern basis for ministerial responsibility is now found in the **Ministerial Code**. This states that:
- Ministers have a duty to Parliament to account for the policies, decisions and actions of their departments;
- Ministers must give accurate and truthful information and correct errors at the earliest opportunity. Ministers that knowingly mislead are expected to offer their resignation to the PM;
- Ministers should be as open as possible with Parliament, refusing to disclose information only when not in the public interest;
- Ministers should require civil servants who give evidence on their behalf to a Parliamentary Committee under their direction to be as helpful as possible in providing accurate, truthful and full information; and
- Ministers must ensure that no conflict arises, or appears to arise, between their public duties and their private interests.

10.2.2 In July 2011 the following addition to the Ministerial Code (2010) was approved by the Prime Minister, David Cameron:

> 'The Government will be open about its links with the media. All meetings with newspaper and other media proprietors, editors and senior executives will be published quarterly regardless of the purpose of the meeting.'

10.2.3 This latest amendment to the expectations placed on Government Ministers by the Code is a move to highlight the need for accountability for ministerial involvement with particular sections of the news media, in particular, who may be swayed or biased toward particular coverage of ministerial policy, for example.

10.2.4 However, the Code has no legal force and there is no independent method of enforcing it. Instead the Code states that Ministers remain in office only as long as they have the confidence of the PM. It is therefore the PM that is 'the ultimate judge of the standards of behaviour expected of a Minister and the appropriate consequences of a breach of those standards'.

10.2.5 It appears that, in the case of responsibility for departmental maladministration or mismanagement, there are no clear rules on when a Minister should resign but three influential factors: whether they have the support of the Prime Minister; whether they have the support of their political Party; and whether they have any support in the media for their continuation in their post.

10.2.6 There are no provisions requiring Ministers to hold particular qualifications or a formal vetting process to identify their appropriateness to hold public office; appointment is purely at the discretion of the PM.

10.2.7 Personal conduct may lead to resignation, and indeed seemingly more so than in cases where there is acceptance of departmental responsibility.

10.2.8 The Ministerial Code provides that Ministers must scrupulously avoid any danger of an actual or apparent conflict of interest between their ministerial position and their private financial interests.

10.2.9 The Code no longer requires Ministers to resign any directorships they hold on assuming office, although if a Minister does have a financial interest he or she must not be involved in any decision-making relating to it.

10.3 Local authorities

10.3.1 Local government, carried out in the United Kingdom by bodies often known collectively as local authorities, is the creation of Parliament – specifically, certain Acts of Parliament.

10.3.2 Local government is the responsible layer of government for huge swathes of State operation in the social care, town planning, commercial licensing, development and environment, local transport and many education functions.

10.3.3 The Local Government Act 2000, the Local Government and Public Involvement in Health Act 2007 and the Localism Act 2011 between them have created a series of newer potential structures than the older county- or district-level authorities under the Local Government Act 1972, which were built around locally elected ward councillors, each representing a specific local area.

10.3.4 Local wards and the notion of electing councillors to represent specific councillors still exist under the newer arrangements.

10.3.5 These newer arrangements now include the possibility of a local authority being governed, according to Elliott and Thomas, in one of four distinct ways (in England):

- Firstly, an indirectly elected leader of a council body is chosen by the councillors whose Party has the most number of seats in the council governing that particular local authority. The leader of the council then appoints a cabinet around them to help them manage the affairs of the local authority, creating a council executive. The cabinet is challenged when necessary by 'overview and scrutiny' committees, modelled on parliamentary committees, and as such are comprised by 'backbench' councillors who are not part of the council cabinet.

- Secondly, there is the possibility of a local authority being headed by a mayor, who is directly elected by the local voters, who also still vote on the particular councillors to represent their wards. Here, the mayor selects the cabinet to take the lead on governance of the local authority – again creating a council-level executive. Under the Local Government Act 2000 as amended there must be a local referendum to legitimise the switch to this model of local authority government.

- Thirdly, councils can still be arranged along committee lines, with a nominal leader selected by ward councillors from amongst their own number, according to the dominant Party after a local election – but where there is no cabinet, only committees, which are meant to represent the political hue of all the councillors as a whole. This system means that, in theory, one highly successful Party following an election does not entirely dominate all of council business.

- Fourthly, and finally, central Government can again, when requested by a local authority itself, stipulate some other kind of system that may be a fusion of elements of any or all of the above models, using powers again under the Local Government Act 2000.

10.3.6 Powers and responsibilities afforded to local authorities as public bodies with oversight in a particular area can be allotted and delegated internally, within the local authority itself, to an array of committees, subcommittees and officers, under section 101 of the Local Government Act 1972.

10.3.7 Elliott and Thomas have observed that, when compared with government by Westminster, or the devolved national legislatures in Edinburgh, Belfast and Cardiff, it can be the case that people 'often have only a rudimentary awareness of the role of local government and this inhibits the development of the strong sense of connection with local authorities that might guard against central government interference'.

10.3.8 Ultimately, while local authorities often have enormous responsibilities in co-ordinating social care in the community, under the Care Act 2014 and other pieces of legislation, and child protection and other social work roles under the Children Act 1989, for example, their budgetary allocations, and their ability to levy local funds in the form of council tax, are all central-Government controlled.

10.3.9 The powers of local authorities have been nominally expanded under provisions of the Localism Act 2011, which provides local authorities with a 'general power of competence'. The 'plain English guide' to the 2011 Act, produced by the Department of Communities and Local Government (in 2011), explains that:

'Instead of being able to act only where the law says they can, local authorities will be freed to do anything – provided they do not break other laws . . . The new, general power gives councils more freedom to work together with others in new ways to drive down costs . . . The general power of competence does not remove any duties from local authorities – just like individuals they will continue to need to comply with duties placed on them. The Act does, however, give the Secretary of State the power to remove unnecessary restrictions and limitations where there is a good case to do so, subject to safeguards designed to protect vital services.'

10.3.10 It is vital to note, however, as Elliott and Thomas have observed, that 'where councils have specified, restricted powers to do things, the general power cannot be used to circumvent such restrictions'.

10.3.11 In May 2015, following its success in the General Election that month, the Conservative Government announced plans for a Cities Devolution Bill, which would create a system of regional government on an unprecedented scale for the UK constitution. City regions, as centres of local government based in larger cities, with various towns around them included in that region, would be the recipients of much greater taxation, spending and borrowing powers – significantly reducing the control of the central,

Westminster Government over the priorities and strategies for developing local or regional economies.

10.4 Police structures

10.4.1 It may be that many elements of the course you are studying in the areas of constitutional law and/or administrative law will have a focus on the roles, powers and legal duties of the police (if indeed you are studying a particular course). As such it is useful to highlight basic policing structures in the United Kingdom today.

10.4.2 England and Wales between them are served by 43 separate police bodies at the time of writing in May 2015, whilst Police Scotland and the Police Service of Northern Ireland carry out policing functions in Scotland and Northern Ireland respectively.

10.4.3 Complaints about the police and policing operations can be made by members of the public to the **Independent Police Complaints Commission**, if it cannot be fairly or finally addressed by the local police force complaints procedure.

10.4.4 Police standards are investigated and upheld, in theory, by **Her Majesty's Inspectorate of Constabulary** – while police training and policy development is monitored and promulgated by the national-level **College of Policing**.

10.4.5 Importantly, while the **Home Office** and the relevant Government Minister, the Secretary of State for the Home Department (the **Home Secretary**), have a large role in developing and setting police practices and a policy and funding agenda for policing on a national level, at the regional level, the Police Reform and Social Responsibility Act 2011 has created the role of a **Police and Crime Commissioner** for every police body.

10.4.6 The office of Police and Crime Commissioner is designed to hold to account each force-level **Chief Constable**, in whose person legal authority for particular operational policing decisions and practices often rests (and who will be the defendant in much judicial review litigation connected to policing as a result). Police and Crime Commissioners are supported in their aim to ensure and increase policing accountability and transparency by local **Police and Crime Panels** comprised of local councillors drawn from local authorities within the relevant force area (e.g. from local authorities in Sheffield, Rotherham, Barnsley and Doncaster in relation to South Yorkshire Police).

10.4.7 Police and Crime Panels in turn also scrutinise the work and competence of Police and Crime Commissioners, and the Commissioners' **Police and Crime Plans**, which steer the priorities of Chief Constables of particular police forces.

10.5 Different types of public body

10.5.1 For the purposes of much of your studies of public law, and particularly of administrative law, the pertinent issue in relation to defining *public bodies* is measuring whether they are amenable to judicial review of their actions and decisions.

10.5.2 To that end, broader concepts of what constitutes a public body for the purposes of judicial review are discussed at 12.4.

10.5.3 However, aside from central Government departments, headed by Government Ministers, local authorities and the police, there are three other main types of executive body.

10.5.4 As Elliott and Thomas have highlighted, these three categories are:

> Firstly: Non-ministerial departments such as Her Majesty's Revenue and Customs (HMRC) – structured in such a way to place them outside of ministerial control to try and enhance their political independence.
>
> Secondly: The extremely broad category of non-departmental public bodies (NDPBs). These, Elliott and Thomas note, include:
>
> - Bodies with executive powers (itself an enormously broad category, including the NHS Commissioning Board, known as 'NHS England', the Health and Safety Executive (HSE) and the Environment Agency.
> - Advisory bodies created to advise the work of Ministers and their central Government departments; for example, as Elliott and Thomas note, the Social Security Advisory Committee advises the Department of Work and Pensions and so the Secretary of State for Work and Pensions.
> - Tribunals which determine individuals' rights, obligations and entitlements in relation to the roles and responsibilities of central Government departments.
> - Independent monitoring boards – such as those that inspect the standards and conditions in UK prisons.

Thirdly: Executive agencies, headed by chief executives. These are created to try and make Government more efficient and expert in certain areas – for example, the National Offender Management Service (known as 'NOMS') oversees the work of dozens of newly formed private probation companies which win contracts from the Ministry of Justice to supervise and rehabilitate criminal offenders in the community.

10.5.5 As Elliott and Thomas note, the term 'quango' has been coined to describe 'quasi-autonomous non-governmental organisations' as a kind of catch-all term for a range of types of public bodies that fall outside of clear central Government. The Public Bodies Act 2011, as Elliott and Thomas describe it, enables Minsters to abolish and merge public bodies using secondary legislation. But the 'bonfire of the quangos', which the Coalition Government sought in order to try to reduce costs of government across what it perceived as a bloated range of executive agencies. But the 'bonfire', as the press termed it, has so far only 'smouldered', as Tonkiss and Dommett have observed, and claims of overall costs saved are doubtful, as the work of abolished quangos has often needed to be re-assigned to re-structured, continuing Government bodies.

10.6 Prerogative powers today: the Monarch and Ministers exercising power

The royal prerogative

10.6.1 The royal prerogative is a source of constitutional law (see Chapter 2). It derives from common law powers that have transferred from the monarchy to the executive, which is discussed below.

10.6.2 The significance in constitutional law of the prerogative is that it provides the executive with considerable power to act without following 'normal' parliamentary procedures. As Dicey explained, the prerogative is 'every act which the executive government can lawfully do without the authority of an Act of Parliament'.

10.6.3 In constitutional terms it is therefore important to explore the means by which the UK constitution secures the accountability for the exercise of prerogative powers by the executive.

10.6.4 No new prerogative powers can be created according to the case of *Entick v Carrington* (1765).

Examples of prerogative powers

10.6.5 Prerogative powers originated in the powers of the Monarch, who could act in his or her own inherent right.

10.6.6 Historically, the Monarch's powers included:

- appointment and dismissal of Ministers;
- law-making by proclamation;
- establishing Royal Courts without judges;
- raising taxation;
- deploying forces in defence of the realm;
- immunity from suit; and
- the grant of honours.

10.6.7 By the reign of James I (1603–25) the Monarch was faced with an increasingly effective Parliament, culminating in the temporary abolition of the monarchy in 1625. Consequently, the monarchy's powers were eroded by both revolution and by legal challenges, including the following:

- *Case of Proclamations* (1611) – the Monarch could not change the law by proclamation. The law of the land, which required that law be made by Parliament, limited the prerogative.
- *Prohibitions del Roy* (1607) – the Monarch had no right to act as a judge.
- *The Ship Money Case* (1637) – although the court declared it to be within the Monarch's power to determine a state of emergency, requiring tax-raising, the Ship Money Act 1637 was passed, making it illegal for the Monarch to raise taxation.

10.6.8 The Bill of Rights 1688, however, crystallised the transfer of legislative (and chiefly taxation) powers from the monarchy to Parliament, and as well as providing for the restoration of the monarchy under the legal control of Parliament.

10.6.9 Certain prerogative powers remain in the hands of the Monarch to the present day but convention requires that the Monarch act only on the advice of Government Ministers. Hence, in theory, the Monarch may appoint and dismiss Ministers and veto legislation by refusing the Royal Assent, yet in practice these prerogatives are now exercised by the Government.

10.6.10 Modern prerogative powers may be defined as the legal powers inherent in Government, which do not require the approval of Parliament for their exercise.

10.6.11 It has traditionally been difficult to identify and assess the extent of prerogative powers with no codified list of those that exist.

10.6.12 In October 2009 the Government published a review of executive prerogative powers which provides the most comprehensive modern examination of the various prerogative powers (although it did not extend to prerogatives related to devolved matters). The report categorises them as follows:

Ministerial prerogative powers	Powers concerning . . .
1. Government and the Civil Service	***machinery of government*** including the power to set up a department or a non-departmental body establish certain specified bodies, appoint members and grant powers (e.g. House of Lords Appointments Committee) appointment and regulation of the Civil Service prohibit civil servants and certain other Crown officials from issuing election addresses or announcing themselves as Parliamentary candidates set nationality rules for non-aliens concerning eligibility to work in the Civil Service require security vetting of contractors working alongside civil servants
2. Justice system and law and order	• grant mercy • keep the peace • appoint Queen's Counsel • provisional and full order extradition requests to countries not covered by Part 1 of the Extradition Act 2003
3. Foreign affairs	recognition of States make and ratify treaties acquire and cede territory governance of British Overseas Territories issue, refuse and withdraw passport facilities responsibility for the Channel Islands and Isle of Man conduct diplomacy send ambassadors abroad and receive them from foreign States grant diplomatic protection to British nationals abroad

(*Continued*)

4. Armed forces, war and times of emergency	make war or peace or institute hostilities falling short of war deployment and use of armed forces overseas use of armed forces within the United Kingdom to maintain the peace control, organisation and disposition of armed forces powers in the event of grave national emergency, including those to enter, take and destroy property maintenance of the Royal Navy requisition of British ships in times of national emergency commissioning of officers armed forces pay certain armed forces pensions closed to new members war pensions for death or disablement due to services before 6 April 2005 Crown's right to claim Prize (enemy ships or goods captured at sea) regulation of trade with the enemy appropriation of the property of a neutral within the realm when necessary
5. Miscellaneous	establish corporations by Royal Charter and to amend existing ones ownership of treasure trove hold public inquiries control of HM Stationery Office sole right to print or license printing of the Bible, Book of Common Prayer, State papers and Acts of Parliament issue certificates of eligibility for inter-country adoption in non-Hague Convention cases powers in respect of pre-paid postage stamps

Prerogative powers of others	Powers concerning . . .
1. Monarch's constitutional or personal prerogatives (exercised under recommendations from Ministers under convention)	appointment and removal of Ministers and PM dismiss Government summon, prorogue and dissolve Parliament assent to legislation legislate by Order in Council or Letters Patent appoint privy counsellors appoint judges and holders of public office that are non-statutory posts grant special leave to appeal from certain non-UK courts to the Privy Council grant honours, decorations, arms and regulating matters of precedence Queen's honours

Prerogative powers of others	Powers concerning . . .
	grant civic honours and dignities approve certain uses of the Royal name and titles require the personal services of subjects in case of imminent danger
2. Legal prerogatives of the Crown	not bound by statute save by express words or necessary implication immunities in litigation including being not directly subject to contempt jurisdiction and the Sovereign has personal immunity from prosecution or being sued for a wrongful act tax not payable on income received by the Sovereign preferred creditor in a debtor's insolvency no prescriptive rights run against the Crown priority property rights in some circumstances
3. Attorney General	in respect of charities in respect of criminal proceedings in respect of civil proceedings

Limitations to the exercise of prerogative powers

10.6.13 **Royal prerogative and the courts:** the exercise of prerogative powers was originally not susceptible to judicial review.

10.6.14 However, since the landmark judgment in *CCSU v Minister for the Civil Service* (1985) (otherwise known as the *GCHQ Case*) the exercise of certain prerogative powers is now capable of being reviewed by the courts and can be challenged on the basis that the Minister:

- did not have the power to act in such a way;
- acted unreasonably; or
- acted in a procedurally unfair way.

10.6.15 However, only certain prerogatives are capable of being reviewed. Whether a prerogative power is susceptible to judicial review will depend on its nature/subject matter. Lord Diplock in the *GCHQ Case* (1985) suggested that ministerial decisions exercising prerogative powers could be difficult to challenge because they would 'generally involve the application of government policy'. In other words, they would be non-justiciable prerogative powers.

10.6.16 Lord Roskill identified some non-justiciable prerogative powers in the *GCHQ Case*, including:

- making treaties;
- defence of the realm;
- prerogative of mercy;
- granting honours;
- dissolution of Parliament; and
- appointment of Ministers.

Since the *GCHQ Case*, however, the courts have appeared willing to examine a range of prerogative powers, including some of the below.

Treaty-making powers

10.6.17 In *R v Secretary of State for Foreign and Commonwealth Affairs, ex parte Rees-Mogg* (1994) the Court of Appeal discussed the prerogative of treaty-making but concluded it was a non-reviewable power. Though Parliament now has the ability to scrutinise treaties before their ratification under the Constitutional Reform and Governance Act 2010 (see Chapter 5 and Chapter 9 for more details and context).

Mercy/granting of pardons

10.6.18 This prerogative was traditionally non-reviewable (*DeFreitas v Benny* (1976)) but in *R v Secretary of State for the Home Department, ex parte Bentley* (1994) the court considered 'some aspects' of the prerogative of mercy to be reviewable. The court did not make any formal order in the case but invited the Home Secretary to reconsider the issues. In 1998 the Criminal Cases Review Commission referred the case to the Court of Appeal, where the conviction was held unsafe and quashed (see also *Attorney-General of Trinidad and Tobago v Lennox Phillip* (1995)).

Issuing passports

10.6.19 In *R v Secretary of State for Foreign and Commonwealth Affairs, ex parte Everett* (1989) the Court of Appeal held the issuing of passports to be a reviewable prerogative on the basis that it is a 'matter of administrative decision, affecting the rights of individuals and their freedom of travel': see also *R v Secretary of State for the Home Department, ex parte Al Fayed* (1997).

Declaring war and deployment of troops

10.6.20 In *Campaign for Nuclear Disarmament v Prime Minister* (2002), CND challenged the decision of the Government to send troops to Iraq. This was considered to be a 'classic example' of a non-reviewable prerogative power.

Power to make ex gratia payments

10.6.21 In *R v Criminal Compensation Board and Another, ex parte P* (1995) the prerogative power of making *ex gratia* payments to the victims of crime was held to be reviewable. In *National Farmers Union v Secretary of State for the Environment, Food and Rural Affairs* (2003), the NFU was able to challenge *ex gratia* payments made to farmers on the culling of their livestock as a result of the foot and mouth epidemic.

Defence of the realm

10.6.22 Considered non-reviewable in the *GCHQ Case*, even this prerogative has in certain contexts been scrutinised by the courts, aided by the passing of the Human Rights Act 1998. For example, in *A (FC) v Secretary of State for the Home Department* (2005) the House of Lords set aside a derogation order made on the grounds of State emergency as being disproportionate to the objective.

Orders in council

10.6.23 In *R (Bancoult) v Secretary of State for Foreign and Commonwealth Affairs* (2008) the House of Lords held that prerogative Orders in Council do not share all of the characteristics of an Act of Parliament, and that an exercise of the prerogative in such a way could be subject to judicial review.

Royal prerogative and statute

10.6.24 Because of the doctrine of parliamentary supremacy, Parliament can legislate to **modify, abolish** or **put on a statutory footing** any particular prerogative power. For example, the prerogative of issuing warrants for telephone tapping was replaced by the legal framework of warrants and authorisations under the Regulation of

Investigatory Powers Act 2000, and more recently the Data Retention and Investigatory Powers Act 2014.

10.6.25 If the royal prerogative and statute exist on the same subject matter and the statute does not expressly abolish the prerogative, the prerogative power must be suspended: *AG v De Keyser's Royal Hotel Ltd* (1920).

10.6.26 Prerogative powers can only be used in such circumstances if the statute **expressly** provides so. If this is the case any subsequent use of the prerogative power must conform to the terms of the statute: *Laker Airways v Secretary of State for Trade* (1977).

10.6.27 A Minister must also not seek to rely on prerogative powers to create new regulations in order to override statutory provisions according to the case of *R v Secretary of State for the Home Department, ex parte Fire Brigades Union* (1995).

10.6.28 The case of *Entick v Carrington* (1765) determined that the range of prerogative powers was at that date closed – in other words, that no new prerogative powers could be created. This was confirmed 200 years later in *BBC v Johns* (1965).

10.6.29 It appears that an established prerogative may be exercised in a new or modern context where it is a logical inference from the powers conferred: *R v Secretary of State for the Home Department, ex parte Northumbria Police Authority* (1988).

10.6.30 It should be noted, however, that drawing the line between using an existing prerogative in a new or modern context and creating what is in effect a new prerogative is a thin one. The constitutional issue is therefore the potential for the executive to abuse such powers yet justify such action on the basis that it is merely the exercise of an existing prerogative in a new context.

Royal prerogative and Parliament

10.6.31 As well as by statute, Parliament may exert some control over the use and exercise of prerogative powers as follows:

- Ministers are **accountable** to Parliament for all their actions, including those taken under the prerogative. This may include scrutiny by select committee.

- The PM is also subject to twice-yearly questioning by the Liaison Committee.

- In addition, parliamentary approval is required where use of the prerogative involves the incurring of expenditure.

Reform of the prerogative

10.6.32 The existence and extent of prerogative power is a matter of common law. Hence the courts are the final arbiter of whether or not a particular type of prerogative power exists: *Case of Proclamations* (1610).

10.6.33 The problem is that for the vast majority of prerogative powers there are no recent cases or indeed any judicial authority. This means that we have to turn to old Government practice and legal textbooks to identify their existence and extent. In terms of academic opinion, the most comprehensive text on prerogatives was written by Chitty in 1820.

10.6.34 This uncertainty has been criticised and there has been demand for:

- a codified list of the range of prerogatives that exist (e.g. Brazier states that this is of 'practical importance'); and
- that certain prerogatives be surrendered or limited on the basis that in a modern democracy they should not be exercised exclusively by the executive.

10.6.35 The following set of tables summarises the recent approach to the reform of key controversial prerogative powers.

	Ratification of treaties
Green Paper 2007	Whether the process of ratifying treaties under the convention known as the 'Ponsonby Rule' could be replaced by formal arrangements or statutory provisions
	(Ponsonby Rule: treaties that come into force at a date later than their signature must be laid before Parliament for at least 21 days)
White Paper 2008	Proposed that the Rule be on a statutory basis
Constitutional Reform and Governance Act 2010	Puts parliamentary scrutiny of treaty ratification on a statutory footing and gives legal effect to a resolution of the House that a treaty should not be ratified

(Continued)

War-making powers/deployment of armed forces	
Green Paper 2007	Proposed that Government should seek approval of the Commons for significant non-routine deployments into armed conflict Commons retains sufficient powers so it could deploy for reasons of urgency or operational security
White Paper 2008	To be achieved through **resolution** of the Commons but future legislation not ruled out

10.7 Proper scrutiny of the executive branch of Government by Parliament

10.7.1 To ensure executive accountability and responsibility, and consequently the operation of the conventions of ministerial responsibility, is Parliament's most constitutionally significant role. Parliament in the form of both Houses has at its disposal a number of mechanisms to scrutinise executive action.

10.7.2 In the 19th century, John Stuart Mill described the Commons as the 'sounding board of the nation'. It remains the case today that one of Parliament's major roles is to undertake debates. The Government generally controls the subject of debate, but the Opposition Parties can do so for 20 days in each parliamentary session.

10.7.3 Debates take place at various stages as a Bill proceeds through Parliament. The most in-depth debate of proposed legislation takes place at the second reading. The debates that take place at the report stage are generally more brief, although there have been exceptions to this (e.g. Police and Criminal Evidence Act 1984).

10.7.4 Any MP, or group of MPs, may request an Early Day Motion, which is a written motion tabled in Parliament for a debate on any subject matter. At the end of the parliamentary day, backbenchers may initiate short debates on matters of their choice known as Daily Adjournment debates. These involve the MP speaking for 15 minutes and the relevant Minister being able to respond for 15 minutes. Any MP can apply to the Speaker for an emergency debate, which will be a three-hour debate held the following day.

10.7.5 The effectiveness of debates in the House of Commons as a means of scrutinising the executive is varied and can depend on a number of factors, including:

- the size of the Government majority;
- the strength and experience of the Opposition parties; and
- whether 'backbenchers' (non-mainstream MPs who are more on the fringes of the political Party of which they are members) are prepared to challenge the Government.

10.7.6 The use of ministerial Question Time provides a rota so that different Ministers answer questions in Parliament during weekly sessions. Answers to questions can be requested in either oral or written format. However, not all oral questions can be answered within parliamentary time, in which case a written answer is provided. The oral question process includes the ability of an MP to ask a supplementary question, for which no notice has to be given. Urgent oral questions can be raised for immediate discussion after Question Time but must be approved by the Speaker by noon on the day the question is to be asked. The Speaker has discretion as to whether to permit it.

10.7.7 Question Time can be effective in that it achieves a great deal of publicity and the responses, whether oral or written, being published, can provide a wealth of information. However, there are also a number of limitations.

10.7.8 Rules have been created, enforced by the Speaker, which limit the range of questions that can be asked. The following matters cannot be part of Question Time:

- matters pertaining to the Monarch;
- certain matters of the prerogative; and
- questions that do not relate to the responsibility of the individual Minister.

10.7.9 There is also a wide range of subjects that questions cannot be asked on, including:

- local authorities;
- personal powers of the Monarch;
- internal affairs of other countries;
- defence and national security;
- Cabinet business;
- advice given to Ministers by civil servants;
- nationalised industries; and
- matters that are *sub judice* (that is, matters that are currently listed to be heard or being heard before a court or tribunal of any kind).

10.7.10 The Speaker will also reject questions that are:
- too broad to be answered within the time constraints;
- trivial or irrelevant;
- critical of the judiciary; and
- not phrased in proper parliamentary language.

10.7.11 In addition to the above limitations:
- answers to questions may be refused because of their disproportionate cost;
- urgent questions are often made to the Speaker but very few are accepted; and
- notice of three sitting days must be given which, although justified on the basis of giving Ministers appropriate time to prepare, significantly reduces the spontaneity of the process.

10.7.12 Prime Minister's Question Time takes place on Wednesdays, is routinely televised and lasts for 30 minutes, and is a very visible (though sometimes overly boisterous affair) means of increasing Government accountability:
- The process requires the asking of an 'open' question before the MP may ask up to two supplementary questions.
- The supplementary questions can be on any matter for which the PM is responsible, or matters that fall outside the responsibility of an individual Minister.
- The Leader of the Opposition can ask up to six questions on almost any aspect of governmental policy.
- Since Prime Minister's Question Time is televised it attracts considerable attention. Its effectiveness is enhanced by the fact that there is no advance notice of the questions to be asked.

10.8 The work of the parliamentary committees

10.8.1 The current system of departmentally related select committees was created in 1979. Their functions are to examine matters within Government departments and to report to the House of Commons.

10.8.2 Select committees have discretion on what matters to investigate and the evidence required. They have the power to call for persons, papers and records. They can also appoint specialist advisers.

10.8.3 Membership of select committees is of a cross-Party nature but is reflective of the strength of each Party in the House. According to convention, they are largely made up of backbenchers.

10.8.4 However, select committees do not have the power to compel Ministers to give evidence (although failure to do so may amount to contempt of Parliament) and there can be difficulties in securing governmental and other co-operation.

10.8.5 Another potential limitation on the effectiveness of select committees is that only approximately one-third of reports produced are debated in the House of Commons. This is a reflection of the considerable pressure on parliamentary time. Reports are, though, published and therefore provide considerable and extensive information that is in the public domain.

10.9 Wider controls on the power of the executive: judicial review, the media and the electorate

10.9.1 In addition to the above, there are a range of other bodies and/or mechanisms that may secure the accountability of the executive. In brief these include the following.

10.9.2 **Judicial review**: operating under the rule of law, judicial review can be extremely effective in securing the accountability of the executive. However, there can be some difficulty in securing an effective remedy

10.9.3 **The media**: good-quality investigative journalism can generate public awareness of Government and/or individual deficiencies, maladministration etc. In some cases this can be limited, by, for example, libel laws, but freedom of expression is an ECHR right.

10.9.4 **The electorate**: free elections provide the public or electorate with the opportunity to elect a different political Party into power, thereby showing its dissatisfaction with a previous administration. The effectiveness of this is, however, limited by a range of factors including: the fact that the PM decides the timing of a General Election; the method of voting, the first past the post system, can disenfranchise the electorate (see Chapter 9); and the process often results in large Government majorities – though not in the General Elections of May 2010 and May 2015.

10.10 The traditional role of the Civil Service and the growth of 'special advisers' to Ministers

The definition of a civil servant

10.10.1 A civil servant is a servant of the Crown but not a holder of political or judicial office, who is employed in a civil capacity and whose remuneration is paid wholly and directly from monies voted by Parliament.

10.10.2 It is extremely difficult to assess the number of civil servants, primarily because of problems in defining whether particular roles are within the public service. The size of a Civil Service staff for a department will depend on its relative size. The terms and conditions of a civil servant's employment are regulated under the prerogative.

Constitutional principles and the Civil Service

Permanency

10.10.3 Civil servants hold permanent posts. This is justified on the basis that expertise can develop and be maintained from one Government to the next. This is in contrast to other constitutions where the Civil Service is semi-permanent and senior posts change with a change of Government, such as in the United States.

Political neutrality

10.10.4 The Civil Service must be loyal to the Government of the day, regardless of which political Party it is comprised of. This is justified on the basis of ensuring a lack of political bias. There has though been constant criticism of whether the Civil Service is indeed politically neutral.

Anonymity

10.10.5 The Civil Service is traditionally anonymous and protected from public inquiry – instead the Minister should be seen to be responsible and accountable. This is justified as a means of ensuring impartiality.

10.10.6 The Civil Service is not accountable to Parliament, thereby protecting its anonymity. Instead, by convention, it is the Minister in charge of the particular Government department that is responsible to Parliament for the conduct of civil servants.

10.10.7 Ensuring accountability has become increasingly difficult for a number of reasons:

(a) departments have massively increased in size, to the extent that it could be questioned whether the Minister is indeed making decisions;

(b) Ministers change on an increasingly frequent basis, with numerous Cabinet reshuffles;

(c) at a practical level the work of Ministers means that they spend what has been estimated to be only one-third of their time on departmental business; and

(d) the proliferation of Government agencies – hence Ministers are distanced from operational matters.

10.10.8 Each Civil Service agency, supporting a particular Government department, has independence in how it meets its objectives. There is a Head of Agency who should be directly responsible for operational matters, whilst the Minister remains responsible for policy (see the Ministerial Code discussed above). Ministers are therefore no longer expected to have an in-depth knowledge of operations on a day-to-day basis.

10.10.9 More recently there has been a move towards privatising previously State bodies so that they become non-departmental public bodies or quangos. A number of bodies have been sold into private ownership including British Rail, British Telecom and most recently the Royal Mail. Questions remain on the extent to which Ministers exert control over such bodies and whether Parliament can secure their accountability for the way in which such bodies implement policy.

10.10.10 Government Ministers have also increasingly appointed 'special advisers' (commonly known as 'spads'). These are Crown servants and temporary civil servants, and are paid from public funds, but not formally part of any department.

10.10.11 The Code of Conduct for Special Advisers states that special advisers are to help Ministers on matters 'where the work of Government and the work of the Government Party overlap' and it would be inappropriate for permanent civil servants to become involved.

10.10.12 The Code describes the types of work 'spads' do as including:

- reviewing ministerial papers and giving advice on departmental business;
- checking facts and research findings from a Party viewpoint;
- preparing policy papers and contributing to Party planning within a department;
- liaising with the Party;
- briefing Party MPs and officials on issues of Government policy;
- liaising with outside interest groups;
- speechwriting;
- representing the views of the Ministers to the media where authorised to do so;
- providing expert advice as a specialist in a particular field;
- attending Party functions; and
- participating in Party reviews organised by the Party.

10.10.13 Special advisers should, according to the Code, act with integrity and honesty but are exempt from the general rule to be impartial and objective. They should not misuse their position to:

- further private interests;
- receive benefits of a compromising nature;
- disclose official information communicated in confidence; or
- use official resources for Party political activity.

10.10.14 However, there are accusations that the increasing use of special advisers has 'politicised' the Civil Service and that there is insufficient scrutiny and control over their activities. As part of a move to ensuring better future accountability of the Civil Service and special advisers, Part 1 of the Constitutional Reform and Governance Act 2010 establishes the following:

- a statutory Civil Service Commission;
- creation of a code of conduct for civil servants that specifically requires them to have regard to the values of integrity, honesty, objectivity and impartiality; and a code of conduct for special advisers (a response to the Damian McBride 'email smear' scandal in April 2009); and
- under section 8 of the Constitutional and Governance Act 2010 special advisers cannot exercise any power in relation to the management of the civil service, save for the work of other appointed special advisers.

10.11 The executive, public records and freedom of information law in the United Kingdom and Europe

10.11.1 For many years there were increasing demands for more open government and a right to access information. In 1997 the new Labour Government promised to generate greater openness and produced the Freedom of Information Act 2000, which applied to central Government from November 2002 and which came into force fully in 2005. (The relevant Scottish legislation is the Freedom of Information (Scotland) Act 2002.)

10.11.2 The Act replaced the Code of Practice on Access to Government Information and amended the Data Protection Act 1998 and the Public Records Act 1958 (see below).

10.11.3 Under section 1, the Act created a legal right for citizens to access data held by public authorities including local government, National Health Service bodies, schools, colleges and the police.

10.11.4 Requests for information must be in writing; the body receiving the request is obligated to reply within 20 working days of its receipt. A fee must be paid and the duty to disclose the information does not arise until that fee is paid.

10.11.5 A public authority may refuse to disclose information where the costs exceed prescribed limits. The Act is enforced by the Information Commissioner who has investigative and enforcement powers.

10.11.6 The effectiveness of the Act is weakened by a list of exempted information. There are two categories – information that is absolutely exempt and information that requires examination to see whether it is in the public interest to disclose it.

10.11.7 The following is information that can be deemed exempt from disclosure (often on the basis of the 'public interest'):

(a) information that is accessible by using other means;

(b) information that is due to be published;

(c) information relating to the security services or the Royal household;

(d) personal information or information provided to the authority in confidence;

(e) information that is professionally privileged;

(f) information that may prejudice the following:

- national security, defence or the effectiveness of the armed forces;

- international relations or relations between the administrations within the United Kingdom;

- the country's economic interests; and

- criminal investigations or proceedings.

10.11.8 The Public Records Acts 1958 and 1967 provided access to public records at the Public Records Office after 30 years (the '30-year rule'). Records could be kept closed for longer under section 5 of the 1958 Act or withheld if there is justification for so doing.

10.11.9 Under the Acts, the Lord Chancellor has power to order release of documents sooner, if in the public interest.

10.11.10 Under the Freedom of Information Act, a statutory regime was created for access to public records, which replaced the provisions of the Public Records Act 1958 in respect of discretionary disclosure. The period of embargo of public records will be 20 years when the reforms provided by the Constitutional Reform and Governance Act 2010 are fully in effect.

10.11.11 The Data Protection Act 1998 provides that personal data should be made available to individuals who request it using a subject access request, primarily so that its accuracy may be checked.

10.11.12 Section 1 provides that you have the right to be informed if personal data is being held and to be told what that information is; as well as that the information is held lawfully, for no longer than necessary, and securely – under the 'data protection principles' (which actually stem, at the time of writing in May 2015, from the EU Data Protection Directive of 1995). Personal data includes that held both on computer and in manual records.

10.11.13 Under sections 28 and 29, data may be more easily withheld (or indeed shared with other bodies) on the part of the data controller (the body holding the data about you) in the interests of national security, taxation, the prevention or detection of crime and the apprehension or prosecution of offenders.

10.11.14 The Data Protection Act is again enforced by the Information Commissioner, who has the power to issue an enforcement notice on any data controller that fails to act in accordance with the Act. An enforcement notice can reach as much as £500,000 per sanction.

10.11.15 The Freedom of Information Act 2000 extended the Data Protection Act 1998 in respect of access and data accuracy on information held by public authorities, and to personal data processed by or on behalf of Parliament.

10.11.16 For handy overview materials describing freedom of information and data protection law, see the website of the Information Commissioner's Office: www.ico.org.uk.

Key Cases Checklist

Cases highlighting Executive powers and duties

Statutory powers and duties

Carltona Ltd v Works Commissioners (1943): a decision taken by a junior/subordinate official is regarded as being the decision of the Minister in charge of the department and they must answer for it in Parliament

Common law powers and duties

Campaign for Nuclear Disarmament v PM (2002): sending troops to fight overseas is considered to be a classic exercise of the prerogative, and non-reviewable

R v Secretary of State for Foreign and Commonwealth Affairs, ex parte Rees-Mogg (1994): Court of Appeal discussed the prerogative of treaty-making but concluded it was a non-reviewable

Exercise of the royal prerogative

Entick v Carrington (1765): no new prerogative powers can be created (but even by May 2015 prerogative powers still exist in some areas concerning foreign affairs, the armed forces, making war, and keeping the peace in the context of law and order)

CCSU v Minister for the Civil Service (1985) (otherwise known as the *GCHQ Case*): the exercise of certain prerogative powers is now capable of being reviewed by the courts and can be challenged on the basis of some unlawfulness, through judicial review

R (Bancoult) v Secretary of State for Foreign and Commonwealth Affairs (2008): Orders in Council do not share all of the characteristics of an Act of Parliament, and that an exercise of the prerogative in such a way could be subject to judicial review (see 10.6)

10.6.20 *Campaign for Nuclear Disarmament v Prime Minister* [2002] EWHC 2777 (HC)

Key Facts

CND challenged the legality of the decision of the Government to send troops to Iraq.

Key Law

Such matters are not reviewable by the courts.

Key Judgment

Richards J
'... it is unthinkable that the national courts would entertain a challenge to a government decision to declare war or to authorise the use of armed forces against a third country. That is a classic example of a non-justiciable decision.'

10.6.17 ## R v Secretary of State for Foreign and Commonwealth Affairs, ex parte Rees-Mogg [1994] 2 WLR 115 (HC)

Key Facts

Rees-Mogg challenged the authority of the Government to ratify the Treaty on European Union (Maastricht Treaty).

Key Law

The application for judicial review was rejected; treaty-making was a non-reviewable prerogative power.

10.6.14 ## CCSU v Minister of State for the Civil Service [1985] AC 374 (GCHQ Case) (HL)

Key Facts

Prerogative empowered the Minister to issue instructions in respect of the conditions of service for civil servants. Following industrial action at the Government Communication Headquarters (GCHQ) the Minister issued instructions that barred membership of a trade union. Contrary to usual practice, the Minister did not consult with the trade union before issuing the instruction.

Key Law

An exercise of prerogative power is susceptible to judicial review. In the case at hand, while the union had a legitimate expectation to be consulted, on the facts this was outweighed by the interests of national security.

Key Judgment

Lord Roskill

'If the executive ... acts under a prerogative power ... so as to affect the rights of the citizen, I am unable to see ... that there is any logical reason why the fact that the source of the power is the prerogative and not statute should today deprive the citizen of that right of challenge to the manner of its exercise which he would possess were the source of the power statutory.'

Key Comment

This landmark decision extended judicial review to acts of the prerogative. However, the application of judicial review is limited or qualified. Whether a particular prerogative power is amenable to review depends upon its nature and subject matter. Lord Roskill identified a number of significant prerogative powers that by their very nature are not capable of being reviewed in terms of their use by the courts. These included:

- making treaties;
- defence of the realm;
- granting mercy;
- granting honours;
- dissolution of Parliament; and
- ministerial appointment.

However, Lord Roskill also stated that 'other' prerogatives could also be non-reviewable.

11 The contemporary role and powers of the courts

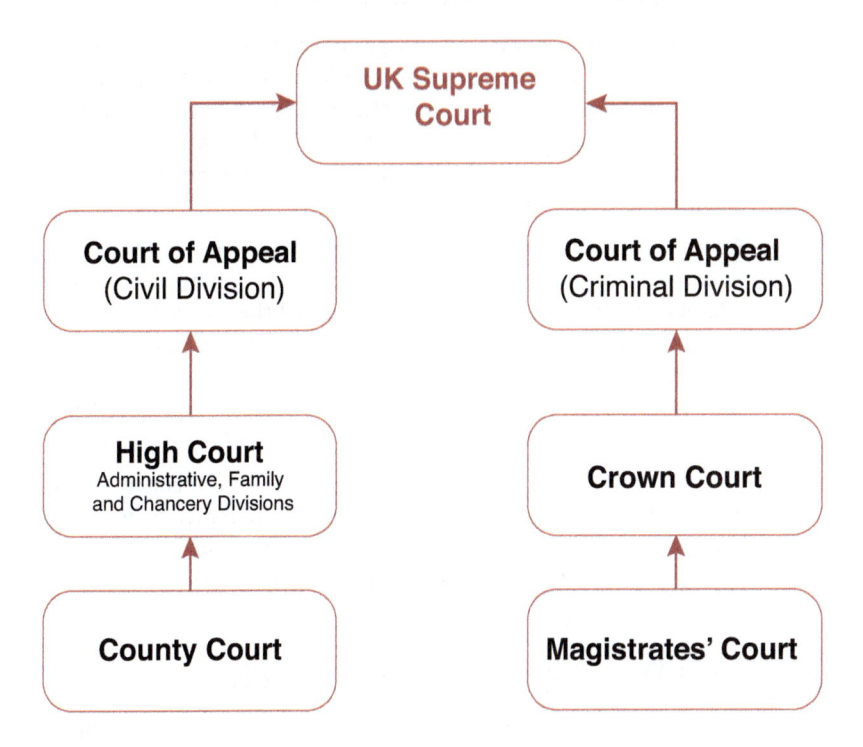

```
                    ┌──────────────┐
              ┌────▶│ UK Supreme   │◀────┐
              │     │    Court     │     │
              │     └──────────────┘     │
              │                          │
    ┌─────────────────┐          ┌─────────────────┐
    │ Court of Appeal │          │ Court of Appeal │
    │ (Civil Division)│          │(Criminal Division)│
    └─────────────────┘          └─────────────────┘
              ▲                          ▲
    ┌─────────────────┐                  │
    │   High Court    │          ┌─────────────────┐
    │ Administrative, │          │   Crown Court   │
    │ Family and      │          │                 │
    │ Chancery Divisions│         └─────────────────┘
    └─────────────────┘                  ▲
              ▲                          │
    ┌─────────────────┐          ┌─────────────────┐
    │  County Court   │          │Magistrates' Court│
    └─────────────────┘          └─────────────────┘
```

▶ 11.1 The role of the courts in the UK constitution

11.1.1 The role of the courts is to offer **redress** – that is, to be a way for parties to legal disputes to *resolve* those disputes. The courts are arranged in a structured hierarchy – generally divisible between **courts of first instance** and **appeal courts**. The courts are also readily divisible along **criminal justice** and **civil justice** lines.

11.1.2 This chapter, however, looks at the less traditional avenues and opportunities for redress: **inquiries** and **ombudsmen**, as well as the development of the system of **tribunals** that more directly support the work of the courts.

11.2 The importance of the separation of powers doctrine in assigning the courts a role in the UK constitution

11.2.1 The separation of powers, as a legal and political doctrine, is the traditional means of explaining the role of the courts in the UK constitution. Under this principle, the courts are not only a place for people to seek legal redress in the event of legal disputes (or for the State to transparently and publicly prosecute and punish criminal offenders).

11.2.2 According to the idea of the separation of powers as outlined in an earlier chapter of this book (Chapter 2), the courts also have a role of checking and balancing the power of the executive (in the United Kingdom, the Government of the day and an array of public bodies – see Chapter 10). Both of these key roles for the courts, and the judiciary in the United Kingdom today, are considered below.

11.2.3 But the courts in the United Kingdom also have a fundamental role in the UK constitution: the creation and maintenance of common law doctrines, or rules – through the steady development of case law, as determined by the senior courts at an appellate level.

11.3 Developing the common law

11.3.1 The judiciary, in determining the outcomes of cases in the courts, both apply the common law, in the form of case law precedent, and also develop that body of case law into the common law itself.

11.3.2 There is no area of the law to which decided cases do not contribute in the form of common law.

11.3.3 The doctrine of precedent ensures that only the most senior judiciary have a role in significantly shaping the common law – since it is the case law produced by the more senior, appellate courts which are the most persuasive or binding precedent.

11.3.4 The Supreme Court, the most senior of the UK courts, determines the direction of the development of the common law on any particular doctrinal issue; that is, on any criminal or civil point of law.

11.4 Engaging in dialogue with Parliament, the Government and European legal structures

11.4.1 The constitutional role of the courts revolves around the work of the judiciary: judges themselves.

11.4.2 More than 21,000 **lay magistrates**, also known as 'Justices of the Peace' or 'JPs' sit in panels to try more minor criminal cases in the magistrates' courts of the United Kingdom, and are assisted by legally qualified professionals in observing court procedure and determining the relevant law. Matters of fact, including the guilt of a defendant 'beyond reasonable doubt' – the **criminal standard of proof** – are determined by the magistrates themselves after hearing evidence from the prosecution and defence.

11.4.3 **Juries** find defendants guilty 'beyond reasonable doubt' in Crown Court trials, overseen by **circuit judges**. The Judicial Office (as part of the Ministry of Justice) lists more than 600 current circuit judges, who can hear criminal or civil cases, depending on the court in which they sit. Many circuit judges sit in County Courts to try civil cases, without the need for a jury, and where cases are determined on the 'balance of probability' – the civil standard of proof.

11.4.4 As noted by the Judicial Office, circuit judges are appointed 'by the Queen, on the recommendation of the Lord Chancellor, following a fair and open competition administered by the Judicial Appointments Commission'.

11.4.5 The majority of judges working in the County Court are **district judges**, however. As such, the Judicial Office notes, the 'work of district judges involves a wide spectrum of civil and family law cases such as claims for damages and injunctions, possession proceedings against mortgage borrowers and property tenants, divorces, child proceedings, domestic violence injunctions and insolvency proceedings'.

11.4.6 High Court judges, as their title implies, sit in the High Court and deal with the most significant cases.

11.4.7 The Judicial Office gives an overview of the structures of the work of the High Court as follows.

The Family Division

'*The Family Division, which deals with family law and probate cases, consists of about 19 judges headed by the President of the Family Division.*'

The Chancery Division

'The Chancery Division deals with company law, partnership claims, conveyancing, land law, probate, patent and taxation cases, and consists of 18 High Court judges, headed by the Chancellor of the High Court. The division includes three specialist courts: the Companies Court, the Patents Court and the Bankruptcy Court. Chancery Division judges normally sit in London, but also hear cases in Cardiff, Bristol, Birmingham, Manchester, Liverpool, Leeds and Newcastle.'

The Queen's Bench Division

'The Queen's Bench Division deals with contract and tort (civil wrongs), judicial reviews and libel, and includes specialist courts: the Commercial Court, the Admiralty Court and the Administration Court. It consists of about 73 judges, headed by the President of the Queen's Bench Division.'

11.4.8 It is the Administration Court as part of the Queen's Bench Division of the High Court which is the guardian and the forum for applications for judicial review – the core focus of many of the following chapters in this book.

11.4.9 The Lords Justices of Appeal sit in panels to hear cases in the **Criminal and Civil Divisions of the Court of Appeal** respectively.

11.4.10 The Judicial Office notes that:

'The Civil Division hears appeals from the High Court, county courts and certain tribunals such as the Employment Appeal Tribunal and the Immigration Appeal Tribunal. Its President is the Master of the Rolls. Cases are generally heard by three judges, consisting of any combination of the Heads of Division and Lords Justices of Appeal.'

'The Criminal Division hears appeals from the Crown Court. Its President is the Lord Chief Justice. Again, cases are generally heard by three judges, consisting of the Lord Chief Justice or the President of the Queen's Bench Division or one of the Lords Justices of Appeal, together with two High Court Judges or one High Court Judge and one specially nominated Senior Circuit Judge.'

11.4.11 The 12 Supreme Court Justices decide cases on appeal before the **Supreme Court**, sitting in panels of five, seven or nine – with a greater number of these most senior of the UK judiciary the more important the matter in the case(s) to be decided.

11.4.12 Given the nature of the Supreme Court as a *de facto* or next-best-thing to a true constitutional court (which would, unlike the UK Supreme Court, have the power to strike down or undo legislation in breach of a written constitution), it is the Supreme Court, and the 12 Justices of the Supreme Court, who have the most important constitutional role in safeguarding those people whose rights are affected by the work of the UK Government from unfairness, abuses of due process or other unlawfulness.

11.4.13 The next few sections of this chapter, for this reason, look at some basic elements of the relationship between the senior judiciary, in their work in both the Court of Appeal and the Supreme Court, and Parliament, the Government, and supranational courts like the **Court of Justice of the European Union** and the **European Court of Human Rights**.

11.5 Engaging with Parliament

11.5.1 The relationship between the Supreme Court and Parliament is a necessary and subtle exercise in back-and-forth law-making and decision-making, and involves no small amount of political awareness on the part of the most senior judges in the UK court system.

11.5.2 Paterson has acknowledged different forms of 'judicial activism' – the political concept of judges consciously and purposefully developing the law in line with their own political views through making decisions which shape the development of the common law in a particular direction.

11.5.3 *R (Yemshaw) v London Borough of Hounslow* (2011) is arguably an example of such a case. In *Yemshaw*, the phrase 'domestic violence' in a section of the Housing Act 1996 was construed with a much broader meaning relating to direct and indirect forms of abuse *per se*. This was a move to open up more support from Government bodies to those who suffered not just physical violence from their partners but also 'abusive psychological behaviour'.

11.5.4 The Supreme Court regularly decides cases like *Yemshaw* that have enormous repercussions for many individuals.

11.5.5 As Paterson has noted in his book *Final Judgment*: 'When it comes to law-making, Parliament has the authority and the power to act, but sometimes lacks the will. The Supreme Court, on the other hand, cannot decide not to decide.'

11.5.6 Mark Elliott has noted a different kind of judicial activism in cases such as *Kennedy v Charity Commission* (2014) and *R (HS2 Action Alliance Ltd) v Secretary of State for Transport* (2014) – where, in Elliott's view, the Supreme Court 'has placed very specific emphasis on the common law, as opposed to the Human Rights Act 1998 and the European Convention on Human Rights, as a source of fundamental rights and values'.

11.5.7 What Elliott and other academics have called 'common law constitutionalism' as evidenced in cases such as *Kennedy* and *HS2*, is a currently highly relevant trend, because particular judges, or groups of judges sitting in an appellate panel, appear to be both intellectually and doctrinally paving the way for potential repeal of the Human Rights Act 1998, for example, under the current Conservative Government.

11.5.8 The stance on the issue of 'open justice', as discussed in *Kennedy*, being driven by the common law as much as by, or independently of, Article 10 of the European Convention on Human Rights, is tantamount to a stance that the removal of the ability to rely on ECHR-based case law might not make such difference. In short, 'common law constitutionalism' is the notion that the common law will still be the guardian of fundamental democratic rights, even without the influence of the ECHR directly through the Human Rights Act 1998.

11.5.9 The argument that we should explicitly recognise that the senior judiciary are politically opinionated, and even politically motivated, in their work in determining important cases in the senior courts is known as **legal realism**. Legal realism is not an idea which sits comfortably with a constitution built around an aspiration to a working separation of powers.

11.5.10 If the senior judiciary recognisably stray beyond the constitutional role assigned to them, that is, the role of applying the (primary and secondary) legislation created by Parliament, and in monitoring and scrutinising the work of the executive in implementing those laws whilst in government; then the **political impartiality** of the judiciary, an important feature of the rule of law, as well as the concept of natural justice, and the doctrine of due process, all become threatened. See Chapter 12.

11.5.11 **Public confidence** in the judiciary should not be allowed to become precarious as a result of the judiciary being seen to abandon impartiality, since people should feel that cases are fairly dealt with by the judiciary when they seek redress, in order that redress is sought by recourse to the law and not by recourse to other, more unlawful means.

11.6 Engaging with the Government

11.6.1 If people would want and expect the judiciary to remain politically impartial, then they would equally also expect the judiciary to intrude into political matters of government only rarely and when necessary, due to the constitutional position of an elected Government in a democratic society.

11.6.2 However, the judiciary do indeed monitor the fairness, and challenge the unfairness of Government decision-making when called upon to do so, and when either statute or the common law relating to judicial review empowers them to do so. (Judicial review is the subject of the next several chapters in this book.)

11.6.3 It is appropriate, before the parts of this book that deal directly with judicial review, to give some examples of the manner in which the Supreme Court has directly re-corrected the Government stance on a matter of fundamental rights.

11.6.4 In *R (HJ and HT) (Iran and Cameroon) v Secretary of State for the Home Department* (2010) the Supreme Court unanimously determined that homosexuals are protected under provisions of the UN Convention Relating to the Status of Refugees, and, in the words of Alan Paterson, 'to compel such a person to pretend that their sexuality does not exist', because the Home Office seeks to return them to their country of origin after they have claimed asylum in the United Kingdom, 'is to deny him his fundamental right to be who he is'.

11.6.5 In the related decision of *R (RT) (Zimbabwe) v Secretary of State for the Home Department* (2012), also concerning the UN Convention Relating to the Status of Refugees, the Supreme Court found that not only were homosexuals protected from potential harm or loss of dignity by the prevention of returning them to their home country (known as the principle of *non-refoulement* under international law), but so were people who faced violence in their home countries due to their support for opposition to the Government.

11.6.6 As such, the decision of the Supreme Court in *RT* expanded the application of this particular kind of political asylum in direct conflict with what central UK Government and Home Office policymakers had wanted or possibly anticipated.

11.7 Engaging with European legal structures: the European Union

11.7.1 The nature of EU law is such that, depending on the exact nature of the legal instrument concerned, it can take direct effect either vertically (empowering citizens to take up legal claims against Government bodies) or horizontally (allowing the legal rules concerned to be deployed in disputes between two or more private bodies).

11.7.2 Although a dedicated chapter of this book deals with more detail on EU law-making, and the manner in which EU law takes effect in the United Kingdom (see Chapter 6), it should be noted at this juncture that it was a decision of the judicial House of Lords, the forerunner to today's UK Supreme Court, in *R v Secretary of State for Transport, ex parte Factortame (No. 2)* (1989) which determined that where UK law and EU law are in conflict then the EU law concerned takes precedence over the UK law.

11.7.3 This naturally leads to cases where the particular provisions of Acts of Parliament (otherwise the most important source of law in the UK constitution) are actually disapplied, because of the way that the House of Lords determined that provisions of the European Communities Act 1972 realigned this element of parliamentary sovereignty in the United Kingdom.

11.7.4 Further to this, the case law of the Court of Justice of the European Union, due to this feature of interpretation resulting in the domestic primacy of EU law, will actually act as binding precedent on particular points of EU law in application in UK cases and by UK judges.

11.7.5 The relationship between the UK courts and European law is therefore relatively straightforward: EU law is effectively binding supranational law, as the constitutional arrangements of the United Kingdom currently stand, and while the European Communities Act 1972 is unreformed and in force as it is now.

11.8 Engaging with European legal structures: a relationship with the European Court of Human Rights

11.8.1 European human rights law, promulgated and observed by the Council of Europe member States (including the United Kingdom) under the European Convention on Human Rights, and developed and defined by the case law of the European Court of Human Rights, however, has a much more loosely defined status with regard to the work of the UK courts.

11.8.2 Academics Francesca Klug and Helen Wildbore have outlined the way that the position of the senior UK courts with regard to the case law of the European Court of Human Rights can be summarised, with regard to the treatment of a particular legal dispute over a human rights issue, into one of:

- **The 'mirror approach'** – where the senior UK courts will simply transpose and apply directly a decision of the European Court of Human Rights to a relevant point of law in a domestic human rights dispute. This is more likely to result in a frustrating result for the UK Government than the following two approaches.

- **The 'municipal approach'** – where the senior UK courts determine that the UK legal position is not sufficiently well understood by the European Court of Human Rights on a particular point of law, involving a domestic application of a Convention right from the ECHR. This approach is the least likely to result in a frustrating outcome for the UK Government, since it is inevitably the most respectful of the Government policy position at a local, that is, national level – hence the term 'municipal approach'.

- **The 'dynamic approach'** – where the UK courts and the European Court of Human Rights decide cases in a 'back and forth' process, each taking into account the decisions of the other body of case law, arriving at a compromise position of sorts after this 'judicial dialogue'. This may not be a position favourable, necessarily, to UK Government policy, however.

11.8.3 Lord Bingham in the case of *R (Ullah) v Special Adjudicator* (2004) summarised this pressure on the UK courts to be mindful of case law of the European Court of Human Rights (which is a result of the requirement to 'take into account' that same body of case law under section 2 of the Human Rights Act 1998). Lord Bingham famously wrote, encapsulating the 'mirror approach' in a formulation that has come to be known as the 'Ullah principle', that:

> 'It is of course open to member states to provide for rights more generous than those guaranteed by the Convention, but such provision should not be the product of interpretation of the Convention by national courts, since the meaning of the Convention should be uniform throughout the states party to it. **The duty of national courts is to keep pace with the Strasbourg jurisprudence as it evolves over time: no more, but certainly no less.**'

11.9 The growth of the landscape of administrative justice

11.9.1 As well as considering a developing position of the senior courts with regard to their relationship with Parliament, Government, and supranational courts and systems of law, this chapter must also now address another area of considerable academic study in the field of constitutional and administrative law: the growth of what can be considered broadly as 'administrative justice'.

11.9.2 'Administrative justice' is a term that has been subject to a number of attempts at definition of late. The UK Administrative Justice Institute has proffered the following definitions for us to consider – that 'administrative justice' is:

- 'The interaction between citizen and state, from rule-making to decision-making to challenge to resolution.'
- 'Decision-making by public bodies.'
- 'Citizen-versus-state conflicts.'
- 'Administrative justice includes initial decision making, dispute resolution, and feedback processes related to the interaction between citizen and state.'
- 'The means by which good administration is ensured for citizens.'
- 'The idea that citizens should be treated fairly by those in power and the processes that make this aspiration a reality.'

11.9.3 We will take the penultimate of these definitions of 'administrative justice' as the most workable, given the aims and scope of the rest of this chapter: that 'administrative justice' is 'the means by which good administration is ensured for citizens'.

11.9.4 New avenues of address outside of the traditional courts structures have opened up to provide greater means by which good administration (or sound government) is ensured for citizens; in the form, considered in the next three sections of this chapter, of a system of tribunals, a set of ombudsmen and regulators, and the development of a system of inquiries.

11.10 A system of tribunals

11.10.1 As Elliott and Thomas have noted, 'an enormous number of cases are adjudicated upon not by courts, but by tribunals'.

11.10.2 Tribunals, aside from employment tribunals, typically consider disputes between individuals and public bodies in areas of the law connected with immigration and asylum, welfare and benefits, mental health and tax disputes.

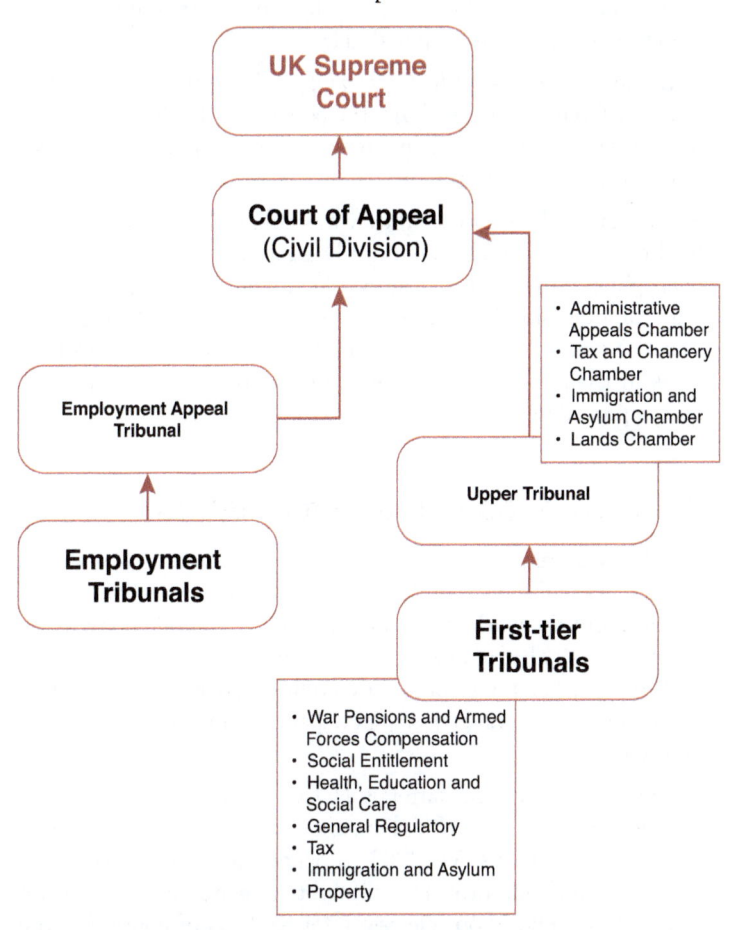

```
                    UK Supreme
                      Court
                        ▲
                        │
                  Court of Appeal
                  (Civil Division)  ◄──────┐
                        ▲                  │
                        │          • Administrative
                        │            Appeals Chamber
                        │          • Tax and Chancery
                        │            Chamber
  Employment Appeal     │          • Immigration and
      Tribunal          │            Asylum Chamber
                        │          • Lands Chamber
        ▲               │
        │           Upper Tribunal
        │                 ▲
        │                 │
   Employment         First-tier
   Tribunals          Tribunals

                    • War Pensions and Armed
                      Forces Compensation
                    • Social Entitlement
                    • Health, Education and
                      Social Care
                    • General Regulatory
                    • Tax
                    • Immigration and Asylum
                    • Property
```

11.10.3 The legislative basis for the system of tribunals in the diagram shown above is the Tribunals, Courts and Enforcement Act 2007.

11.10.4 As Leyland and Anthony have explained, to a lesser or greater extent, a system of tribunals not only allows for a large number of legal disputes about Government decision-making to be resolved outside the more costly traditional courts system, but may have distinct advantages when it comes to:

- encouraging applicants to bring cases due to their potentially speedier resolution;

- a greater flexibility of approach in terms of hearing procedure;
- the possibility of inquisitorial rather than adversarial procedure, which is less intimidating for applicants; and
- specialised and more expert jurisdictions, attracting more specialist advocates and tribunal judges.

11.10.5 In the important case of *R (Cart) v Upper Tribunal* (2011), the UK Supreme Court determined that the possibility of judicial review of decisions of the Upper Tribunal remained open to the High Court's Administrative Division.

11.10.6 As Leyland and Anthony put it, it was held in *Cart* that 'decisions by the Upper Tribunal should not be subjected to routine judicial oversight but, in principle, they would be amenable to review'. The important decision in *Cart* helps more broadly retain the principle that the courts have the ability under the common law to hear cases in their role of scrutinisers of Government, under judicial review procedure.

11.11 Ombudsmen and regulators

11.11.1 The key difference between an ombudsman and a regulator is that an ombudsman handles complaints from members of the public about the work, decision or actions of a public body, and a regulator typically handles complaints from members of the public about the behaviour of private bodies such as companies, like utility providers, advertisers, newspapers, telecoms companies and so on.

11.11.2 As an example of the latter, OFCOM is the communications regulator in the United Kingdom, and has a statutory power under the Communications Act 2003 to operate a Content Board, for instance, which monitors the suitability of material broadcast, for example, by radio or on television, for public consumption in the United Kingdom, covering 'matters principally concerning harm and offence, accuracy and impartiality, fairness and privacy'.

11.11.3 There are, say Leyland and Anthony, now a 'series of public sector ombudsmen, each with their own jurisdiction'. There are also a number of private sector ombudsmen whose roles overlap those of statutory sector regulators such as OFCOM.

11.11.4 A list of ombudsmen in the United Kingdom, and their descriptions, is provided by the Ombudsman Association on its website: http://www.ombudsmanassociation.org/.

The Parliamentary and Health Service Ombudsman (PHSO)

11.11.5 The best-known ombudsman is the Parliamentary and Health Service Ombudsman (PHSO), first introduced (and originally as a Parliamentary Commissioner for Administration) under the Parliamentary Commissioner Act 1967. It has considerable statutory powers (see below). A statutory basis is a considerable strength for an ombudsman, whether they regulate in the public or private sector, given that some ombudsmen operating in the private sector rely on operators or businesses in their industry consenting to regulation by the ombudsman concerned, for example.

11.11.6 The PHSO investigates complaints made by members of the public – though these complaints must be referred to it by a Member of Parliament – about the decisions, actions or workings of a central Government department, or a particular non-departmental public body (for descriptions of these bodies, see Chapter 10).

11.11.7 If some poor practice or 'maladministration' is found by the PHSO using its investigative powers, the PHSO will make recommendations as to how the complaint could be resolved – and these complaints are typically followed by the body concerned, to preclude other legal action etc.

11.11.8 The investigative powers of the PHSO stem from section 5 of the Parliamentary Commissioner Act 1967; and the PHSO can obtain information relating to a matter under investigation using a statutory power under section 7 of the 1967 Act.

11.11.9 The courts cannot compel the PHSO to investigate a complaint if the PHSO has already reviewed the complaint and decided on the basis of the following criteria that an investigation is not appropriate (following the House of Lords decision in *Re Fletcher's Application* (1970)):

- Is the complaint about a central Government department, or a non-departmental public body, which the PHSO can investigate?
- Is there some evidence of administrative failure?
- Is there some form of personal redress which is necessary?
- Is the investigation able to lead to a recommendation of some kind of remedy or redress to be awarded?

11.12 Inquiries

11.12.1 While tribunals and ombudsmen are largely about dispute resolution, and act, in effect, like a less-formal or 'substitute' court system, inquiries are sometimes part of a decision-making process, or the process of policy formation by Government.

11.12.2 As such, inquiries are best seen as an exercise in establishing facts themselves, rather than ascertaining how the law should apply in a particular case. And as Leyland and Anthony have noted, aside from being 'part of the decision-making process, inquiries assume many forms and have very disparate functions and aims'.

11.12.3 *Ad hoc* inquiries can be set up by Government Ministers on the basis of their powers under the royal prerogative, or using their statutory powers.

11.12.4 The statutory framework for the ministerial creation of inquiries is found in the Inquiries Act 2005.

11.12.5 Ministers have the power to order an inquiry under section 1 of the Inquiries Act 2005 on the basis of 'public concern'.

11.12.6 Section 2 of the 2005 Act stipulates that inquiries do not determine criminal or civil liability for actions investigated by the inquiry (but that does not mean that criminal or civil action cannot be commenced under other processes).

11.12.7 Section 9 of the 2005 Act requires that only impartial individuals, without a connection to or interest in the matter being investigated under the inquiry, are to be appointed by a Minister to the panel conducting the inquiry.

11.12.8 Section 17 of the Inquiries Act 2005 informs us that the 'procedure and conduct of an inquiry are to be such as the chairman of the inquiry may direct', but that in 'making any decision as to the procedure or conduct of an inquiry, the chairman must act with fairness and with regard also to the need to avoid any unnecessary cost (whether to public funds or to witnesses or others)'. The chair of the inquiry panel may also compel and take evidence from witnesses under oath.

Role and powers of the courts 193

Key Cases Checklist

Operation of the UK Courts – Key Principles in Case Law

R (Yemshaw) v London Borough of Hounslow (2011): legislation is sometimes interpreted broadly to give effect to the rights of the vulnerable in society (see 11.5.3)

R (HJ and HT) (Iran and Cameroon) v Secretary of State for the Home Department (2010): the courts can develop the common law so as to protect the rights of the vulnerable in line with (incorporated) international law (see 11.6.4 and 11.6.5)

Kennedy v Charity Commission (2014) and *R (HS2 Action Alliance Ltd) v Secretary of State for Transport* (2014): the Supreme Court shows that there are fundamental rights in the common law

R (Ullah) v Special Adjudicator (2004): 'The duty of national courts is to keep pace with [ECHR] jurisprudence as it evolves over time: no more, but certainly no less.' (see 11.8.3)

R v Secretary of State for Transport, ex parte Factortame (No. 2) (1989): the UK courts have determined that where UK law and EU law are in conflict then the EU law concerned takes precedence over the UK law (Chapters 1 and 6)

R (Cart) v Upper Tribunal (2011): the UK Supreme Court determined that the possibility of judicial review of decisions of the Upper Tribunal remained open to the High Court's Administrative Division (see 11.10.5)

11.5.6 Kennedy v Charity Commission [2014] UKSC 20 (SC)

Key Facts

The Freedom of Information Act 2000 places an absolute duty not to disclose any information that relates to an ongoing inquiry, if a request is made under the Act seeking such information. This 'complete exemption' was challenged by Kennedy in the case of information held by the Charity Commission, which was undertaking an inquiry into the accounts of a particular charity appeal.

Key Law

The Supreme Court determined that the absolute exemption applied to the records held by the Charity Commission, and that the records could as such only be released when they became public records years from now, falling under the regime established under the Constitutional Reform and Governance Act 2010. The Supreme Court did not find that Article 10 ECHR, and the right to obtain information as part of the right to freedom of expression, required any reading down of the absolute exemption concerned, as found in the language of the Freedom of Information Act 2000. In addition, it was noted by some members of the Supreme Court that common law rights can be shown to give effect to and be the equivalent to rights typically thought of as ECHR rights.

Key Judgments

Lord Mance
'Since the passing of the Human Rights Act 1998, there has too often been a tendency to see the law in areas touched on by the Convention solely in terms of the Convention rights. But the Convention rights represent a threshold protection; and, especially in view of the contribution which common lawyers made to the Convention's inception, they may be expected, at least generally even if not always, to reflect and to find their homologue in the common or domestic statute law.'

'Greater focus in domestic litigation on the domestic legal position might also have the incidental benefit that less time was taken in domestic courts seeking to interpret and reconcile different judgments (often only given by individual sections of the European Court of Human Rights) in a way which that Court itself, not being bound by any doctrine of precedent, would not itself undertake.'

Lord Toulson
'What we now term human rights law and public law has developed through our common law over a long period of time. The process has quickened since the end of World War II in response to the growth of bureaucratic powers on the part of the state and the creation of multitudinous administrative agencies affecting many aspects of the citizen's daily life. The growth of the state has presented the courts with new challenges to which they have responded by a process of gradual adaption and development of the common law to meet current needs. This has always been the way of the common law and it has not ceased on the enactment of the Human Rights Act 1998, although since then there has sometimes been a baleful and unnecessary tendency to overlook the common law. It needs to be emphasised that it was not the purpose of the Human Rights Act that the common law should become an ossuary.'

Key Comment

Mark Elliott has noted that in this case the Supreme Court has placed very specific emphasis on the role of the common law, *in addition to* the Human Rights Act 1998 and the European Convention on Human Rights, as a source of fundamental rights and values.

Key Link

In *R (HS2 Action Alliance Ltd) v Secretary of State for Transport* [2014] UKSC 3 it was determined that it was lawful for the development of the plans for the High Speed 2 railway project to be undertaken in a parliamentary process; a process used at the same time to create the primary legislation which would give effect to the plans in law. This was a lawful departure from the normal process of using only local executive planning processes for large construction projects – and did not contravene EU law on the rights of individuals and groups to take part in public discussion of project plans, as contained in Article 7 of the Aarhus Convention. In their judgment, members of the Supreme Court commented that key constitutional principles can be identified in the developing common law (as developed by the courts, of course) as well as in prominent 'constitutional statutes' (as created by Parliament).

12 The constitutional role and configuration of judicial review

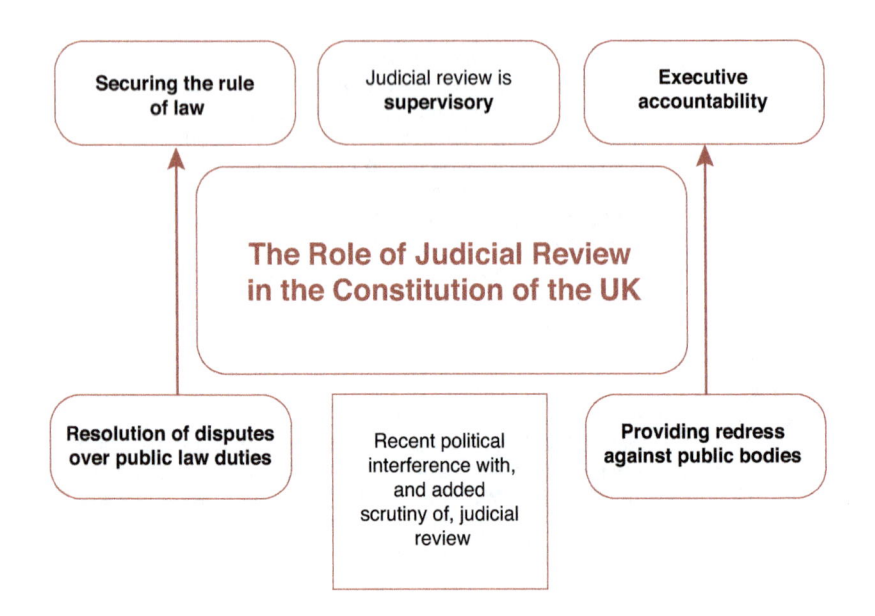

The Role of Judicial Review in the Constitution of the UK

- Securing the rule of law
- Judicial review is supervisory
- Executive accountability
- Resolution of disputes over public law duties
- Recent political interference with, and added scrutiny of, judicial review
- Providing redress against public bodies

12.1 Defining the role of judicial review

12.1.1 Judicial review is the process whereby the judiciary examines the legality of the actions of the executive. Hence it represents the means by which the courts may control the exercise of governmental power.

12.1.2 Judicial review is closely aligned with **securing the rule of law**.

12.1.3 For example, Lord Hoffmann in *R (Alconbury) v Secretary of State for the Environment, Transport and the Regions* (2001) described the significance of judicial review in terms of the constitution in the following terms: 'The principles of judicial review give effect to the rule of law. They ensure that administrative decisions will be taken rationally in accordance with a fair procedure and within the powers conferred by Parliament.'

12.1.4 Wade describes judicial review as 'an essential process if the rule of law is to be observed in a modern democracy'.

12.1.5 Judicial review is not an appeals process. In finding that a public body has exceeded its lawful authority, the court will not inquire into the subjective correctness of the decision, but only into the process by which the decision was reached. Unlike in an appeal, the court will therefore not substitute its own assessment of the merits.

12.1.6 The process of judicial review is therefore procedural in nature and determines whether a public body has acted within its powers (*intra vires*) or outside of its powers (*ultra vires*). If a body is determined to have acted *intra vires* its decision is not open to challenge under the process of judicial review.

12.1.7 Judicial review can consequently be described as a **supervisory**, rather than an appellate, jurisdiction.

12.1.8 Judicial review cannot be used for private law matters (see below). Where the matter is one of public law, judicial review must be used: *O'Reilly v Mackman* (1983). This is known as the 'exclusivity principle'. However, where there is a combination of private and public law matters, the courts may be willing to generate exceptions to the exclusivity principle: see, for example, *Roy v Kensington and Chelsea Family Practitioner Committee* (1992); *Mercury Communications Ltd v Director-General of Telecommunications* (1996); and *Clark v University of Lincolnshire and Humberside* (2000).

12.1.9 As a matter of procedure in judicial review, cases are brought by the Crown on behalf of the applicant against a defendant public body.

12.2 A (problematic) growth in judicial review, or scrutiny of the Government we can be proud of?

12.2.1 In December 2012, the Ministry of Justice published a public consultation paper ('Judicial Review: Proposals for reform') which set out the argument that there had 'been a significant growth in the use of Judicial Review to challenge decisions of public authorities, in particular over the last decade'. 'In 1974', claimed the Ministry of Justice, 'there were 160 applications for Judicial Review, but by 2000 this had risen to nearly 4,250, and by 2011 had reached over 11,000.'

12.2.2 The Ministry of Justice, during the recent Coalition Government, used this apparently significant and dramatic rise in applications for judicial review as evidence to support its argument that it should be more difficult to challenge the decisions of public bodies in certain areas, and advocated a series of relevant reforms.

12.2.3 Two key suggestions by the Ministry of Justice were that time limits to bring an application for judicial review should be enforced more strictly, and that the required permission of the High Court to proceed to a judicial review hearing should be harder to obtain (see Chapter 13).

12.2.4 Legal academics Varda Bondy and Maurice Sunkin have challenged the use of bare statistics, such as the ones mentioned above, to argue that too many judicial review applications are being made against Government bodies.

12.2.5 Bondy and Sunkin have argued that 'there has been little change in the volume of JR [judicial review] claims over the last 10 years or so'. 'Since the mid 1990s', they note, 'the volume of non-immigration/asylum JRs has remained fairly stable at just over the 2,000 per annum mark', highlighting that immigration and asylum law claims are responsible for the largest proportion of the growth in judicial review applications to the stated level observed by the Ministry of Justice at more than 11,000 per year by 2011.

12.2.6 But immigration and asylum law claims are now dealt with more efficiently, claimed Sunkin and Bondy under the newly established First-tier Tribunal (Immigration and Asylum Chamber) (see Chapter 11), which the two legal academics hoped, from 2013 onwards, would perhaps 'reduce significantly the volume of JRs in the Administrative Court [part of the High Court]'.

12.2.7 Sunkin and Bondy concluded as a result that (in early 2013 at least) it was potentially 'misleading [of the Ministry of Justice] to rely on data relating to immigration/asylum JRs in order to justify reforms to the JR system as a whole'.

12.3 Judicial review and the Human Rights Act 1998

12.3.1 The Human Rights Act 1998 has had a significant impact on judicial review. Public bodies have a legal duty to act in accordance with Convention rights; failure to do so may result in judicial review proceedings.

12.3.2 The application of judicial review under the Act differs from traditional judicial review in a number of ways including:

- the interpretation of a public body (and therefore which bodies are 'amenable' or subject to judicial review of their actions or decisions; and
- the standing or 'sufficient interest' required to apply for judicial review.

These aspects will be discussed further below.

12.3.3 In addition, judicial review on human rights claims may result in a 'declaration of incompatibility', which could result in reform of the law (see Chapter 7 and Chapter 16).

12.3.4 Human rights-based review of actions or decisions by public bodies is often something that supplements pre-existing common law-based judicial review approaches. For example, the Human Rights Act 1998 also supplements the traditional judicial review requirements of natural justice by incorporating Article 6 of the ECHR in respect of the right to a fair trial.

12.4 Defining public bodies: amenability to judicial review

12.4.1 Judicial review is only available to challenge decisions made by public bodies. If the body is a private body, private law must be used.

12.4.2 There is no single test to identify a public body and the courts will examine a number of factors.

12.4.3 If a body is set up under statute or by delegated legislation then the source of its power means it is a public body and subject to judicial review.

12.4.4 However, where the matter is unclear, the courts should examine the 'nature of the power' being exercised. In *R v City Panel on Takeovers and Mergers, ex parte Datafin Ltd* (1987) it was held that if the body is exercising public law functions or if the exercise of its functions has public law consequences, it may be a public body and subject to judicial review.

12.4.5 Conversely, a body holding extensive regulatory powers may be concluded to be a private body, on the basis that such powers are based exclusively on contract or some other agreement to submit to their jurisdiction, for example, disciplinary powers exercised by sporting or professional bodies: *R v Jockey Club, ex parte Aga Khan* (1993) and *R v Football Association, ex parte Football League* (1993).

12.4.6 Under the Human Rights Act 1998 challenge through the process of judicial review can be made against decisions of **public authorities**, defined under section 6 to include courts and tribunals and 'any person whose functions are functions of a public nature'. However, definition of a public authority within the context of the Human Rights Act has been narrowly interpreted (see e.g. *R (Julian West) v Lloyd's of London* (2004)). (See in particular the discussion of *YL v Birmingham City Council* (2007) in Chapter 7.)

12.4.7 To determine whether a body is a public authority reference can be made to the following factors (*Aston Cantlow and Wilmcote with Billesley Parochial Church Council v Wallbank* (2003)):

- whether the body is publicly funded;
- whether the body is exercising statutory powers;
- whether the body is taking the place of central Government or local authorities; and
- whether the body is providing a public service.

12.4.8 Sometimes a private body can be deemed to owe duties under section 6 of the Human Rights Act 1998, because the courts themselves (since they are public bodies) have a duty proactively to protect the rights of individuals subject to the actions of private bodies. This is known as the **horizontality** principle: *Campbell v Mirror Group Newspapers* (2004).

12.5 Reviewing crucial matters of policy

12.5.1 Sometimes the courts are called upon to judicially review matters of Government 'high policy' – and these cases are always controversial. This is because the outcomes of such cases can directly or indirectly affect the lives of thousands upon thousands of people – and because they acutely remind us that the courts have duty to be respectful of the policy aims and motivations of a democratically elected Government.

12.5.2 Recent cases where this tension has been illustrated include the case of *R (SG) v Secretary of State for Work and Pensions* (2015) (discussed in Chapter 5), where an (eventually unsuccessful) claim had been brought by way of judicial review, challenging the lawfulness of the 'benefits cap' introduced by the Conservative and Liberal Democrat

Coalition Government on the basis of a need for 'austerity' in public expenditure. The 'cap', introduced under the Welfare Reform Act 2012, limits the amount of housing benefit, amongst other benefits, which a single household could receive, at a time of Government spending cuts.

12.6 Limitations on judicial review: the concept of justiciability

12.6.1 With regard to claims for judicial review the subject matter must be suitable for review by the courts. If the matter is one of 'high policy' including national security, it may be considered by the courts as being non-justiciable and therefore not amenable to the process of judicial review.

12.6.2 Traditionally, matters of public high policy are determined by the executive and not the courts: *R v Parliamentary Commissioner for Administration, ex parte Dyer* (1994).

12.6.3 The courts will also be cautious in examining exercises of the royal prerogative particularly where issues of national security are involved: *Council for Civil Service Unions v Minister for the Civil Service* (1985).

12.6.4 For example, the courts will not consider whether the executive's prerogative of treaty-making has been exercised unlawfully: *R v Secretary of State for Foreign and Commonwealth Affairs, ex parte Rees-Mogg* (1994). The courts will also not review the content of a treaty: *Blackburn v Attorney-General* (1971).

12.6.5 However, in more recent times the courts have shown an increased willingness to examine exercises of prerogative powers.

12.7 Ouster clauses and other exclusions in relation to judicial review

12.7.1 Statute has been used to attempt to limit the availability of judicial review in two main ways.

12.7.2 **Complete (or finality) ouster clauses** provide that the decision made by the public body is final and hence not subject to any review.

12.7.3 The leading case on such clauses is *Anisminic v Foreign Compensation Commission* (1969). According to this case a court may conclude that judicial review is available regardless of the clause on the basis that the decision itself was not within the powers conferred. In other words it was *ultra vires* and not a decision at all; therefore it fell outside of the ouster clause. It would not be the intention of Parliament to remove the jurisdiction of the courts to judicially review such decisions.

12.7.4 In *R v Medical Appeal Tribunal, ex parte Gilmore* (1957) a statutory provision stating that any decision of the Tribunal was final was held to mean that whilst the decision could not be re-opened by the Tribunal and no other right to appeal could apply, it did not prevent the decision being subject to the supervisory jurisdiction of judicial review.

12.7.5 On a practical basis, the creation of a larger and more comprehensive system of first-tier tribunals and an Upper Tribunal has gone some way toward ensuring that there is a necessary route to challenging a decision by a public body at a more preliminary stage than by seeking judicial review, which is traditionally the purview of the High Court, with appeals from the High Court lying with the Civil Division of the Court of Appeal (in England and Wales) and thence to the Supreme Court.

12.7.6 However, certain clauses may be upheld as preventing judicial review if they are precisely drafted and still provide for some review of the decision. One example of this is a **time limit clause**.

12.7.7 These provide that judicial review can only be applied for within a defined and often short period of time and that thereafter the decision shall not be questioned in a court of law (e.g. statutes relating to planning and compulsory purchase orders).

12.7.8 Such clauses are justified on the basis of the need to ensure particular matters are not delayed or impeded in implementation.

12.7.9 These clauses are generally upheld by the courts. For example, in *R v Cornwall CC, ex parte Huntingdon* (1994) it was concluded that the clause was valid on the basis that it did not completely exclude any possibility of review of the decision and was necessary to meet the purpose of the statute, namely to ensure quick development of the land in question: see also *R v Secretary of State for the Environment, ex parte Ostler* (1976).

12.8 Exhausting other processes: the importance of the availability of other remedies beyond judicial review

12.8.1 In deciding whether to grant leave to seek judicial review to the claimant (see Chapter 13) the court may also take into account whether alternative remedies are available: *R v Inland Revenue Commissioners, ex parte Preston* (1985).

12.8.2 For example, if there are statutory rights of appeal these should be exhausted prior to any action for judicial review: *R v Secretary of State for the Home Department, ex parte Swati* (1986).

12.8.3 Generally, the court will exercise its discretion and, if an alternative appeals process is considered satisfactory, will decline to grant leave for judicial review (*Leech v Deputy Governor of Parkhurst Prison* (1988)) unless there are exceptional circumstances (*R (Sivasubramaniam) v Wandsworth County Court* (2003)).

Key Cases Checklist

If a body is set up under statute or by delegated legislation then the source of its power means it is a public body and subject to judicial review

R v City Panel on Takeovers and Mergers, ex parte Datafin Ltd (1987): if the body is exercising public law functions or if the exercise of its functions has public law consequences, it may be a public body and subject to judicial review

R v Jockey Club, ex parte Aga Khan (1993): a body holding extensive regulatory powers may be concluded to be a private body, on the basis that such powers are based exclusively on contract or some other agreement to submit to their jurisdiction

Amenability

Case law helping to define the limits of judicial review

Justiciability

With regard to claims for judicial review: the subject matter must be suitable for review by the courts. If the matter is one of 'high policy' including national security, it may be considered by the courts as being non-justiciable and therefore not amenable to the process of judicial review

Council for Civil Service Unions v Minister for the Civil Service (1985): The courts will be cautious in examining exercises of the royal prerogative particularly where issues of national security are involved: (see Key cases in Chapter 10)

R v Parliamentary Commissioner for Administration, ex parte Dyer (1994): Matters of public high policy are determined by the executive and not the courts

Anisminic v Foreign Compensation Commission (1969): **complete (or finality) ouster clauses** provide that the decision made by the public body is final and hence not subject to any review. According to this case a court may conclude that judicial review is available regardless of the clause on the basis that the decision itself was not within the powers conferred

12.4.4 *R v Panel on Takeovers and Mergers, ex parte Datafin* [1987] QB 815 — CA

Key Facts

Judicial review is only available against public bodies. If the body whose decision is being challenged is considered a private body, the remedy will lie in private law. The applicants sought judicial review of the Panel's rejection of their complaint. The Panel contended that its actions were not subject to judicial review because it was not a public body; its powers did not derive from statute or prerogative.

Key Law

The Panel was a public body because it was performing public functions that would otherwise be performed by Government.

Key Judgment

Lloyd LJ
'. . . if a body in question is exercising public law functions, or if the exercise of its functions have public law consequences, then that may be sufficient to bring the body within the reach of judicial review.'

12.4.5 *R v Disciplinary Committee of the Jockey Club, ex parte Aga Khan* [1993] 1 WLR 909 — CA

Key Facts

The Aga Khan sought judicial review of the decision of the Jockey Club to disqualify his horse.

Key Law

The Jockey Club was not a public body because its powers derived from agreement between the parties and it was not an organ of state. Hence, it was a private law matter.

Key Judgment

Sir Thomas Bingham
'. . . the Jockey Club is not in its origin, its history, its constitution or . . . its membership a public body.'

12.6.2 R v Parliamentary Commissioner for Administration, ex parte Dyer [1994] 1 All ER 375 [HC]

Key Facts

Dyer sought judicial review of a decision by the Parliamentary Commissioner not to re-open an investigation into the mishandling over her welfare benefit entitlements. The Commissioner had powers to conclude investigations by means of a report and recommendations under the Parliamentary Commissioner Act 1967 and refused to do more than recommend an apology and some voluntary compensation, which Dyer received. In particular, the Commissioner refused to re-investigate the matter.

Key Law

While, as a public body, the decisions of the Commissioner were susceptible to judicial review, the Commissioner exercised his powers with a wide margin of discretion as to how investigations could be brought to a close with particular recommendations, and as to how investigations were directed, as a matter of public policy – and in this case those recommendations were within that margin of discretion.

12.7.3 Anisminic v Foreign Compensation Commission [1969] 2 AC 147 [HL]

Key Facts

Anisminic's claim to the Foreign Compensation Commission failed. The Foreign Compensation Act 1950, section 4(4) stated that no decisions of the FCC 'could be called in question in any court of law' (an ouster clause).

Key Law

The House of Lords held that the jurisdiction of the courts could not be ousted – if a decision has been made *ultra vires* (without jurisdiction) it is not a decision, and therefore the court retains the jurisdiction to examine it under judicial review. The court concluded that the FCC had misunderstood its legal powers when making its decision and the courts could therefore intervene.

Key Judgment

Lord Wilberforce

'What would be the purpose of defining by statute the limits of a tribunal's powers, if by means of a clause inserted in the instrument . . . those limits could safely be passed?'

Key Comment

This important judgment effectively renders complete ouster clauses ineffective. It also protects the operation of the rule of law (see Chapter 2).

13 Process, standing and remedies in judicial review

- Supreme Court Act 1831
- Part 54 Civil Procedure Rules
- Elements of judicial discretion over procedural matters

Judicial review procedure

- Time limits
- Permission stage: consideration of a substantially different outcome
- Pre-action protocol

'Standing' on the basis of 'sufficient interest', an Article of the ECHR being engaged, or on some 'representative' basis

Prerogative Remedies:
Quashing orders; Mandatory orders; Prohibiting orders

Other Remedies:
Injunctions; Damages (in human rights cases); Declaratory relief

Deference and comity in judicial review

13.1 Procedural requirements in applying for permission for judicial review

13.1.1 The procedural basis for judicial review is found in the:
- Supreme Court Act 1981; and
- Civil Procedure Rules (Part 54)

13.1.2 Both of these set out procedural requirements in relation to judicial review – the key elements of which are set out in this chapter.

13.1.3 Claims for judicial review are made to the Administrative Court and have two main stages:
- the permission stage (request for leave); and
- the substantive hearing.

13.1.4 Prior to the permission stage there is the pre-action protocol whereby the applicant is to write to the body identifying the issues and the body is to reply. Because this process can ensure a settlement, thereby removing the need for litigation, the court will usually expect the parties to comply with it. The procedural requirements are then as follows.

13.1.5 The Supreme Court Act 1981, section 31 states that 'no application for judicial review shall be made unless the leave of the High Court has been obtained'.

13.1.6 The requirement of **leave**, or **permission**, acts as a filter to remove unmeritorious claims.

13.1.7 Judicial review is therefore not available as a right since it is discretionary on the acceptance of the court.

13.1.8 Prior to 2000, leave was previously sought *ex parte* (without the other side) but it is now *inter partes* so the court is aware of both sides of the argument.

13.1.9 This part of the process is mostly based on written submissions, though the court may convene an oral hearing.

13.1.10 In early 2015, the Coalition Government sought to limit the number of cases which proceeded to hearings in the judicial review process by making it harder to obtain leave/permission – purportedly out of concern that the growth in judicial review cases over a period of decades has been very great; and that this level of regular scrutiny of the work of Government in the courts has been something that has stalled or slowed the progress of efficient government. This argument, that the courts should be respectful of the work of Government, and the difficulties and pressures Governments face to implement policies in the face of strong public opposition, has been scathingly called 'the tyrant's plea' by Timothy Endicott.

13.1.11 The effect of section 84 of the Criminal Justice and Courts Act 2015 is to create a new test for leave/permission. This is a determination by the court as to whether there would be the 'highly likely' outcome of no 'substantial difference' following judicial review, if a hearing were to take place.

13.1.12 If it is highly likely that there would be no substantial difference in the eventual action or decision by the public body concerned, even if there were a judicial review hearing in which the claimant were successful, then there will be no leave/permission granted for judicial review, therefore.

13.1.13 When these reforms were passing through Parliament as the Criminal Justice and Courts Bill, there was much criticism that this legislation was an attempt by the Government to reduce the scrutiny that judicial review claims put upon the Government itself.

13.2 The pre-action protocol in relation to claims for judicial review

13.2.1 Parties as the claimants seeking judicial review are expected engage with the pre-action protocol, prior to filing their claim for judicial review.

13.2.2 This is not a strict requirement, however. For one thing, it may be too late for the claimant to follow the pre-action protocol and still comply with the expected time limit to bring their claim (see 13.3).

13.2.3 The pre-action protocol is in essence the supply of a draft claim form to the defendant, along with the factual details underpinning the claim, as the claimant understands them.

13.2.4 This gives the defendant an opportunity to resolve the issue with the claimant without the need for the claim to even reach the High Court. It also allows the defendant to clarify any pertinent factual issues, or dispute them, with regard to the claimant's version of events.

13.3 Time limits

13.3.1 Under the Civil Procedure Rules 1998, rule 54.5, an action (filing of the claim form) must be brought 'promptly' and in any event no later than **three months** after the grounds to make the claim first arose (rule 54.5(1)(b)).

13.3.2 This may be reduced by statute in specific areas (see above). Conversely, it may also be extended by the court at its discretion.

13.4 'Sufficient interest' standing

13.4.1 Section 31 of the Supreme Court Act 1981 provides that 'the court shall not grant leave . . . unless it considers that the applicant has a sufficient interest in the matter to which the application relates'. Sufficient interest is also known as *locus standi* or standing.

13.4.2 **Sufficient interest** will be assessed by the court at both the leave stage and at the substantive hearing: *R v Inland Revenue Commissioners, ex parte National Federation of Self-employed and Small Businesses* (1982).

13.4.3 The need for sufficient interest prevents what Lord Scarman described in the above case as 'abuse by busybodies, cranks and other mischief makers'. It therefore ensures cases are genuine and avoids unnecessary interference with administrative decisions and processes.

13.4.4 Applicants for judicial review are generally of four types:

- individuals whose personal rights and interests are affected by a decision;
- individuals concerned that a decision has affected the interests of society as a whole;
- pressure or interest groups who believe a decision affects the rights or interests of their members or society as a whole; and
- individuals claiming for judicial review for a breach of human rights under the Human Rights Act 1998.

Individual personal 'sufficient interest'

13.4.5 This will depend on the facts of the case and is determined by the court exercising its discretion. It will be relatively easy to establish sufficient interest if the individual is directly or indirectly affected by the decision. There will, for example, be clear indication of sufficient interest if a person's property or livelihood will be affected.

13.4.6 Some examples of individual personal sufficient interest include:
- An individual being excluded the right to enter the country (*Schmidt v Secretary of State for Home Affairs* (1969)); and
- a traveller trying to ensure his local authority provided an adequate site for him as required by statute (*R v Secretary of State for the Environment, ex parte Ward* (1984)).

Individuals representing the interests of society as a whole

13.4.7 In some cases an individual may be granted sufficient interest because they are representing the public interest in a matter.

13.4.8 Some examples of sufficient interest in this context include:
- an individual concerned with the budget of the European Union, on the basis that the person was a taxpayer (*R v HM Treasury, ex parte Smedley* (1985));
- an individual challenging the executive's treaty-making power in respect of the Treaty on European Union, on the basis that they were a concerned citizen (*R v Secretary of State for Foreign and Commonwealth Affairs, ex parte Rees-Mogg* (1994)); and
- and an individual wishing to challenge the decision of a health authority, in this case relating to contraception for girls, since she was the mother of a young daughter (*Gillick v West Norfolk and Wisbech Area Health Authority* (1986)).

13.5 Standing in human rights claims

13.5.1 **Individuals claiming for judicial review for a breach of human rights under the Human Rights Act 1998 must satisfy the requirements of section 7 of the HRA 1998.**

13.5.2 A new test for human rights-based standing for judicial review was created by the Human Rights Act 1998. Under section 7 of the Act a claim can only be brought by a 'victim' of an alleged breach of Convention rights.

13.5.3 Pressure or interest groups do not have sufficient interest unless they can establish that one or more of their actual members are, in fact, a 'victim' of an infringement of ECHR rights: for example, *R (Swami Suryananda) v Welsh Ministers* (2007).

13.6 Representative standing

13.6.1 Pressure or interest groups may be able to claim sufficient interest if a decision affects their interests or those of their members. Some examples include:

- an association of taxi operators wishing to challenge a decision to increase the number of taxi licences available (*R v Liverpool Corporation, ex parte Liverpool Taxi Operators' Association* (1972));
- the Royal College of Nursing wishing to challenge a decision of the Department of Health in respect of the role of nurses in terminations (*Royal College of Nursing v Department of Health and Social Security* (1981)); and
- the Equal Opportunities Commission wishing to challenge statutory provisions that discriminated against female employees (*R v Employment Secretary, ex parte EOC* (1995)).

13.6.2 The granting of sufficient interest for pressure or interest groups in respect of matters that affect society as a whole has been a more complex issue.

13.6.3 In *R v Secretary of State for the Environment, ex parte Rose Theatre Trust Company Ltd* (1990) the court found that the group, formed to save Shakespeare's Rose Theatre from being built upon, did not have sufficient interest; its mere assertion of an interest did not suffice.

13.6.4 However, the court has taken a more inclusive or liberal approach in cases since. For example:

- *R v Poole Borough Council, ex parte BeeBee* (1991) – the court ruled that the World Wildlife Fund had sufficient interest to challenge the decision to grant planning permission for the development of land of special scientific interest.
- *R v Inspectorate of Pollution, ex parte Greenpeace Ltd (No. 2)* (1994) – the court held that Greenpeace had sufficient interest to challenge the decision in respect of the location of a nuclear processing plant. This was because it was a large organisation with the prime objective of protecting the environment; had members residing within the area; and had invested both money

and expertise so that a properly mounted challenge could be made. It was therefore in the public interest to grant Greenpeace sufficient interest.

- *R v Secretary of State for Foreign and Commonwealth Affairs, ex parte World Development Movement* (1995) – the court held that the WDM had sufficient interest to challenge the decision to grant financial aid to Malaysia for the building of the Pergau Dam. The WDM had considerable expertise in the matter of providing such aid and, the court emphasised, there was no other means of challenging the decision.
- *R (Al-Haq) v Secretary of State for Foreign and Commonwealth Affairs* (2009) – the court identified the claimant as being a non-governmental organisation protecting human rights in the Palestinian territories, and that the test for standing was a liberal one that extended to responsible, expert groups; albeit not in this case.

13.7 Prerogative remedies in judicial review – and the influence of the Human Rights Act 1998

13.7.1 Generally there are two types of remedy applied for in cases of judicial review: (i) prerogative orders and, under private law, (ii) the remedies of **declarations**, injunctions and damages.

13.7.2 Application can be made for more than one remedy and the court has the discretion to order any of the remedies in combination, or an alternative one to that actually applied for: section 31(4) of the Supreme Court Act 1981.

13.7.3 Prerogative orders cannot be used against the Crown. However, they can be issued against individual Ministers.

Quashing orders (previously an order of *certiorari*)

13.7.4 These quash or set aside the original decision and therefore act retrospectively. Where only part of a decision is *ultra vires* that part can be severed and quashed whilst the rest of the decision stands.

Mandatory orders (previously orders of *mandamus*)

13.7.5 These order the body to act and if it then fails to do so, the body will be in contempt of court.

Prohibiting orders (previously orders of *prohibition*)

13.7.6 These prevent the body from making a decision that would, if it made it, be susceptible to a quashing order. In other words this order acts prospectively in that it prevents a body acting *ultra vires* in the future. Failure to comply with such an order will amount to a contempt of court.

13.7.7 Damages under the Human Rights Act 1998 are dealt with by section 8 of the Act. Section 8 provides for the court to award a remedy or 'make such order within its jurisdiction as it considers just and appropriate'.

13.7.8 Section 12(4) of the Human Rights Act 1998 provides that in the case of an injunction, the court is to have particular regard to the right of freedom of expression.

13.7.9 Damages will not be awarded unless the court is satisfied they are necessary: *R (on the application of Anufrijeva) v Southwark LBC (2003)*. Damages cannot be claimed against the courts, except where a judicial body has been in breach of right to liberty (Article 5 ECHR).

13.7.10 Damages cannot be awarded for a breach of human rights caused by an Act of Parliament – instead a declaration of incompatibility should be made, given section 4 of the Human Rights Act 1998. (See Chapter 7.)

13.8 Other remedies used in judicial review

13.8.1 These are made up of private law-type remedies. Private law remedies include the following.

Injunction

13.8.2 This restrains a body or person from doing something unlawful (a negative injunction) or orders them to undo something that was done unlawfully (a positive injunction). Injunctions may also be interim or permanent.

13.8.3 Injunctions cannot be issued against the Crown. They can be issued against an individual Minister but only as an action of last resort: *M v Home Office* (1994). If the Minister fails to comply with the injunction he or she may be held in contempt of court.

Damages

13.8.4   A claim for damages must be attached to a claim for one of the other remedies above. Damages will only be awarded though where they would have been granted if the action had been a private law action; or where damages would satisfy the need for 'just satisfaction' for an infringement of a human right protected by an Article of the ECHR, given the requirements of section 8 of the Human Rights Act 1998.

13.9 Declaratory relief

13.9.1   Declaratory relief comes in the form of a declaration by the court in judicial review.

Declaration

13.9.2   A declaration is a statement of the legal position of the parties so is not in the full sense a remedy. Declarations cannot be enforced but it is unlikely that a body would ignore one. In contrast to prerogative orders, a declaration can be made against the Crown.

13.10 Judicial deference and comity: refusal of a remedy

13.10.1   All remedies are granted at the **discretion** of the court. Thus a remedy may be refused, even when the applicant has established their case when:

- there has been a delay in commencing proceedings;
- the applicant has acted unreasonably; and/or
- the public interest of ensuring efficient administration would be harmed.

13.10.2   Legal academics will sometimes describe the refusal by the courts of a remedy, even when a claimant has established that the action or decision of a public body has been unlawful, as an issue of 'judicial deference', or 'comity'.

13.10.3   This can be easily seen, for example, in the case of R *(Hurley & Moore) v Secretary of State for Business, Innovation and Skills* (2012), where the claimant established that the consultation process surrounding the increase of student tuition fees at English and Welsh universities, to a then maximum fee of £9,000 per year, had been unlawful.

13.10.4 Despite this acknowledgement of a strong legal argument by the claimants, Hurley and Moore, the court declined the opportunity to afford the claimant a remedy such as a quashing order, since the plans to implement the new higher education fees system for universities was well underway, and in the words of Elias LJ, to halt this process because of the claimant's legal arguments would only produce 'administrative chaos' – while the lawful introduction of the new higher fees would simply have been delayed.

Key Cases Checklist

Key cases guiding judicial review procedure

Standing

R v Inland Revenue Commissioners, ex parte National Federation of Self-employed and Small Businesses (1982): **sufficient interest** will be assessed by the court at both the leave stage and at the substantive hearing

R (Suryananda) v Welsh Ministers (2007): pressure or interest groups do not have sufficient interest unless they can establish that one or more of their actual members are, in fact, a 'victim' of an infringement of ECHR rights (see 13.5.3)

R v Secretary of State for Foreign and Commonwealth Affairs, ex parte World Development Movement (1995): representative standing is obtained if a group bringing a JR claim has prominence in the relevant field, recognised expertise, and the matter is important to the public

Comity and deference in relation to remedies

R (Hurley & Moore) v Secretary of State for Business, Innovation and Skills (2012): a remedy may be refused even where there is some ground for judicial review, taking into account the 'administrative chaos' which would otherwise result from a decision being overturned (13.10.3)

Anufrijeva v London Borough of Southwark (2003): the Court of Appeal concluded that damages should be considered a last resort under the Act – other remedies such as injunctions are more meaningful

13.4.2 R v Inland Revenue Commissioners, ex parte National Federation of Self-employed and Small Businesses [1982] AC 617

`HL`

Key Facts

The applicants sought judicial review of the decision of the Inland Revenue to grant a tax amnesty to casual workers in the newspaper industry.

Key Law

The applicants had no sufficient interest; in general a taxpayer did not have sufficient interest to challenge decisions made relating to other taxpayers' matters. *Locus standi* must be considered in two stages: it should be assessed at the leave stage but a court may revise its decision when reviewing the merits of the case.

Key Judgment

Lord Scarman
The assessment of sufficient interest at the leave stage 'prevents abuse by busybodies, cranks and other mischief makers'.

13.6.4 R v Secretary of State for Foreign and Commonwealth Affairs, ex parte World Development Movement [1995] 1 All ER 611

`HC`

Key Facts

In 1988 the UK Government agreed to sell arms to Malaysia. In 1989 the UK offered £234 million towards the building of the Pergau Dam. (Linking arms with aid is prohibited under international law.) Section 1 of the Overseas Development and Co-operation Act 1980 empowered the Foreign Secretary to grant aid 'only for the purpose of promoting the development or maintaining the economy of a country . . . or the welfare of its people'.

Key Law

The organisation World Development Movement was found to have sufficient interest because it played a significant role in giving advice and assistance in relation to the granting of foreign aid and because it would be unlikely that any other body would have the necessary interest, that is, it was the public interest to grant the WDM *locus standi*.

The High Court held that the Foreign Secretary had acted unlawfully in that the aid did not promote the development of the country's economy.

13.7.9 *R (on the application of Anufrijeva) v Southwark LBC* [2003] EWCA Civ 1406 (CA)

Key Facts

Asylum seekers sought damages on the basis of unlawful maladministration by the local authority in Southwark – which they claimed had not provided them the support to which they were entitled under statute. The Court of Appeal determined that where Articles of the European Convention on Human Rights were infringed, other remedies were more appropriate in order to bring the unlawful maladministration to an end, and obtain the support to which the claimants were entitled.

Key Law

Damages are not awarded unless the court is satisfied they are necessary. In *Anufrijeva* the Court of Appeal concluded that damages should be considered a last resort under the Act. The scale of damages for any maladministration has to be modest.

14 Substantive grounds for judicial review

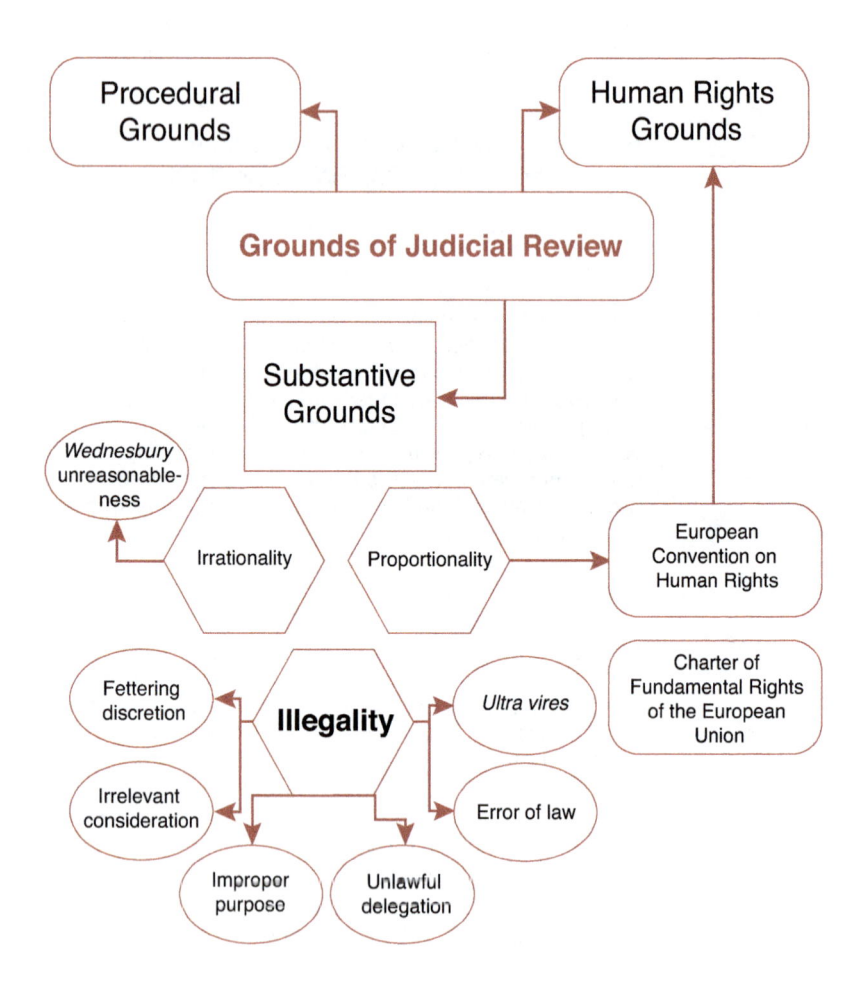

Grounds of Judicial Review

- Procedural Grounds
- Human Rights Grounds
- Substantive Grounds

Substantive Grounds

- **Irrationality**
  - *Wednesbury* unreasonableness
- **Proportionality**
  - European Convention on Human Rights
  - Charter of Fundamental Rights of the European Union
- **Illegality**
  - Fettering discretion
  - Irrelevant consideration
  - Improper purpose
  - Unlawful delegation
  - Ultra vires
  - Error of law

14.1 An overview of grounds for judicial review

14.1.1 It is extremely difficult to classify the grounds for judicial review since they are broad and can overlap. This was recognised by the House of Lords in *Boddington v British Transport Police* (1998).

14.1.2 The way this book breaks down grounds of judicial review is to take them in three particular categories:

- **Substantive grounds** *(dealt with in this chapter)*;
- **Procedural grounds** *(dealt with in Chapter 15)*; and
- **Human rights grounds** *(dealt with in Chapter 16)*.

14.1.3 This chapter is mainly concerned with substantive grounds. Substantive grounds are those grounds of judicial review that purport to criticise the overall basis or substance of a decision by a public body – while procedural grounds are concerned with addressing flaws in the manner in which a decision by a public body was actually made.

14.1.4 'Human rights grounds' are what we might call the basis of a claim for an infringement with a human right protected by an Article of the ECHR – in a sense, each protected human right, if breached, can be a distinct human rights-based ground of judicial review in that regard.

14.1.5 A useful starting point (in terms of examining how grounds of judicial review are and have been typically classified) is the classification in *Council for Civil Service Unions v Minister for the Civil Service* (1985) (the *GCHQ Case*) where Lord Diplock referred to the following three grounds (however, Lord Diplock recognised that these grounds may overlap and that others may be developed to supplement them):

- illegality;
- irrationality; and
- procedural impropriety.

14.1.6 The first two of these are different groups of substantive grounds, using the classification in this book – and accordingly are dealt with in this chapter. Procedural impropriety makes up the mainstay of the group of procedural grounds – dealt with in Chapter 15.

14.1.7 Grounds that have developed since the decision in the *GCHQ Case* include:

- **proportionality**, particularly since the passing of the Human Rights Act 1998;

- the particular means of acting unlawfully, on the part of a public body (or 'hybrid public body') by **contravening section 6 of the Human Rights Act 1998**, in breach of an individual's human rights; and
- the newer procedural ground of **'legitimate expectation'**.

14.1.8 Figure 14A at the start of this chapter should therefore be used as a guide in identifying the grounds for judicial review, and is based on the three grounds in the *GCHQ Case*.

14.2 Types of illegality and the importance of statutory interpretation in deploying arguments about illegality in claiming judicial review

Narrow or simple *ultra vires*

14.2.1 A body will act in this way when it acts outside of the powers conferred on it: in other words it lacks the necessary jurisdiction.

14.2.2 Lord Diplock in the *GCHQ Case* defined this as where 'the decision maker must understand correctly the law that regulates his decision-making power and give effect to it'.

14.2.3 Examples of bodies acting in such a way include:
- *Attorney-General v Fulham Corporation* (1921) – in this case statute granted local authorities the power to provide a washhouse for local people. The Corporation interpreted this as granting it the power to provide a laundry service. According to the court this was unlawful because a washhouse was where someone did their own laundry.
- *Bromley London Borough Council v Greater London Council* (1983) – the House of Lords held that an obligation on the GLC to provide an 'efficient and economic' public transport service did not give the Council the power to subsidise the London Underground for social reasons.
- *R v Lord Chancellor, ex parte Witham* (1998) – the Lord Chancellor, under the Supreme Court Act 1981, removed the exemption for payment of court fees for litigants receiving income support. The court found that the Act did not expressly provide for the

removal of access to justice and hence the Lord Chancellor had acted *ultra vires*.

14.2.4 In contrast, in *Akumah v Hackney London Borough Council* (2005) the House of Lords held that the Council had statutory power to manage, regulate and control 'dwelling houses' and this should be interpreted widely to include regulation of car parking. Consequently the Council's action to clamp cars in a car park attached to a block of flats was held *intra vires*.

14.2.5 *Illegality as a failure to act* is where a body has a statutory duty to act and fails to do so. Whether the duty to act is enforceable by the courts will depend on the wording of the statute: if the obligation to act is clear and precise the court will hold it enforceable. Conversely, if the duty is not specific the court will not hold it enforceable. If, under statute, the Secretary of State has default powers to intervene to ensure the duty to act takes place, the courts will generally not intervene: *R v Secretary of State for the Environment, ex parte Norwich City Council* (1982).

14.3 Illegality as an excess of powers (*ultra vires*)

14.3.1 The various grounds as types of illegality as considered below are concerned with the way in which bodies exercise their discretion; regardless of how wide a body's discretion may be, the court can examine whether it has been exercised ultra vires: for example, in relation to an **improper purpose**: *Padfield v Minister for Agriculture, Fisheries and Food* (1968).

14.4 Illegality as an improper purpose

14.4.1 This is where the body uses its powers to achieve a purpose that it is not empowered to do: see *Padfield v Minister for Agriculture, Fisheries and Food* (1968).

14.4.2 Examples of the application of this ground include:

- *R v Secretary of State for Foreign and Commonwealth Affairs, ex parte World Development Movement* (1995) – where the court held that the Minister had acted unlawfully by granting aid to Malaysia because it did not promote development of the country's economy, as required by statute.

- *Porter v Magill* (2002) – the House of Lords ruled that the power of local authorities to sell property to tenants was unlawfully used to secure electoral votes.

14.5 Illegality as an error of law (or an error of fact)

14.5.1 An error of law can take several forms, including incorrect interpretation, whether discretion has been properly exercised and whether irrelevant considerations have been considered or relevant ones ignored.

14.5.2 Generally all errors of law are reviewable: *Anisminic Ltd v Foreign Compensation Commission* (1969) and *R v Lord President of the Privy Council, ex parte Page* (1992).

14.5.3 Examples of bodies acting in such a way include:

- *Perilly v Tower Hamlets Borough Council* (1973) – the Council had misinterpreted the law so instead of granting stall licences only in order of application, it could grant a licence to the son of a deceased licence holder.
- *R v Secretary of State for the Home Department, ex parte Venables* (1997) – the Home Secretary was held to have misdirected himself as to the law when increasing the tariff for two young murderers on the basis they should be treated as adults.

14.5.4 Errors of fact are not usually reviewable unless they are central to the decision that has been made, for example: if the decision is based on facts for which there is no evidence (*Ashbridge Investments v Minister of Housing and Local Government* (1965)); and where facts are proved incorrect or have been ignored or misunderstood (*R v Criminal Injuries Compensation Board, ex parte A* (1992)).

14.5.5 Where the decision involves a person's individual rights, the courts are more likely to review any error of fact. For example, in *R v Secretary of State for the Home Department, ex parte Khawaja* (1984) the court held that whether the applicant was indeed an illegal immigrant had to be determined as fact before the power to detain or expel could be exercised.

14.6 Illegality as a failure to take into account a relevant consideration, or the taking into account of an irrelevant consideration

14.6.1 In exercising its discretion a body must be seen to take into account all relevant considerations and not be swayed in its decision-making by irrelevant ones. It should be noted that this can overlap with the previous ground of improper purpose.

14.6.2 In *R v Somerset County Council, ex parte Fewings* (1995) three types of consideration were identified:

- considerations that must be taken into account and which are therefore mandatory;
- considerations that must not be taken into account and which are therefore prohibited; and
- discretionary considerations that a decision-maker may have regard to, in which case the court will only intervene if it believes the decision-maker has acted unreasonably.

14.6.3 Examples of the application of this ground include:

- *Wheeler v Leicester City Council* (1985) – the decision of a local authority to refuse to permit a local rugby club to use its playing field was found to have been based on the irrelevant consideration that the club had failed to prevent some of its members from touring South Africa during the apartheid regime.
- *R v Talbot Borough Council, ex parte Jones* (1988) – the decision to grant priority housing to a divorced councillor was decided on the basis of irrelevant factors, with relevant ones, such as the needs of other applicants on the waiting list, ignored.
- *R v Secretary of State for the Home Department, ex parte Venables* (1997) – the Secretary of State, when reviewing the tariff of child murderers, took into account the irrelevant consideration of public opinion. In *R (Bulger) v Secretary of State* (2001) it was also concluded that the Home Secretary had failed to take into account the relevant considerations of the progress and development of the children whilst in detention.
- *R v Liverpool Crown Court, ex parte Luxury Leisure* (1998) – the court found that the local authority had acted on the basis of relevant considerations when it had considered its knowledge of the

area and community when deciding to create a system of permits for amusement arcades.

- *R v Gloucestershire County Council, ex parte Barry* (1997) – a local authority, when exercising its statutory obligation to provide care for disabled persons, could take into account its financial resources as a relevant consideration in determining how to meet those needs (see also *R v Sefton Metropolitan Borough Council, ex parte Help the Aged* (1997)).

14.7 Illegality as an unlawful delegation of power in decision-making

14.7.1 Where powers are conferred under statute they should generally be exercised by the body on which they are conferred, and should not be delegated in an unauthorised manner to another body or person.

14.7.2 Delegation by a Minister to the personnel in their department is not considered unauthorised delegation: *Carltona v Works Commissioner* (1943). For example, in *R v Secretary of State for the Home Department, ex parte Oladehinde* (1991) the court held that decisions in respect of deportation could be legally delegated to an Immigration Inspector.

14.7.3 Examples of the application of this ground include:

- *Barnard v National Dock Labour Board* (1953) – the decision to delegate power of disciplining striking workers by the London Dock Board to a port manager was unauthorised and hence illegal.
- *R v Talbot Borough Council, ex parte Jones* (1988) – the power to allocate council housing had been delegated to an officer when the power to make such decisions rested in the hands of the chair of the housing committee.

14.8 Illegality as an unlawful fettering of discretion in decision-making

14.8.1 This occurs when the decision-maker binds themselves to exercise their discretion in a particular way, sometimes by imposing a rigid rule, so that they are no longer able to exercise discretion in individual cases; where decision-makers have discretion it should be exercised in each case according to its merits: *British Oxygen Co. v Board of Trade* (1971).

14.8.2 Some examples of the application of this ground include:
- *Sagnata Investments v Norwich Corporation* (1971) – the policy adopted by the Corporation of not granting any licences for amusement arcades resulted in it failing to consider any cases on their merits.
- *R v Army Board of the Defence Council, ex parte Anderson* (1992) – the Army Board's policy of never permitting oral hearings amounted to an unlawful fettering of discretion.
- *R v Chief Constable of North Wales Police, ex parte AB* (1997) – the decision publicly to disclose information pertaining to a convicted paedophile was held to have been based on the merits of the case and was not the adoption of any policy on behalf of the police.
- *R v Secretary of State for the Home Department, ex parte Simms* (1999) – the Home Secretary's blanket policy of not permitting professionals (such as journalists) to visit prisoners was held to have been unlawful.

14.9 Unreasonableness and irrationality

14.9.1 Irrationality as a ground is also referred to as **unreasonableness**.

14.9.2 It is a far wider and vaguer ground for judicial review than illegality. Consequently this ground is one where the court comes far closer to examining the merits of the decision.

14.9.3 It is because of this that the courts will generally only accept this ground if a high level of unreasonableness is found and such cases are rare.

14.10 *Wednesbury* unreasonableness

14.10.1 This is seen in the case of *Associated Picture Houses Ltd v Wednesbury Corporation* (1948), in which the court stated that it would only interfere where a decision was 'so unreasonable that no reasonable authority could ever have come to it'.

14.10.2 In the *GCHQ Case*, Lord Diplock referred to this ground as operating only when a decision has no rational basis or 'is so outrageous in its denial of accepted moral standards that no sensible person who has applied his mind to the question to be decided could have arrived at it'.

14.10.3 For example, in *Brind v Secretary of State for the Home Department* (1991) a ban on live media interviews with supporters of the IRA was held not to be unreasonable; it was a rational means of preventing terrorists gaining publicity.

14.10.4 However, if there is interference with a person's human rights the court will require a higher justification before it will consider the decision to be reasonable: *R v Ministry of Defence, ex parte Smith* (1996).

14.10.5 For example, in *R (Rogers) v Swindon NHS Primary Care Trust* (2006) the court found that the decision of the Trust to grant certain breast cancer treatment only in 'exceptional personal or clinical circumstances' to be irrational, particularly since it had the necessary funds to provide such treatment.

14.11 Proportionality: influenced by human rights law

14.11.1 The requirement to act proportionally means that powers must be exercised in a manner that is proportionate to the objective pursued: in other words, no more than is necessary.

14.11.2 Originally the English courts did not accept proportionality as a ground for judicial review: *Brind* (above).

14.11.3 Over time, however, the courts appeared more willing to adopt the concept: see, for example, Lord Diplock's comments in the *GCHQ Case* (above) and *R v Chief Constable of Sussex, ex parte International Trader's Ferry Ltd* (1999).

14.11.4 A need for proportionality is now accepted in the context of decisions impacting on Convention rights as a result of the passing of the Human Rights Act 1998. This is because it is a doctrine favoured by the European Court of Human Rights, and section 2 of the Act requires the jurisprudence of the Court to be taken into account.

14.11.5 An example of the application of proportionality can be seen in *R (Daly) v Secretary of State for the Home Department* (2001). In this case the House of Lords held the policy of permitting the scrutiny of a prisoner's legal correspondence to not be a proportionate means of achieving any objective in the public interest.

14.11.6 In *Daly*, the House of Lords provided a three-part test to examining the proportionality of a measure:

- whether the objective is sufficiently important to justify limiting a fundamental right;

- whether the measures taken are designed to meet the objective and rationally connected to it; and
- whether the means used are no more than is necessary to achieve the objective.

14.11.7 The House of Lords also stressed in *Daly* that in cases involving a human rights element, proportionality was the standard of review that should be applied.

14.11.8 In some cases, a fourth part is sometimes added to this important proportionality test, as we see in the judgment of Wilson LJ in *R (on the application of Quila) v Secretary of State for the Home Department* (2011):

- '(a) is the legislative object sufficiently important to justify limiting a fundamental right?;
- (b) are the measures which have been designed to meet it rationally connected to it?
- (c) are they no more than necessary to accomplish it?
- And (d) do they strike a fair balance between the rights of the individual and the interests of the community?'

14.11.9 The courts have indicated that proportionality extends beyond human rights cases: see, for example, *R (Alconbury Developments Ltd) v Secretary of State for the Environment, Transport and the Regions* (2001). In this case Lord Slynn argued for proportionality to become a separate fourth ground for judicial review (see also *Secretary of State for the Home Department v Rehman* (2003)).

14.11.10 Of late the UK Supreme Court has begun to acknowledge that even if the United Kingdom were not, at some point in the future, to subscribe to and domestically incorporate the Articles of the ECHR through a mechanism like the Human Rights Act 1998, proportionality would still remain a valid substantive ground of judicial review: *R (Pham) v Secretary of State for the Home Department* (2015).

14.11.11 At present, the two tests, *Wednesbury* unreasonableness and proportionality, can be applied in the same claim for judicial review, with the acknowledgement that cases involving human rights will often use proportionality. The courts have recognised the coexistence of the tests: see *R (Association of British Civilian Internees: Far East Region) v Secretary of State for Defence* (2003) and *R (Ann Summers Ltd) v Jobcentre Plus* (2003). However, the courts have also recognised the increasing significance of proportionality and legal academics have mooted the possible eventual doctrinal disappearance of *Wednesbury* unreasonableness in the future.

Key Cases Checklist

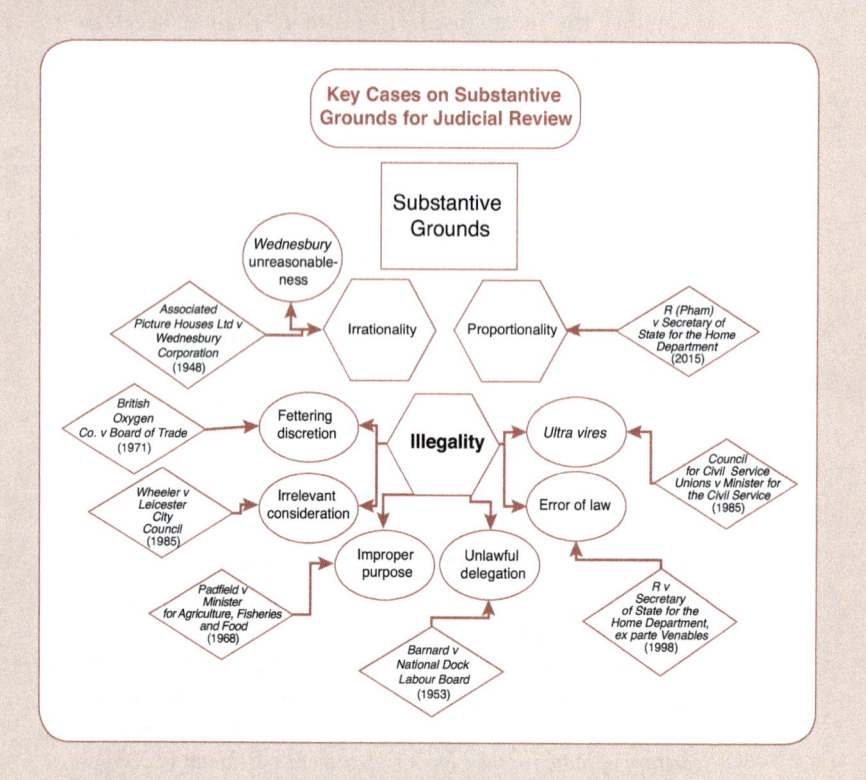

Key Cases on Substantive Grounds for Judicial Review

- Substantive Grounds
  - Irrationality
    - Wednesbury unreasonableness
      - Associated Picture Houses Ltd v Wednesbury Corporation (1948)
  - Proportionality
    - R (Pham) v Secretary of State for the Home Department (2015)
  - Illegality
    - Fettering discretion
      - British Oxygen Co. v Board of Trade (1971)
    - Irrelevant consideration
      - Wheeler v Leicester City Council (1985)
    - Improper purpose
      - Padfield v Minister for Agriculture, Fisheries and Food (1968)
    - Unlawful delegation
      - Barnard v National Dock Labour Board (1953)
    - Ultra vires
    - Error of law
      - Council for Civil Service Unions v Minister for the Civil Service (1985)
      - R v Secretary of State for the Home Department, ex parte Venables (1998)

14.10.1 Associated Provincial Picture Houses v Wednesbury Corporation [1948] 1 KB 223 (CA)

Key Facts

The court had to consider the legality of a condition imposed under statute. The statute permitted 'such conditions as the authority think fit to impose'. In this case the condition was that no children under the age of 15 could be admitted to the cinema on a Sunday.

Key Law

The condition was not unreasonable. A court may set aside a decision for unreasonableness only when the authority

Substantive grounds for judicial review   231

has come to a conclusion (in the words of Lord Greene MR) 'so unreasonable that no reasonable authority could ever have come to it'.

Key Comment

In the *GCHQ Case* (see below) Lord Diplock stated that the courts would only apply this ground when the decision has no rational basis or 'is so outrageous in its denial of accepted moral standards that no sensible person who has applied his mind to the question . . . could have arrived at it'.

Many have criticised the *Wednesbury* test as too difficult to meet when challenging executive discretion and have argued that there should be adoption of the European concept of 'proportionality' as a free-standing ground of judicial review, not dependent on the application, for example, of the ECHR or any particular EU law. (See below with regard to *Pham*.)

14.1.5 *CCSU v Minister of State for the Civil Service* [1985] AC 374 *(the 'GCHQ Case')*   (HL)

Key Facts

Prerogative empowered the Minister to issue instructions in respect of the conditions of service for civil servants. Following industrial action at the Government Communication Headquarters (GCHQ) the Minister issued instructions that barred membership of a trade union. Contrary to usual practice, the Minister did not consult with the trade union before issuing the instruction.

Key Law

An exercise of prerogative power is susceptible to judicial review. In the case at hand, while the union had a legitimate expectation to be consulted, on the facts this was outweighed by the interests of national security.

In this case, however, in the context of judicial review, the House of Lords summarised the three grounds for review as being illegality, irrationality and procedural impropriety.

Key Judgments

Lord Roskill
'If the executive . . . acts under a prerogative power . . . so as to affect the rights of the citizen, I am unable to see . . .

that there is any logical reason why the fact that the source of the power is the prerogative and not statute should today deprive the citizen of that right of challenge to the manner of its exercise which he would possess were the source of the power statutory.'

Lord Diplock
'Judicial review has I think developed to a state today when . . . one can conveniently classify under three heads the grounds on which administrative action is subject to control by judicial review. The first ground I would call "illegality", the second "irrationality" and the third "procedural impropriety".'

'By "illegality" . . . I mean that the decision maker must understand correctly the law that regulates his decision making power and give effect to it.'

'By "irrationality", I mean what can now be succinctly referred to as *Wednesbury* unreasonableness. It applies to a decision which is so outrageous in its defiance of logic or of accepted moral standards that no sensible person who had applied his mind to the question to be decided could have arrived at it.'

'I have described the third head as "procedural impropriety" rather than failure to observe basic rules of natural justice or failure to act with procedural fairness . . . This is because susceptibility to judicial review under this head covers also failure by an administrative tribunal to observe the procedural rules that are expressly laid down in the legislative instrument by which its jurisdiction is conferred.'

Key Comment

Lord Diplock also recognised that further grounds could be accepted in the future, referring particularly to the concept of proportionality (see below).

14.8.1 *British Oxygen Co. v Board of Trade* [1971] AC 610

(HL)

Key Facts

A scheme provided for discretionary grants to industries. The Board of Trade adopted a policy of not paying for items costing less than £25. BOC sought to challenge the Board's decision to refuse a grant for gas cylinders costing £20 each (BOC had spent over £4 million in total).

Key Law

Policies or rules may be adopted but they must not be applied in a blanket manner or as automatically binding; discretion to discuss the merits of each case must be available.

14.6.3 *Wheeler v Leicester City Council* [1985] AC 1054 (HL)

Key Facts

Wheeler challenged the decision of Leicester City Council under the Race Relations Act 1976 to prohibit the rugby club of which Wheeler was a member from using particular council-owned training facilities, arguing that this was a politically motivated decision, since the council had concerns over some players who were members of the club also playing rugby in South Africa during the period of racist apartheid Government in that country. (At the time there was great popular and political opposition to British sportspeople playing in South Africa during apartheid, since refusal to play in South Africa was a way of putting indirect political pressure on the apartheid regime – especially in the case of rugby, since this is a particular passion for South Africans, and remains so today.)

Key Law

It was determined that while it was appropriate for the city council to take into account race relations when deciding who should use its training facilities, in the absence of any wrongdoing by the rugby club concerned, mere failure by a handful of its members to show indirect political support for the campaign against apartheid, because they were willing to play rugby in South Africa, was an irrelevant consideration to take into account, and so the decision was unlawful.

14.4.1 *Padfield v Minister for Agriculture, Fisheries and Food* [1968] 2 WLR 924 (HL)

Key Facts

The then Minister for Agriculture, Fisheries and Food was asked by Padfield to start an investigation into failures by the Milk Marketing Board to promote the interests of certain dairy producers in the south-east region of England.

Other producers in other parts of the country were better able to control the practices of the Board, since they had elected members to represent their interests on the Board itself. The Minister had the power to investigate and rectify any inconsistencies in the practices of the Board carrying out a milk marketing and production programme, under the Agricultural Marketing Act 1958.

Key Law

The Act of Parliament in question conferred a statutory power on the Minister to intervene to redress such inconsistencies and unfairness as complained of by Padfield and others, and so to refuse to intervene was an unlawful use of that discretion, frustrating the purpose of the Act concerned.

Key Judgment

Lord Denning
'When Parliament has set up machinery for that very purpose, it is not for the Minister to brush it on one side.'

14.7.3 *Barnard v National Dock Labour Board* [1953] 2 QB 18

(CA)

Key Facts

The National Board lawfully delegated disciplinary functions to local boards but one local board then unlawfully sub-delegated the functions to the port manager.

Key Law

A delegation of power, to be lawful, should be expressly or impliedly a feature of a legislative regulatory scheme, or occur through some rule of the common law.

Key Commont

This case can be contrasted with *Carltona v Works Commissioners* **[1943] 2 All ER 560**. In that case, under wartime regulations Carltona's property was requisitioned, but the order was signed by a civil servant. This was ultimately deemed to be lawful, as an element of the common law. The *Carltona* decision, as a result, established that a

Minister may lawfully delegate power but remains accountable to Parliament for any decision.

14.5.3 *R v Secretary of State for the Home Department, ex parte Venables* [1998] AC 407 (HL)

Key Facts

The Home Secretary increased the tariff period for two young murderers to 15 years, on the basis that they should be treated in the same way as adults.

Key Law

The Home Secretary had misdirected himself as to the law, rendering the decision unlawful.

Key Judgment

Lord Steyn
'His legal premise was wrong: the two sentences are different. A sentence of detention during Her Majesty's pleasure requires the Home Secretary to decide from time to time . . . whether detention is still justified. The Home Secretary misunderstood his duty. This misdirection by itself renders his decision unlawful.'

14.11.10 *R (Pham) v Secretary of State for the Home Department* [2015] UKSC 19 (SC)

Key Facts

Pham, a Vietnamese-born individual, had been denied British citizenship under the British Nationality Act 1981 by the Home Secretary. Pham argued this rendered him stateless, in breach of binding international law, as the Vietnamese Government did not recognise him as a citizen. However, at the time of the decision by the Home Secretary it was recognised by the Supreme Court that the Home Secretary had not known that the Vietnamese Government would refuse to recognise Pham's citizenship – entailing that the decision of the Home Secretary to deny Pham British citizenship had not been unlawful.

Key Law

In its judgment in this case, the Supreme Court recognised that the proportionality principle had become part of the common law of the United Kingdom, and so a proportionality test could be applied to determine the lawfulness of actions or decisions by UK public bodies without particular recourse to EU law, or the application of the ECHR even, for example.

Key Judgment

Lord Sumption

'. . . although English law has not adopted the principle of proportionality generally, it has for many years stumbled towards a concept which is in significant respects similar, and over the last three decades has been influenced by European jurisprudence even in areas of law lying beyond the domains of EU and international human rights law. Starting with the decision of the House of Lords in *R v Secretary of State for the Home Department, Ex p Bugdaycay* [1987] AC 514 it has recognised the need, even in the context of rights arising wholly from domestic law, to differentiate between rights of greater or lesser importance and interference with them of greater or lesser degree. This is essentially the same problem as the one to which proportionality analysis is directed. The solution adopted, albeit sometimes without acknowledgment, was to expand the scope of rationality review so as to incorporate at common law significant elements of the principle of proportionality.'

15 Procedural grounds for judicial review

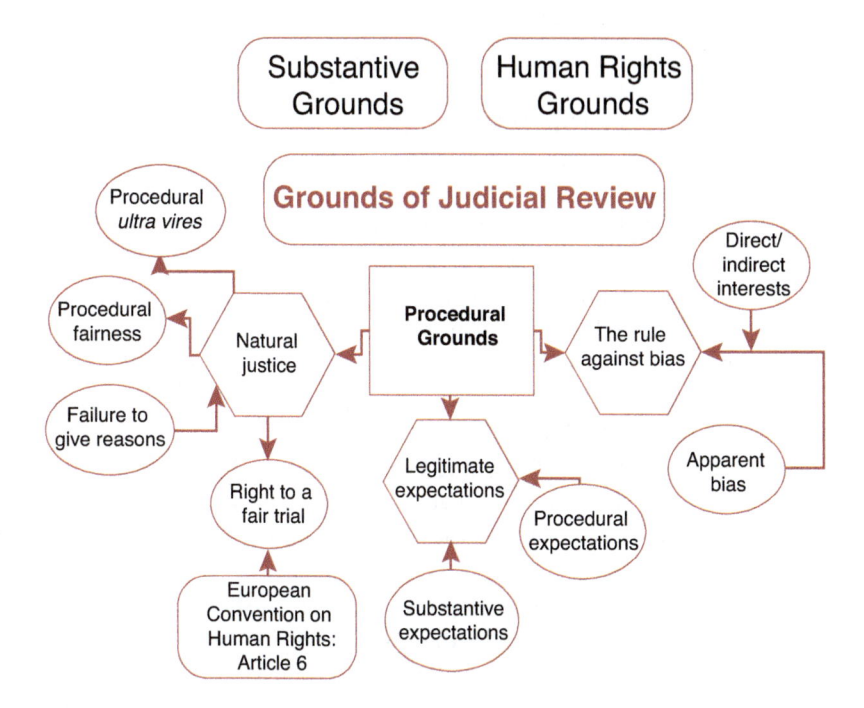

Grounds of Judicial Review

- Substantive Grounds
- Human Rights Grounds
- Procedural Grounds
  - Procedural ultra vires
  - Natural justice
    - Procedural fairness
    - Failure to give reasons
    - Right to a fair trial
      - European Convention on Human Rights: Article 6
  - The rule against bias
    - Direct/indirect interests
    - Apparent bias
  - Legitimate expectations
    - Procedural expectations
    - Substantive expectations

15.1 An overview of procedural grounds for judicial review

15.1.1 Lord Diplock in the *GCHQ Case* (discussed above) described procedural impropriety as ground of judicial review to include 'the failure to observe basic rules of natural justice or failure to act with procedural fairness' and also 'failure . . . to observe procedural rules expressly laid down in . . . legislative instrument'.

15.1.2 This chapter considers the different procedural grounds that taken as a collective whole can be said to encompass the fuller concept of procedural impropriety.

15.2 Natural justice

15.2.1 The origin of the 'natural justice' **principles** of procedure is found in the **common law**. They effectively require a public body to act fairly.

15.2.2 With the passing of the Human Rights Act 1998, Article 6 of the ECHR, which requires 'a fair and public hearing within a reasonable time by an independent and impartial tribunal established by law', is now enforceable in English courts.

The right to a fair hearing (*audi alteram partem*)

15.2.3 Traditionally the courts would only apply the right to a fair hearing to judicial decisions: *Local Government Board v Arlidge* (1915).

15.2.4 In *Ridge v Baldwin* (1964), however, it was concluded that irrespective of whether a decision is judicial or administrative there is, in principle, **a right to be heard**. Judicial proceedings will attract a higher procedural standard of the right to a fair hearing than administrative decisions.

15.2.5 One exception to the right to be heard is where there are overriding factors in the interests of national security: *GCHQ Case* (above). (See also *R v Secretary of State for Transport, ex parte Pegasus Holdings Ltd* (1989).)

15.2.6 Failure to permit a hearing may also not invalidate the decision when the court concludes that the outcome of the decision would have been the same regardless. For example, in *Glynn v Keele University* (1971) the court dismissed an application by a student against their expulsion from the university on the basis that no representation by them would have affected the decision.

15.2.7 Whether a hearing is itself fair is not subject to fixed requirements, although the more serious the consequences for the individual, the higher the standard required for the hearing to be fair.

15.2.8 A fair hearing could require one or more of the following requirements therefore, depending on the facts of the case:

- notification of a hearing/advance notice;
- to be informed of the case against;
- the opportunity to respond to evidence;

- an oral hearing;
- legal representation before and at the hearing; and
- the ability to question witnesses.

15.2.9 For example, there is no absolute right to an oral hearing. According to *R v Army Board of the Defence Council, ex parte Anderson* (1992), whether an oral hearing is required for the hearing to be fair will depend on the subject matter and circumstances of the particular case. Consequently the question is whether any written proceedings are sufficient to ensure a fair hearing.

15.2.10 Arguments that an oral hearing is an entitlement of a person who may be deprived or may continue to be deprived of a fundamental right, such as their liberty, will be well received by the courts however: see *Osborn v Parole Board* (2013). The right to cross-examine any witnesses will only arise if there is an oral hearing.

15.2.11 Similarly, the right to legal representation will depend on the nature of the hearing and the rights that will be affected. In *R v Secretary of State for the Home Department, ex parte Tarrant* (1985) the criteria to be applied in determining whether legal representation is necessary include:

- the seriousness of the charge and potential penalty;
- whether any points of law are likely to be raised;
- the ability of the person to present their own case;
- the complexity of the procedure to be applied; and
- whether there is need for reasonable speed in making the decision.

15.2.12 There does, however, appear to be no such discretion when the matters are 'criminal' – for example, in *Ezeh v UK* (2002) a prison governor's decision not to allow legal representation at a disciplinary hearing was a breach of the right to a fair trial (Article 6 ECHR).

15.3 Bias: the rule against bias (*nemo judex in causa sua*)

15.3.1 Impartial and independent decision-making is a fundamental aspect of the rule of law.

15.3.2 The rule against bias is described as being strict in that the risk or appearance of bias will suffice. As stated by Lord Hewart in *R v*

Sussex Justices, ex parte McCarthy (1924), 'justice must not only be done but must manifestly and undoubtedly be seen to be done'.

15.3.3 If a decision-maker becomes aware that they may be biased, they should remove themselves from the decision-making process: *AWG Group v Morrison* (2006).

15.3.4 A financial interest, however small, will automatically indicate bias: *Dimes v Grand Junction Canal Co.* (1852) and *Metropolitan Properties Co v Lannon* (1969).

15.3.5 This principle, of automatic disqualification because of a direct interest, was extended in *R v Bow Street Metropolitan and Stipendiary Magistrate, ex parte Pinochet Ugarte* (1999). In this case extradition proceedings were challenged on the basis that Lord Hoffmann had links with Amnesty International, which had provided evidence. Whilst there was no evidence of actual bias, it was concluded that there could be the appearance of bias and therefore the case was re-heard. The House of Lords stated that any direct interest whether financial, proprietary or otherwise would lead to automatic disqualification.

15.3.6 In other instances, where there is no direct personal interest but a non-direct interest that may give the appearance of bias, the court will examine whether in the view of a 'fair minded and informed observer' taking into account all the circumstances there is a 'real possibility' of bias: *Porter v Magill* (2002).

Failure to give reasons as a potential ground of judicial review?

15.3.7 Numerous statutes impose a duty to provide reasons. For example, there is a duty to give reasons on request in tribunals and public inquiries: Tribunals and Inquiries Act 1992.

15.3.8 There is no absolute duty to give reasons under the common law rules of natural justice, although there is a strong presumption that they should be provided: *R v Secretary of State for the Home Department, ex parte Doody* (1993).

15.3.9 There have been developments in the common law though where reasons must be provided. These include, for example:

- Where decisions are analogous to those of a judicial body: *R v Civil Service Appeal Board, ex parte Cunningham* (1991) and *R v Ministry of Defence, ex parte Murray* (1998).

- Where the decisions involve very important interests so that the individual would be at a clear disadvantage if reasons were not provided. For example, in *ex parte Doody* (above) reasons were required as the applicant otherwise had no knowledge of the case against them; the decision at hand was the fixing of a minimum sentence for a life prisoner (see also *Stefan v General Medical Council* (1999)). In *R v Secretary of State for the Home Department, ex parte Fayed* (1997) the court ruled that some indication of the Home Secretary's objections to the application for a British passport should have been given.

- Where the decision is unusual or a severe penalty can be applied. For example, in *R v DPP, ex parte Manning* (2000) reasons should have been provided for the decision not to prosecute after a coroner's finding of unlawful killing.

15.3.10 Conversely, there are situations where there will be no duty to provide reasons. This may occur where to do so would be extremely costly or particularly onerous on the decision-maker, or where the reasons for a range of potential decisions are laid out in advance of a final decision by the decision-maker: see *R v Higher Education Funding Council, ex parte Institute of Dental Surgery* (1994) and *R (Asha Foundation) v Millennium Commission* (2003).

15.3.11 Where a Minister fails to provide reasons for a decision, the court may infer that there were in fact no proper reasons for that decision: *Padfield v Minister of Agriculture, Fisheries and Food* (1968).

15.3.12 Where reasons are required, they must enable the parties to understand the basis for the decision, but this does not necessarily mean they have to be detailed or comprehensive. The level of detail necessary will depend on the facts of the case: *South Buckinghamshire DC v Porter* (2004).

15.3.13 Article 6 of the ECHR does not explicitly require the giving of reasons. However, it could be implied because of the need to have reasons in order to be able to exercise any right to appeal. Article 5 of the Convention, however, expressly states in the context of the right to liberty and security that arrested persons shall be informed promptly and in a language they understand of the reasons for their arrest.

15.4 Legitimate expectations

15.4.1 Legitimate expectation is a well-accepted principle of EU law, and has been increasingly recognised by the English courts. It occurs when the decision-maker, by either their words or actions, creates a reasonable and therefore legitimate expectation that certain procedures will be followed in reaching a decision.

15.4.2 If such expectations have been created, the decision-maker is not able to ignore them when coming to a decision on the matter unless there are good reasons not to do so: *R (Nadarajah) v Secretary of State for the Home Department, R (Abdi) v Secretary of State for the Home Department* (2005).

15.4.3 Whether a legitimate expectation has been created will depend on the circumstances. According to Lord Diplock in the *GCHQ Case* (above) a legitimate expectation may arise in two circumstances:

- from either an **express promise** given on behalf of the decision-maker; or
- from the existence of a **regular practice** that the applicant can reasonably expect to continue.

15.4.4 For a promise to create a legitimate expectation it must be clear, unambiguous and precise: *R v Inland Revenue Commissioners, ex parte MFK Underwriting Agents Ltd* (1990). However, the individual does not have to be aware of it, since it is the decision-maker who should be aware of any expectation created: *R (Rashid) v Secretary of State for the Home Department* (2005).

15.4.5 Some examples of where there was a clear, unambiguous and precise promise, creating a legitimate expectation, include:

- *R v Liverpool Corporation, ex parte Liverpool Taxi Fleet Operators Association* (1972) – the Corporation had given an express representation that licences would not be revoked without prior consultation. This created a legitimate expectation which could be relied on when the Corporation then failed to carry out that consultation.
- *Attorney-General for Hong Kong v Ng Yuen Shiu* (1983) – it was concluded that an illegal immigrant had a legitimate expectation of an interview prior to deportation and for his case to be considered on its individual merits because of an express undertaking given by the British Government.
- *R v Secretary of State for the Home Department, ex parte Asif Mahmood Khan* (1984) – the issuing of a circular providing the criteria under which a child would be permitted entry into the United Kingdom was held to have created a legitimate expectation that those criteria would be applied.

- *R (Bibi) v Newham LBC* (2001) – it was held that promises made by the local authority had created a legitimate expectation that the applicants (refugees) would be provided with accommodation with security of tenure.

15.4.6 Examples of where the promise was not considered sufficiently clear, unambiguous and precise enough to create a legitimate expectation include:

- *R v Secretary of State for the Home Department, ex parte Behluli* (1998) – the applicant argued that in the case of their expulsion they had a legitimate expectation that the Dublin Convention would be applied. The court held that the statements being relied upon did not create a sufficiently clear intention on behalf of the Government to create a legitimate expectation.

- *R v DPP, ex parte Kebeline* (1999) – four applicants sought to rely on a legitimate expectation that the DPP would exercise its discretion to prosecute only in accordance with the ECHR. They based their argument on the ratification of the Convention by the Government; the enactment of the Human Rights Act 1998; and from public statements made by Ministers. However, the Act whilst passed had not yet come into force. The court concluded that no legitimate expectation had been created.

- *R v Secretary of State for Education and Employment, ex parte Begbie* (2000) – a Labour Party pre-election promise that children benefiting from the assisted-places scheme would continue to receive this until the end of their education was held not to create a legitimate expectation. This was because Labour was in opposition at the time the statement was made and could not know of all the complexities of the matter until in office; consequently the promise was unclear. Thus, as a consequence of this decision, a pre-election promise cannot bind a new Government.

15.4.7 It should be noted that a legitimate expectation cannot arise from a promise or representation that is unlawful: *R v Ministry of Agriculture, Fisheries and Food, ex parte Hamble (Offshore) Fisheries Ltd* (1995) and *R (Bibi) v Newham LBC* (2001).

15.4.8 The question of whether there is an enforceable legitimate expectation is more complex when it involves a situation where there has been a change of policy.

15.4.9 Whilst legitimate expectation as a ground for judicial review promotes certainty and trust in executive authority, thus upholding the rule of law, it must also be recognised that the executive must be able to develop, adapt and change policies particularly if in the public interest.

15.4.10 In *North and East Devon Health Authority, ex parte Coughlan* (1999) the Court of Appeal identified three such situations involving legitimate expectation:

(a) Where a body changes policy, it should consider previous policy and representations made, before changing that policy. Thereafter, in cases of claims of legitimate expectation, review will take place on the basis of whether the decision is *Wednesbury* unreasonable (see above). For example, *R v Secretary of State for the Home Department, ex parte Hargreaves* (1996) – there was an agreement between prisoners and prison authorities that, subject to good behaviour, prisoners could apply for home leave after serving one-third of their sentence. The Home Secretary then changed this to having served half of the sentence. The court held that the agreement did not give rise to a legitimate expectation and that in any case the Home Secretary's change of policy was reasonable.

(b) If there is a legitimate expectation of being consulted prior to a decision (a procedural legitimate expectation), the court will examine closely any change in that policy to ensure that any decision is made fairly. For example, in *R v Secretary of State for Health, ex parte US Tobacco International Inc.* (1992) the company, using a Government grant, opened a factory in 1985 producing snuff. In 1988 the Government was provided with additional evidence of the health risks of snuff and decided to ban it. It was held that whilst there was a legitimate expectation created by the Government's prior actions, that expectation could not override the need to change the policy in the public interest.

(c) Where undertakings, representations or promises by a decision-maker create a substantive legitimate expectation, the court will very closely examine any change of policy. The court will balance carefully the interests of fairness given the individual's legitimate expectation against any overriding need to change the policy in the public interest. For example, in *R v North and East Devon Health Authority, ex parte Coughlan* (1999) the applicant lived in a home for the severely disabled and had been told by the Health Authority that it would be her home for life. She was then informed that the home was to be closed and she would be transferred. The court held that a legitimate expectation had been created, which no public-interest factor could override.

15.5 Procedural fairness

15.5.1 Following case such as *Coughlan* (discussed above), the common law has developed to such a point that we can surmise a 'procedural fairness' doctrine.

15.5.2 Academic writers Bradley and Ewing have noted that with regard to 'procedural fairness', in cases 'where no misconduct is alleged (for example, in the case of school or residential home closures, where parents or residents must in fairness be consulted by the local authority), then':

'(a) consultation must take place at a time when the proposals are at a formative stage;

(b) sufficient reasons must be given for the proposal to permit intelligent consideration and response;

(c) adequate time must be allowed; and

(d) the product of consultation must be conscientiously taken into account.'

15.5.3 These principles of procedural fairness have been endorsed as existing in the common law by the UK Supreme Court in *Moseley v Haringey London Borough Council* (2014) but they are often principles that run in parallel to, and add little beyond statutory duties in relation to fair decision-making, often referred to as the notion of procedural *ultra vires* as a ground of judicial review.

15.6 Procedural *ultra vires*

15.6.1 Failure to comply with a procedural requirement set out in statute could render a decision *ultra vires* and hence void. Such procedural requirements could include, for example:

- time limits;
- consultations;
- providing specific information; and
- providing notice.

15.6.2 The courts have traditionally distinguished between rules that are mandatory and those that are discretionary. This is ascertained by examining the statute. Failure to comply with a mandatory requirement will render a decision void; failure to abide by a discretionary requirement may not invalidate the decision.

15.6.3 However, more recently the courts have been less inclined to make a distinction on such a basis: see *London and Clydeside Estates Ltd v*

Aberdeen DC (1980) and *R v Immigration Appeal Tribunal, ex parte Jeyeanthen* (2000).

15.6.4 According to *AG's Reference (No. 3 of 1999)* (2001) the issue of validity is determined with reference to the purpose of the legislation, in that an act in breach of the provision was intended to be invalid. In turn, to determine the purpose regard must be had to the language of the relevant provision and the scope and object of the legislation as a whole.

15.6.5 Examples of the application of this ground include:
- *Ridge v Baldwin* (1964) – regulations under the Police Act 1964 required a formal inquiry before a chief constable could be dismissed, hence failure to do so rendered the dismissal invalid.
- *Bradbury v Enfield London Borough Council* (1967) – failure to give notice on the closing of schools and the creation of new ones invalidated the decision since it was a requirement under the Education Act 1944.
- *Agricultural, Horticultural and Forestry Industry Training Board v Aylesbury Mushrooms Ltd* (1972) – when making a decision the respective Minister had failed to consult the Mushroom Growers Association, which was held to be a breach of a statutory duty of consultation.

In recent years, the fastest growing area of case law around the notion of breaches of a duty to consult is centred on the public sector equality duty in the Equality Act 2010.

15.7 The general public sector equality duty (or duties)

15.7.1 The general public sector equality duty (PSED) reformed previously existing anti-discrimination procedural requirements adopted in various statutes – something that took effect through the Equality Act 2010.

15.7.2 The PSED is imposed upon public authorities by section 149 of the Equality Act 2010 which provides, in part, that:

'(1) A public authority must, in the exercise of its functions, have due regard to the need to —

(a) eliminate discrimination, harassment, victimisation and any other conduct that is prohibited by or under this Act;

(b) advance equality of opportunity between persons who share a relevant protected characteristic and persons who do not share it;

(c) foster good relations between persons who share a relevant protected characteristic and persons who do not share it; . . .'

15.7.3 Section 149(7) of the Equality Act 2010 determines that relevant 'protected characteristics' are 'age; disability; gender reassignment; pregnancy and maternity; race; religion or belief; sex; sexual orientation'.

15.7.4 The scope of this PSED is enormous, since it applies to the exercise of functions of public authorities, and as such the PSED is becoming a distinct ground of judicial review that is used to challenge decisions to withdraw funding from services where the supply of a particular service or quality of service is a 'function' or legislative duty of a public body.

15.7.5 The duty to consult to ensure that issues of equality are given 'due regard' in making difficult decisions on the supply or quality/level of public services in health, social care, education and housing is the main thrust of the PSED.

15.7.6 Below are 13 principles from the relevant case law as it stands today, at the time of writing in May 2015.

(1) **Equality duties are an integral and important part of the mechanisms for ensuring the fulfilment of the aims of anti-discrimination legislation** (*R (Elias) v Secretary of State for Defence* (2006)). The duty to have 'due regard' to issues of equality (e.g. equality of opportunity between different groups with or without 'protected' characteristics) must be 'exercised in substance, with rigour, and with an open mind'. It is not a question of 'ticking boxes'; while there is no duty to make express reference to the regard paid to the relevant duty, reference to it and to the relevant criteria reduces the scope for argument: *R (Brown) v Secretary of State for Work and Pensions* (2008).

(2) **The duty applies to the exercise of all public authority functions** even where the relevant decision relates to a public authority's private law arrangements such as the termination of a private contract or licence: see, for example, *Barnsley Borough Council v Norton* (2011) relating to possession proceedings in relation to residential property.

(3) An important evidential element in the demonstration of the discharge of the duty is the recording of the steps taken by the decision-maker in seeking to meet the statutory requirements: *R (BAPIO Action Ltd) v Secretary of State for the Home Department* (2007). **It is good practice for a decision-maker to keep records demonstrating consideration of the duty** as per *R (Brown) v Secretary of State for Work and Pensions* (2008).

(4) (There is a rebuttable presumption that) the relevant duty is upon the Minister or other decision-maker personally. What matters is what he or she took into account and what he or she knew. Thus, the Minister or decision-maker cannot be taken to know what his or her officials know or what may have been in the minds of officials in proffering their advice – *R (National Association of Health Stores) v Department of Health* (2005). **The PSED as a legal duty is non-delegable**: *R (Brown) v Secretary of State for Work and Pensions* (2008).

(5) A decision-maker must assess the risk and extent of any adverse impact and the ways in which such risk may be eliminated before the adoption of a proposed policy and not merely as a 'rearguard action', following a concluded decision: *Kaur & Shah v LB Ealing* (2008). **The duty must be fulfilled before and at the time when a particular policy is being considered**: *R (Brown) v Secretary of State for Work and Pensions* (2008).

(6) The public authority decision-maker must be aware of the duty to have 'due regard' to the relevant matters; and that **the duty is a continuing one**: *R (Brown) v Secretary of State for Work and Pensions* (2008).

(7) **'General regard to issues of equality is not the same as having specific regard, by way of conscious approach to the statutory criteria'**: *R (Meany) v Harlow DC* (2009).

(8) Those reporting to or advising Ministers/other public authority decision-makers, on matters material to the discharge of the duty, as **officials must not merely tell the Minister/decision-maker what he or she wants to hear** but they have to be 'rigorous in both enquiring and reporting to them': *R (Domb) v Hammersmith & Fulham LBC* (2009).

(9) Provided the court is satisfied that there has been a rigorous consideration of the duty, so that there is a proper appreciation of the potential impact of the decision on equality objectives and the desirability of promoting them, **it is for the decision-maker to**

decide how much weight should be given to the various factors informing the decision: *R (Hurley & Moore) v Secretary of State for Business, Innovation and Skills* (2012).

[10] 'The concept of "due regard" requires the court to ensure that there has been a proper and conscientious focus on the statutory criteria, but if that is done, the court cannot interfere with the decision simply because it would have given greater weight to the equality implications of the decision than did the decision maker. In short, **the decision maker must be clear precisely what the equality implications are when he puts them in the balance**, and he must recognise the desirability of achieving them, but ultimately it is for him to decide what weight they should be given in the light of all relevant factors': *R (Hurley & Moore) v Secretary of State for Business, Innovation and Skills* (2012).

(11) The duty of due regard under the statute requires public authorities to be properly informed before taking a decision. **If the relevant material is not available, there will be a duty to acquire it** and this will frequently mean that some further consultation with appropriate groups is required: *R (Hurley & Moore) v Secretary of State for Business, Innovation and Skills* (2012).

(12) In a case where large numbers of vulnerable people, very many of whom fall within one or more of the protected groups, the 'due regard' requirement is necessarily very high: see *Hajrula v London Councils* (2011).

(13) A sense of proportionality and reality is required. If a fair reading of the equality analysis makes clear that the decision-maker considered and conscientiously applied his or her mind to the relevant equality impact or impacts of the proposed decision, the court will not micromanage such decisions: *Branwood v Rochdale Metropolitan Borough Council* (2013).

Key Cases Checklist

Grounds of Judicial Review

- Substantive Grounds
- Human Rights Grounds
- Procedural Grounds

Procedural Grounds

- **European Convention on Human Rights: Article 6**
  - Procedural *ultra vires*
    - *Aylesbury Mushrooms Ltd* (1972)
  - Procedural fairness
  - Right to a fair trial

- **Natural justice**
  - Procedural fairness
    - *Moseley v Haringey LBC* (2014)
  - Failure to give reasons
  - *Ridge v Baldwin* (1964)
  - *R (Doody) v Home Secretary* (1993)

- **The rule against bias**
  - Direct/indirect interests
    - *Dimes v Grand Junction Canal Co.* (1852)
  - Apparent bias
    - *Porter v Magill* (2002)

- **Legitimate expectations**
  - Procedural expectations
  - Substantive expectations
    - *US Tobacco International Inc.* (1992)
    - *R (Coughlan) v NEDHA* (1999)

15.5.3 *R (on the application of Moseley) v Haringey LBC* [2014] UKSC 56

(SC)

Key Facts

Moseley claimed that the degree of consultation with the public over a council tax benefit reduction scheme had not been sufficient to ensure it was lawful. These schemes were introduced to realign the level of council tax benefit some people in the local area in London received – unfortunately for some people a reduction in their council tax benefit meant that their accommodation would become unaffordable. There had been a duty to consult under the relevant legislation; and only a single possible means of implementing the reduction in council tax benefit had been offered for consultation in the local community.

Key Law

It had been unlawful to offer up only one principal means for implementing the Government policy target concerned, in cutting council tax benefit in the local area to a certain level. Good consultation requires setting out a number of different options for consideration in the consultation process – ensuring that consultation is compliant with any legislative duty to consult, but also ensuring it is meaningful consultation overall.

Key Link

Agricultural, Horticultural and Forestry Industry Training Board v Aylesbury Mushrooms Ltd [1972] 1 WLR 190: similarly to the reasoning in *Moseley*, in *Aylesbury Mushrooms Ltd*, when making a decision the respective Minister had failed to consult the Mushroom Growers Association, which was held to be a breach of a statutory duty of consultation.

15.2.4 *Ridge v Baldwin* [1964] AC 40

(HL)

Key Facts

A chief constable was dismissed after his trial. Regulations under the Police Act 1919 required a formal inquiry before a chief constable could be dismissed.

Key Law

The regulations applied to the case and hence the formal inquiry should have been heard prior to any decision to dismiss.

In dismissing the chief constable the defendants had not only departed from the applicable regulations but had also acted in breach of the principles of natural justice.

Key Comment

This case marked a change in the law. Prior to this, the rules of natural justice had been applied to only judicial and quasi-judicial decisions. In this case the House of Lords moved away from this limitation and instead focused on the consequences of the action. If the consequences will infringe a person's rights then the rules of natural justice apply. However, certain factors may materially change the nature of the right to a hearing, such as, for example, national security.

15.3.8 *R v Secretary of State for the Home Department, ex parte Doody* [1993] 3 WLR 154 (HL)

Key Facts

The Criminal Justice Act 1991 gave the Home Secretary the power to release, on the direction of the Parole Board, discretionary life prisoners after they had served a tariff period. This period was recommended by the trial judge. The prisoner was not informed of this.

Key Law

The prisoner was entitled to know the length of the tariff period recommended and other relevant factors.

Key Judgment

Lord Mustill
'The giving of reasons may be inconvenient, but I can see no grounds at all why it should be against the public interest: indeed, rather the reverse. That being so, I would ask simply: is refusal to give reasons fair? I would answer without hesitation [in this case] that it is not.'

Key Comment

It has been argued that the scope of natural justice is in fact the requirement that powers are exercised 'fairly'.

This, according to *Doody*, demands that the context of the decision be considered. Fairness will therefore usually require that where a person will be adversely affected by the decision, they should be able to make representations and in order to do so should be informed of the reasons or nature of the case.

Key Link

In *R v Secretary of State for the Home Department, ex parte Al Fayed* [1997] 1 All ER 228 the Home Secretary failed to give reasons for the refusal to grant the applicant a passport, so the decision was quashed (although after the Court of Appeal decision the Home Secretary decided to give reasons and hence Al Fayed withdrew an appeal to the House of Lords). The concept of fairness is also linked to that of legitimate expectation (see below).

15.3.4 *Dimes v Grand Junction Canal Co.* (1852) 3 HL Cas 759 [HL]

Key Facts

Lord Cottenham had adjudicated in a decision involving Grand Junction Canal Ltd but held shares in the company.

Key Law

The mere existence of any financial interest in the decision will constitute unlawful bias.

15.3.6 *Porter v Magill* [2002] 2 AC 357 [HL]

Key Facts

The leader of Westminster Council was alleged to have adopted a policy of selling properties to tenants who would then vote Conservative. The auditor, Magill, was alleged to have prejudged the issue in press announcements and was therefore biased.

Key Law

The test for establishing bias was whether a 'fair minded and informed observer' would conclude that there was a 'real possibility' of bias.

15.4.10 R v Health Secretary, ex p US Tobacco International Inc. [1992] QB 353 (CA)

Key Facts

The company, using a Government grant, opened a factory in 1985 producing snuff. In 1988 the Government was provided with additional evidence of the health risks of snuff and decided to ban it through creating the Oral Snuff (Safety) Regulations 1989.

Key Law

It was held that whilst there was a legitimate expectation created by the Government's prior actions, such a legitimate expectation could not override the need to change the policy in the public interest. (On a separate ground of procedural fairness: the Regulations were, however, quashed due to the lack of consultation over their formulation, given the seriousness of their impact on the commercial undertakings of the company.)

15.4.10 R v North and East Devon Health Authority, ex parte Coughlan [2001] QB 213 (CA)

Key Facts

The applicant was severely disabled and lived in a home that she had been told would be for life. The Health Authority then decided to change policy and as a result closed the home.

Key Law

It was held that a legitimate expectation had been created, and to decide otherwise would be unfair. In addition there was no overriding public interest to justify enforcing the new policy.

Key Judgments

In *Coughlan*, on the issue of duties to consult, as an element of procedural fairness, Lord Woolf famously said:

'It is common ground that, whether or not consultation of interested parties and the public is a legal requirement, if it is embarked upon it must be carried out properly. To be proper, consultation must be undertaken at a time when proposals are still at a formative stage; it must include sufficient reasons for particular proposals to allow those consulted to give intelligent consideration and an intelligent response; adequate time must be given for this purpose; and the product of consultation must be conscientiously taken into account when the ultimate decision is taken . . .'

Though Lord Woolf qualified those words by saying:

'. . . It has to be remembered that consultation is not litigation: the consulting authority is not required to publicise every submission it receives or (absent some statutory obligation) to disclose all its advice. Its obligation is to let those who have a potential interest in the subject matter know in clear terms what the proposal is and exactly why it is under positive consideration, telling them enough (which may be a good deal) to enable them to make an intelligent response. The obligation, although it may be quite onerous, goes no further than this.'

Key Comment

The decision in *Coughlan*, as far as it concerns the power of the doctrine of substantive legitimate expectation, does raise potential problems; a court will have to carefully balance the interests of fairness given the individual's legitimate expectations against the necessity in reality for authorities to be able to change policy should it be necessary.

16 Human rights grounds for judicial review

```
┌─────────────────┐      ┌─────────────────┐
│   Substantive   │      │   Procedural    │
│     Grounds     │      │     Grounds     │
└─────────────────┘      └─────────────────┘
                                   ┌─────────────────┐
      ┌───────────────────────────┐│    European     │
      │ Grounds of Judicial Review││  Convention on  │
      └───────────────────────────┘│  Human Rights   │
                                   └─────────────────┘
                                   ┌─────────────────┐
            ┌──────────────────┐   │    Charter of   │
            │   Human Rights   │   │ Fundamental Rights│
            │     Grounds      │   │ of the European │
            └──────────────────┘   │      Union      │
                                   └─────────────────┘
```

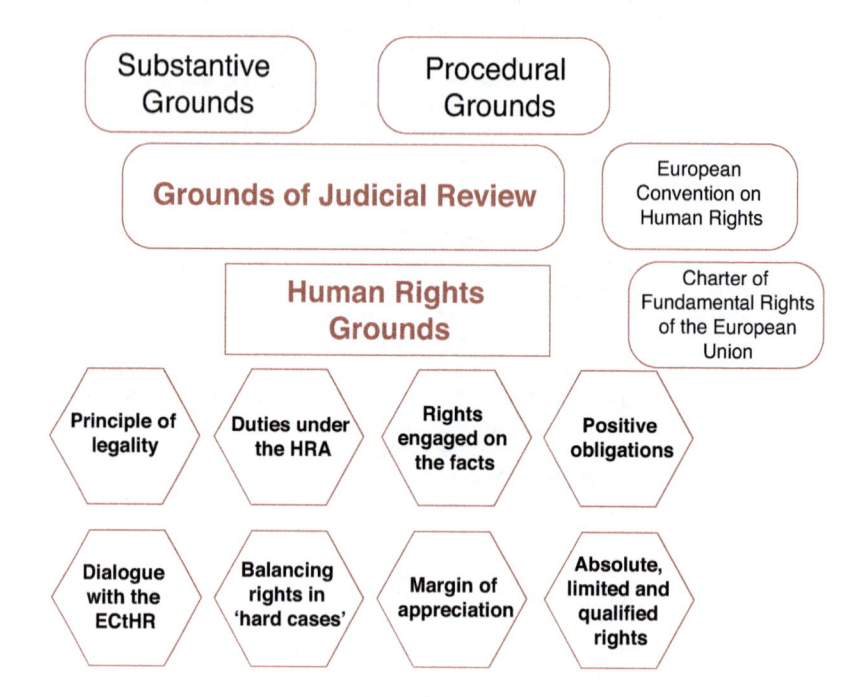

| Principle of legality | Duties under the HRA | Rights engaged on the facts | Positive obligations |
| Dialogue with the ECtHR | Balancing rights in 'hard cases' | Margin of appreciation | Absolute, limited and qualified rights |

▶ 16.1 An overview of human rights grounds for judicial review

16.1.1 This chapter has a slightly different structure and style to Chapters 1–15:

- It begins with the use of **ten key cases** to explore the workings of human rights-based judicial review.
- It should be read in conjunction with Chapter 7 (addressing the operation of the European Convention on Human Rights in the

United Kingdom, through the Human Rights Act 1998); along with Chapter 13 – which discusses issues of process, standing and remedies in judicial review cases.

- The later parts of this chapter focus on and explain how certain human rights-based arguments were used in recent cases involving UK public bodies or the UK Government – broken down by different Articles of the ECHR.

Key human rights principles: Case 1

R v Secretary of State for the Home Department, ex parte Simms [2000] **2 AC 115**

16.1.2 This case features the best exposition of the principle of legality, in the era of human rights law, which has yet been written. In the words of Lord Hoffmann (at 131):

> *'Parliamentary sovereignty means that Parliament can, if it chooses, legislate contrary to fundamental principles of human rights. The Human Rights Act 1998 will not detract from this power. The constraints upon its exercise by Parliament are ultimately political, not legal. But the principle of legality means that Parliament must squarely confront what it is doing and accept the political cost. Fundamental rights cannot be overridden by general or ambiguous words. This is because there is too great a risk that the full implications of their unqualified meaning may have passed unnoticed in the democratic process.'*

Key human rights principles: Case 2

YL v Birmingham City Council [2007] **UKHL 27**

16.1.3 The case which still determines the test as to whether duties under human rights law apply (or not) to a private body carrying out a public function – for example, the difference between arranging personal care under a statutory duty (and so human rights duties exist) or carrying out that care under a contract (where human rights duties were found not to exist).

16.1.4 The outcome of the case (in the House of Lords finding there were no human rights duties owed by a privately run care home as a care provider) caused enough political backlash to see the creation of section 145 of the Health and Social Care Act 2008 to redress the situation, at least in terms of residential social care.

Key human rights principles: Case 3

R v Horncastle and Others [2009] **UKSC 14**

16.1.5 At times the UK Supreme Court fronts up to the direction of a line of Strasbourg case law, and holds its own in taking a position eventually followed by the European Court of Human Rights itself. In *Horncastle*, the rules relating to the admission of 'hearsay' evidence in criminal prosecutions for serious crimes, in particularly controversial circumstances (such as when a witness is too intimidated to give evidence), were deemed compatible with the right to a fair trial, as found in Article 6 ECHR.

16.1.6 The Strasbourg Court in time endorsed this 'municipal' view of the UK court system on this issue of natural justice – meaning *Horncastle* is a strong example of the 'dialogic' relationship between the European Court of Human Rights and the UK courts.

Key human rights principles: Case 4

In re W (Children) (Family Proceedings: Evidence) [2010] **UKSC 12**

16.1.7 In notoriously 'hard' cases, human rights law in the United Kingdom can be all about balancing the rights of two parties or sides to a dispute, or a criminal case. In *W (Children)*, the right to a fair trial of a defendant was relied upon in the 'rebalancing' of that right as against the right to respect for private life of a child complainant in a prosecution for serious sexual offences. Prior to this decision, there had been a presumption that an alleged child victim of a sexual offence would not be cross-examined by defence counsel, but would simply give a statement that would be read to the court in their absence. This presumption was successfully challenged in this case by counsel for a defendant charged with rape of his own stepdaughter.

16.1.8 This ensured that each subsequent application for the prosecution to introduce a statement alone, rather than have such a child complainant cross-examined on the basis of that statement, would need to be examined in the light of the particular facts of the relevant case. This procedural victory of sorts for the right to a fair trial is a morally uneasy one for some, but as Lady Hale reminded us in her judgment in the case: 'A fair trial is a trial which is fair in the light of the issues which have to be decided.'

16.2 Engaging rights: measuring lawful and unlawful interferences with rights

Key human rights principles: Case 5

P v Cheshire West and Chester Council [2014] **UKSC 19**

16.2.1 When considering human rights-based grounds for judicial review, first we must be confident that a right protected by the ECHR is 'engaged'. That is to say, that a right is being negatively affected by the actions or decision of a public body. Tests and analyses of whether a right has been 'unlawfully interfered with', or *violated*, to use the term deployed by the European Court of Human Rights, come as the next stage, once it is established that a Convention right has been engaged by a public body.

16.2.2 In *Cheshire West*, Lady Hale reminds us that 'a golden cage is still a cage'. P, the claimant, who is severely disabled, was placed under a care plan by Chester Council staff which meant that his ability to leave his place of residence, a care home known as Z House, was restricted – and he was sometimes restrained while being fed. In this brilliant judgment, which reminds us of how to measure whether human rights of individuals are 'engaged', we see that we must measure a human rights infringement, done in a person's best interests and in good faith, in the same way as with malice or through neglect: hence the phrase, 'a golden cage is still a cage'.

16.2.3 So a right under the ECHR is still 'engaged' if it is interfered with even for a benevolent purpose.

16.3 Absolute, limited and qualified rights in the language of the ECHR

Key human rights principles: Case 6

S and Marper v United Kingdom [2008] **ECHR 1581**

16.3.1 This case from the European Court of Human Rights shows that the values of the ECHR will not tolerate blanket, inflexible practices that disproportionately affect a (qualified) human right – including the right to respect for private and family life (Article 8 ECHR) in this case. This judgment saw the indefinite retention of DNA profiles on the relevant UK police database deemed to be an unlawful interference with Article 8.

16.4 The concept of 'positive obligations' under the ECHR

Key human rights principles: Case 7
Rabone v Pennine Care NHS Trust [2012] **UKSC 2**

16.4.1 In this case, there was an institutional failing to do enough to prevent the suicide of a person under the care of the National Health Service. *Rabone* shows us that it is not just the actions of a body with human rights duties that can infringe a person's rights under the ECHR, but also failures to act, or the disorganisation of such a body and its work which leads to dangerous failures.

16.4.2 As such, *Rabone* is a case that clearly demonstrates the scope of 'positive obligations' placed on public bodies to uphold the rights of individuals under the ECHR.

16.5 The concept of a margin of appreciation

Key human rights principles: Case 8
S.A.S. v France **Application No. 43835/11 (1 July 2014)**

16.5.1 When Governments interfere with a qualified right under the ECHR, through the creation of a criminal offence in their domestic law, they may do so with greater latitude using their 'margin of appreciation' – meaning that the legal and constitutional culture and conventions of that jurisdiction may make for greater possible restrictions on the scope of some rights than in other jurisdictions across the Council of Europe.

16.5.2 In this case, the so-called '*burqa* ban' was upheld by the Strasbourg Court as being within the French Government's 'margin of appreciation', largely due to the French secular constitutional value of '*laïcité*'.

Key human rights principles: Case 9
Hirst v United Kingdom (No. 2) [2005] **ECHR 681**

16.5.3 But the notion of a Government's 'margin of appreciation' only runs so far. In *Hirst*, the European Court of Human Rights determined that it was unlawful, as a blanket and inflexible ban, to prevent all prisoners in the United Kingdom from voting in any elections at all while they were serving their sentences – of any length, that is, and in relation to offences of all severities.

16.5.4 The judgment in this case has been repeated by the European Court of Human Rights in several others since, leading to David Cameron, UK Prime Minister, claiming that it makes him feel 'physically ill' to contemplate allowing *any* prisoners to vote.

16.6 Preventing the use of ECHR rights to undermine the rights of others

Key Human Rights Principles: Case 10
Norwood v UK [2005] **40 EHRR SE11 (Application No. 23131/03)**

16.6.1 Norwood had displayed an offensively anti-Islamic poster in the window of his property, and was duly convicted of a public order offence. He tried to challenge his conviction before the European Court of Human Rights on the basis that the relevant criminal conviction unlawfully restricted his freedom of expression – but his claim was deemed inadmissible and it therefore failed.

16.6.2 The Strasbourg Court (and the ECHR) cannot tolerate the purported use of a qualified right (freedom of expression) to undermine the rights, safety and well-being of others in society.

16.6.3 The principle that legal arguments based on human rights in the ECHR cannot be used to undermine the rights of others is laid down in Article 17 ECHR.

Key Cases Checklist

More recent cases broken down by ECHR Article

Recent UK Human Rights Cases of Significant Importance

Article 2 ECHR
- *Al-Skeini v UK* (2011)

Article 3 ECHR
- *Vinter v UK* (2013)
- *H and B v UK* (2013)

Article 5 ECHR
- *Austin v UK* (2012)
- *P v Cheshire West* (2014) (see above)
- *Magee v UK* (2015)

Article 6 ECHR
- *Othman v UK* (2012)
- *Hanif and Khan v UK* (2012)

Article 8 ECHR
- *McDonald v UK* (2014)
- *Mosley v UK* (2011)
- *R (Quila) v Home Secretary* (2011)
- *R (T) v Home Secretary* (2014)
- *R (Catt) v Metropolitan Police* (2015)

Article 9 and Article 14 ECHR
- *Eweida v UK* (2013)

Article 11 ECHR
- *The RMT v UK* (2014)
- *Redfearn v UK* (2012)

Article 10 ECHR
- *Gough v UK* (2015)
- *Evans v Attorney General* (2015)

ECHR rights drawn from Protocols
- *Firth v UK* (2014) and *McHugh v UK* (2015)

Overlaps between ECHR rights and the EU CCR
- *Vidal-Hall v Google Inc.* (2015)
- *Bonkharbouche v Embassy of Sudan* (2015)

16.7 Article 2 ECHR

16.7.1 Article 2 ECHR provides individuals with the right to life, which also entails a positive obligation for deaths to be investigated by the Member State which should have safeguarded the lives of individuals that are killed.

16.7.2 *Al-Skeini v United Kingdom* (2011) 53 EHRR 18 — ECtHR

Key Facts

In *Al-Skeini*, the European Court of Human Rights determined that the protections of the ECHR should have been extended to those individuals killed, who were the subjects of security operations in Iraq that were conducted by British armed forces. Accordingly, the positive obligation to investigate the loss of life, which existed under Article 2 ECHR, had been breached by the United Kingdom.

Key Law

Al-Skeini is a reminder that the framework of the ECHR can apply in particular circumstances to the actions of British forces, and institutions, which operate overseas. In the military context of *Al-Skeini* this was true because of the physical control of the Iraqi jurisdiction during a military occupation by the British armed forces at the relevant time.

16.8 Article 3 ECHR

16.8.1 Article 3 ECHR protects individuals from torture, as well as inhuman or degrading treatment. This protection must be extended to even the most reviled or hateful criminal offenders in a society; or as Sir Tom Bingham once noted, those subject to the greatest 'public obloquy', or stigmatisation. It must also be a right extended and used to protect the most vulnerable in society, such as failed asylum seekers unable to return safely to their country of origin.

16.8.2 *Vinter v United Kingdom* 34 BHRC 605 — ECtHR

Key Facts

In *Vinter*, the applicants successfully challenged the 'whole life tariffs' which were their punishments for extremely serious crimes, including murder. It was held by the European Court of Human Rights that a 'whole life tariff' of imprisonment, which meant a prisoner could only be released by the order of the Home Secretary, and then on compassionate grounds, was unlawful; it was tantamount to inhuman or degrading treatment, since there was no guarantee at any point in the future of a review of the appropriateness of the imprisonment of an individual, thus engaging Article 3 ECHR.

Key Law

It should be an important premise in the criminal justice system of a Council of Europe Member State, such as the United Kingdom, that however horrendous or outrageous a crime committed by an individual, the function of the imprisonment of that person should also be rehabilitation as well as punishment, or the safeguarding of the public. An automatic review of the imprisonment of a purported 'lifer' ensured that there was some prospect of release; and enough reason to warrant their personal engagement with a programme of 'rehabilitation work' while in prison.

16.8.3 *H and B v United Kingdom* (2013) 57 EHRR 17

ECtHR

Key Facts

H and B were failed asylum seekers, originally living in Afghanistan, who had worked for the US and UN administrations in their home country, and so were, they felt, targets for Taliban or anti-Western extremists if they were to be returned by the UK Government to Afghanistan. In this case, the European Court of Human Rights dismissed their claim that their forcible return to Afghanistan by the UK Government would constitute a breach of their Article 3 ECHR rights.

Key Law

It was determined by the European Court of Human Rights in this case that it was for the claimants in such circumstances to establish that there was no ability on their part to avoid persecution upon their return, and that there were substantial grounds to believe that they would be subject to torture, or inhuman or degrading treatment upon their return to Afghanistan; which H and B failed to do. Cases such as that of *H and B* will often be decided on the very specific evidence of risk in that particular case.

16.9 Article 5 ECHR

16.9.1 Article 5 ECHR protects the right to liberty and security of the person – and is 'engaged' or affected, in many different sorts of contexts where an individual is bodily or spatially controlled or restrained. In *P v Cheshire West* (2014), discussed in this chapter, above, the UK Supreme Court drew on a great deal of case law from the European Court of Human Rights to determine that the first issue in examining whether there had been an infringement of Article 5 ECHR is to establish the degree to which a person's liberty was actually limited or restricted, even if this was done in their best interests, in the context concerned.

16.9.2 *Austin v UK* (2012) 55 EHRR 14 (ECtHR)

Key Facts

Thousands of demonstrators had been detained within box-shaped police cordons on the streets of London (a police tactic often called 'kettling'), after some of the demonstrators had become more violent and disorderly in their behaviour. Austin had been one of the demonstrators that were 'kettled' for more than five (and up to seven) hours in cold, open streets with no shelter, water or food provided, while the police dispersed the crowd gradually through an opening in one part of their cordon. Austin claimed that the police tactics had been a breach of her Article 5 ECHR rights. The European Court of Human Rights dismissed her claim.

Key Law

The European Court of Human Rights noted in its judgment in *Austin* that the police had faced, in that particular case, exceptional difficulties in possible outbreaks of very serious disorder and violence if they had not intervened.

While there may be positive obligations on the police to use cordon or 'kettling' tactics to safeguard the public from serious risk of harm, given the positive obligation on the police to protect Articles 2 and 3 ECHR rights, those tactics still represented an interference in the most serious cases with Article 5 ECHR rights, and so could only be used in a manner that was reasonable, proportionate, in good faith and in response to an imminent risk of serious public disorder, according to domestic common law.

16.9.3 *Magee and Others v United Kingdom* (2015) (Applications nos. 26289/12, 29062/12 and 29891/12) (ECtHR)

Key Facts

In 2009 the applicants in *Magee* were arrested under provisions of the Terrorism Act 2000, on suspicion of committing a terrorist murder, variously, of a police officer and two British Army soldiers, in Northern Ireland. None of the three applicants in this case were ever convicted – two were not even charged. All three had been detained for a period of up to 12 days, while being questioned and before being charged; the maximum permitted under the relevant statutory scheme *in place at the time* was 28 days. They had been brought before judicial officers (judges in court) at particular points in order that their detention without charge be justified by an independent, court body. The European Court of Human Rights determined that the Article 5 ECHR rights of the three applicants in *Magee* had not be unlawfully interfered with, as their detention was authorised under a statutory scheme that demanded judicial oversight and scrutiny of the purpose for detaining them without charge – and the detention, on the basis of a reasonable suspicion of their involvement in the terrorist murders concerned, was also able to be challenged by the applicants by way of judicial review.

Key Law

It is not simply just the length of detention, or the conditions of detention, before charge or conviction which determine whether a deprivation of liberty is lawful in the pursuit of criminal justice: it is particularly important that there are independently observed procedural safeguards against abuses of the power to detain criminal suspects. This detention should not occur without a sound, ongoing basis in evidence of a 'reasonable suspicion', which must last throughout the period of their pre-charge detention.

16.10 Article 6 ECHR

16.10.1 The UK courts recognise that the right to a fair trial must be flexible and adaptable across the different contexts in which it is invoked, including both civil justice, and criminal trials. However, the case law of both the UK courts and that of the European Court of Human

Rights has determined that there is always an 'irreducible minimum' of the right to a fair trial under Article 6 ECHR which must be afforded to those taking part in, or being subject to, any kind of judicial or decision-making process. As Lady Hale has usefully observed on this point of the flexibility of the right to a fair trial, as mentioned above already, 'A fair trial is a trial which is fair in the light of the issues which have to be decided'.

16.10.2 *Othman v United Kingdom* (2012) 55 EHRR 1

ECtHR

Key Facts

Othman, a Jordanian citizen, had been convicted of terrorist offences in Jordan in his absence, having claimed asylum in the United Kingdom, alleging that he had been tortured when previously detained by State authorities in Jordan. Othman claimed that his deportation to Jordan would be a breach of Article 3 ECHR, since he feared further torture by State authorities in Jordan upon his return. The UK Government had entered into an agreement with the Jordanian Government, which stipulated that Othman would not be subject to any treatment which would infringe Article 3 ECHR and the prohibition of torture, or inhuman or degrading treatment. However, Othman also complained that there was a risk that he would be punished on the basis of convictions secured by evidence extracted through the torture of his fellow defendants – thus breaching his own Article 6 ECHR right to a fair trial. The European Court of Human Rights, after examining the evidence presented, agreed that there was a real risk of a violation of Othman's right to a fair trial in the manner he alleged.

Key Comment

The European Court of Human Rights, in the judgment outlined above, had also concluded that it was possible for an agreement between two states to facilitate the deportation of a terrorist suspect such as Othman, provided there was a sufficient likelihood of it being effective and binding, and had the effect of precluding the breach of the suspect's rights under the ECHR. As a result, the UK Government and the Jordanian Government entered into a second agreement in relation to Othman; this time stipulating that he would not be prosecuted or convicted on the basis of any evidence secured through use of torture of others; thus allegedly better safeguarding Othman's Article 6 ECHR right to a fair trial. It followed that Othman was deported by the UK Government to the custody of the Jordanian authorities in July 2013.

16.10.3 Hanif and Khan v United Kingdom (2012) 55 EHRR 16 (ECtHR)

Key Facts

In this case the European Court of Human Rights determined that it was an unlawful violation of a defendant's right to a fair trial to have a police officer sit as a member of the jury in their trial, where that police officer was also familiar with a police officer giving evidence against the defendant as part of the trial.

Key Comment

This situation would always be an unlawful violation of the Article 6 ECHR right to a fair trial of the defendant.

16.11 Case law on qualified rights under the ECHR

16.11.1 A group of Articles within the ECHR protect what are known as the 'qualified rights':

- Article 8 ECHR: the right to respect for private and family life, and the confidentiality of correspondence;
- Article 9 ECHR: the right to freedom of religion, conscience, thought and belief;
- Article 10 ECHR: the right to freedom of expression; and
- Article 11 ECHR: the right to freedom of association.

16.11.2 In assessing whether an action or decision of a public body is a (potential) violation of a qualified right under the ECHR, as above, regard must first be had to whether the ECHR right itself is sufficiently interfered with to be **'engaged'**.

16.11.3 State policies or actions, as well as legislation, are often termed to be **'intrusions'** into qualified rights – practical limitations on the right to respect for private life, or to manifest a religion, or express oneself, for example. These 'intrusions' are what commonly can be seen to 'engage' a qualified right.

16.11.4 After the degree of limitation/intrusion is established as an interference with the right to an extent sufficient for the court to see the right as 'engaged', then the court must examine whether the right is actually engaged in a manner that is **'justified'**; on the basis of whether it was **'necessary', 'legitimate' and 'proportionate'** to limit or interfere with the Convention right at issue.

16.11.5 The European Court of Human Rights has developed a set of well-versed tests to use to ensure the justifications of interferences with rights as being 'necessary', 'legitimate' (and 'proportionate'), as follows:

- *necessary:* an interference with the qualified right is the result of addressing a 'pressing social need';
- *legitimate:* an interference with a qualified right, in addressing a 'pressing social need', is also done in a manner 'prescribed by law'; and
- *proportionate:* here the UK courts have developed their own multi-part test as to the required proportionality that would complete the justification of an interference with a qualified right under the ECHR (for more details, see Chapter 14).

16.11.6 A frequently cited version of this proportionality test is found in the judgment of Wilson LJ in *R (on the application of Quila) v Secretary of State for the Home Department* (2011):

- '(a) is the legislative object sufficiently important to justify limiting a fundamental right?;
- (b) are the measures which have been designed to meet it rationally connected to it?
- (c) are they no more than necessary to accomplish it?
- And (d) do they strike a fair balance between the rights of the individual and the interests of the community?'

16.12 Article 8 ECHR

16.12.1 *McDonald v UK* (2014) 17 CCL Rep 187 — ECtHR

Key Facts

The applicant in this case, McDonald, claimed that her rights under Article 8 ECHR had been disproportionately interfered with when a local authority removed her package of night-time care, instead offering her only the use of incontinence pads. The European Court of Human Rights dismissed her claim, holding that there was no violation of Article 8 ECHR in this care context if financial constraints in a period of budget pressures were given a careful, proportionate weighting in a detailed and personal assessment of an individual's care needs.

Key Law

Economic costs and pressures can be used to justify the limitation and reduction in the provision of public services without necessarily violating Article 8 ECHR rights, as long as this reduction in services impacts proportionally on the people affected, and there is a context of a 'pressing social need', or necessity, to reduce costs.

16.12.2 *Mosley v UK* (2011) 161 NLJ 703 (ECtHR)

Key Facts

While there was no lawful justification for the publication online, by a UK newspaper, of videos of private sexual activities engaged in by the applicant – which had been a breach of Article 8 ECHR as determined by the domestic UK courts – in this case the European Court of Human Rights held there was no need for the United Kingdom to adopt a domestic law requiring that newspapers notify the subject of an intrusive article before it is published. This matter fell within the 'margin of appreciation' of the UK legal system.

Key Law

There is a fair balance to be struck between the rights to private life possessed by individuals in the public eye, and the rights to freedom of expression possessed by journalists who need to bring public attention to the (sometimes private) acts of individuals; such as politicians, sportspeople, musicians and prominent businesspeople. The degree of intrusiveness into the private life of an applicant or claimant, as well as the exact nature of their public profile, will be the determining factors in adjudging the lawfulness of the publication of particular material.

Key Link

In 2012 the European Court of Human Rights published two decisions with privacy law implications for the United Kingdom. They are clear restatements of the law relating to the publications of photographs and accompanying news articles as these media activities engage the right to respect for private and family life (Article 8 ECHR), while drawing on the right to freedom of expression (Article 10 ECHR) contemporaneously.

In finding there had been no violation of the positive obligations owed under Article 8(1) ECHR following amendments in German law with regard to the publication of photographs that engage right to a private life of an individual, the Grand Chamber of the European Court of Human Rights said at paragraph 106 in *Von Hannover No. 2 v Germany* (2012):

> 'In cases such as the present one, which require the right to respect for private life to be balanced against the right to freedom of expression, the Court considers that the outcome of the application should not, in theory, vary according to whether it has been lodged with the Court under Article 8 of the Convention, by the person who was the subject of the article, or under Article 10 by the publisher. Indeed, as a matter of principle these rights deserve equal respect . . .'

The Grand Chamber then went on to outline **the complex criteria to be used in this balancing exercise concerning the tension between Articles 8 and 10** (paragraphs 108–113):

- **Contribution to a debate of general interest** (typically including political and criminal issues, as well as sporting and entertainment issues or the arts – though not infidelities or financial woes of a private nature).

- **How well known is the person concerned and what is the subject of the report** (considering the potential public role or function of the subject of the photo, or lack thereof, and their public or private nature of the action within the report or photo – with little weight given to mere satisfaction of public curiosity alone)?

- **Prior conduct of the person concerned** (and whether the photo was previously published, though not necessarily previous co-operation or consent to publication).

- **Content, form and consequences of the publication** (including the manner of publication of the photo and the accompanying report, as well as the extent of publication and circulation).

- **Circumstances in which the photos were taken** (including issues of consent, possible subterfuge, the nature or seriousness of the intrusion, the consequences of the publication and the likelihood the subject of the photo was previously unknown to the public).

When considering the proportionality of an injunctive measure or similar sanction against a media entity which has, or is about to publish an image or article that engages Article 8(1) ECHR and the right to respect for a private life, regard must be had to the following headings or criteria (paragraphs 89–95) lest there be a violation of the right to freedom of expression in Article 10(1) ECHR, as in the case of *Axel Springer AG v Germany* (2012):

- **Contribution to a debate of general interest** (including crime, political issues, sport, arts or entertainment – but not merely infidelity or financial difficulties alone).

- **How well known is the person concerned and what is the subject of the report** (considering the potential public role or function of the subject of the photo, or lack thereof, and their public or private nature of the action within the report or photo – with little weight given to mere satisfaction of public curiosity alone)?

- **Prior conduct of the person concerned** (and whether the photo was previously published, though not necessarily previous co-operation or consent to publication).

- **Method of obtaining the information and its veracity** (regard should be had to whether the party obtaining the photo/information was acting in good faith and on an accurate factual basis and whether they could be said to provide 'reliable and precise' information in accordance with the ethics of journalism).

- **Content, form and consequences of the publication** (including the manner of publication of the photo and the accompanying report, as well as the extent of publication and circulation).

- **Severity of the sanction (to be) imposed** (i.e. 'the nature and severity of the sanctions imposed').

These important reciprocal criteria or tests, now laid out more clearly and definitively, have fed themselves into the reasoning of UK courts concerned with claims for remedies in media privacy cases, and appeals against the same by media organisations, due to the duty of inclusion with regard to Strasbourg case law, which sits on UK judges because of section 2 of the Human Rights Act 1998.

16.12.3 R (on the application of Aguilar Quila) v Secretary of State for the Home Department [2011] UKSC 45

Key Facts

The UK Immigration Rules had been amended in such a way to attempt to preclude 'forced marriages', where there was a great disparity in age between a younger and an older partner. It was decided by the Home Secretary to ensure that this amendment would not allow individuals from non-EU countries under the age of 21 to settle in the United Kingdom with their spouse. It was determined by the UK Supreme Court in this case that this age-related rule was a disproportionate interference with the Article 8 ECHR right to private life of the applicant.

Key Law

There had to be a sufficient body of evidence to substantiate the new policy position in the Immigration Rules, and this was lacking at the point the amendment to the Rules was adopted. Having an evidence-base for a new policy or legal position is vital to be able, on the part of Government, to demonstrate the 'fair balance' criteria involved in proportionality assessment.

16.12.4 *R (on the application of T) v Secretary of State for the Home Department* [2014] UKSC 35

Key Facts

T, in his late teens, had applied for jobs working with children, which required him to provide his prospective employers with an Enhanced Criminal Record Certificate (the process commonly known as an 'enhanced DBS check' – since the Disclosure and Barring Service is the key public body involved in the compilation of ECRCs). T's ECRCs would routinely contain information describing his criminal offences from his pre-teen years; for which he had received two police warnings (meaning he was not prosecuted let alone convicted in his younger years). The Supreme Court held in this case that it was disproportionate and unlawful for the police and the DBS in this instance to place such information on T's ECRCs.

Key Law

The retention and disclosure through the ECRC compilation process of criminality information has to be proportionate, which could only be achieved through a more careful approach to filtering out irrelevant or outdated criminality information.

Key Comment

The litigation around the *T* case led to legal reform of the ECRC process, with new filtering rules to be applied by the DBS.

16.12.5 *R (on the application of Catt) v Commissioner of Police of the Metropolis* [2015] UKSC 9

Key Facts

Catt was a regular demonstrator at public protests, events which occasionally led to some violence from members of a group of which he was also a member. However, Catt himself had never been charged or convicted of any criminal offence, and had only been arrested twice in the course of many years of public protest, each time on suspicion of the non-violent offence of obstructing a highway. Catt was a person about whom a specialist surveillance unit of the Metropolitan Police kept a surveillance log, or file, detailing his attendance and activities at different public protests (while many of his fellow protestors would also have such records kept about them). Catt argued that this was a disproportionate and thus unlawful interference with his Article 8 ECHR rights, since he was not a violent protestor. The Supreme Court disagreed, placing a heavy emphasis on the need for police forces in the United Kingdom to base their planning of public order operations on a complete 'jigsaw' of pieces of intelligence about all members of potentially disorderly groups – and in other sensitive and important policing contexts.

Key Judgment

Lord Sumption
'The composition, organisation and leadership of protest groups who are persistently associated with violence and criminality at public demonstrations is a matter of proper interest to the police even if some of the individuals in question are not themselves involved in any criminality. The longer-term consequences of restricting the availability of this resource to the police would potentially be very serious. It would adversely affect police operations directed against far less benign spirits than Mr Catt. Organised crime, terrorism, drug distribution and football hooliganism are all obvious examples. One cannot look at an issue of this kind simply in relation to Mr Catt.'

16.13 Article 9 (and Article 14) ECHR

16.13.1 *Eweida v UK* [2013] IRLR 231 — ECtHR

Key Facts

The judgment by the European Court of Human Rights in *Eweida* actually dealt with several separate cases. Each of the applicants in *Eweida* argued that they had been discriminated against (engaging Article 14 ECHR) in the manner in which their employers allowed them, or did not allow them, to manifest their religious beliefs in the workplace. Their employers, and the employment tribunals which heard their cases against their employers at first instance, owed them duties under the ECHR in UK employment law, given the principle of horizontality.

Eweida had been employed by British Airways, where she wore a uniform at work. British Airways requested that she stop wearing a cross, a symbol of the Christian religion, on the outside of her uniform – and when she persistently refused, suspended her. The European Court of Human Rights determined that Eweida's treatment had been unlawful; the adornment of a cross she wore did not detract from her ability to undertake her duties and in any case was relatively discreet; while other manifestations of other religions, in terms of styles of dress, had been incorporated into the corporate dress code developed by British Airways without any issues.

Three other applicants in the case, however, were not able to establish that their treatment by their employers had been unlawful:

- a Christian nurse had been required to remove a cross when treating and handling or moving patients as a matter of health and safety practice, which was deemed by the European Court of Human Rights to be a proportionate interference with her right to manifest her religious beliefs;

- a Christian registrar had refused to undertake civil partnership ceremonies for gay couples, and so had eventually been dismissed from her post – again deemed to be a proportionate interference with her right to manifest her religious beliefs; and

- a Christian relationship counsellor had refused to provide relationship counselling to same-sex couples, on the basis that it would be against his beliefs, and so was subject to disciplinary processes at work – again this was deemed to be a proportionate interference with his right to manifest his religious beliefs

Key Law

The treatment of the nurse, registrar and counsellor were all deemed to be within the margin of appreciation enjoyed by the UK employment law system in implementing and adopting the principles of anti-discrimination law found within Article 14 ECHR.

16.14 Article 10 ECHR

16.14.1 *Gough v United Kingdom* (2015) SCCR 1 (ECtHR)

Key Facts

Gough had been arrested, convicted and imprisoned a number of times for public nudity while rambling on lengthy walks across the United Kingdom. He had been seeking to stimulate debate about public nudity – and complained to the European Court of Human Rights that his punishment by the criminal justice system was a disproportionate and unlawful interference with his right to freedom of expression under Article 10 ECHR. The European Court of Human Rights disagreed that there had been a violation of his right to freedom of expression as a 'naked rambler'.

Key Law

The tendency of the UK legal system to view Gough's public behaviour as anti-social behaviour was justified, particularly given the wide margin of appreciation enjoyed by Member States under the ECHR when they set limits on scope of anti-social behaviour which can be the vehicle of the expression of personal political or moral views.

16.14.2 *R (on the application of Evans) v Attorney General* [2015] UKSC 21 (SC)

Key Facts

The journalist Rob Evans had sought to obtain copies of correspondence between Prince Charles, the Prince of Wales, and senior Government figures in the last Labour Government, using a request under the Freedom of Information Act 2000. Using his power under section 53 of the Act, the Attorney General had decided to veto the release of these items of correspondence, known anecdotally as the 'black spider memos', due to the Prince's scrawling handwriting. In *Evans*, the UK Supreme Court held that it had been unlawful for the Attorney General to prevent the release of the correspondence on the basis of a purely personal assessment of the public interest issues in their potential disclosure – that personal assessment of the issues by the Attorney General did not constitute the required 'reasonable grounds' to preclude the release of the information.

Key Comment

The decision in *Evans* is an important reminder of several things: firstly, that the rights to freedom of expression in Article 10 ECHR includes the right to obtain and then disseminate information as part of informing public discourse as a journalist, for example; secondly, it is an important reminder that the courts will seek to assert their role in undertaking judicial review of the actions and decisions of public officials where those actions or officials are of constitutional significance, while at the same time respecting Parliamentary legislative supremacy.

As Alison Young has commented in relation to *Evans*:

> 'Protecting both parliamentary legislative supremacy and effective judicial review enables the UK constitution to develop, with institutions interacting effectively to develop legitimate constitutional principles. If either is undermined, this interaction can no longer take place. It is for this reason that courts do and should protect judicial review.'

16.15 Article 11 ECHR

16.15.1 *National Union of Rail, Maritime and Transport Workers ('The RMT') v United Kingdom* [2014] IRLR 467 (ECtHR)

Key Comment

The right to freedom of association under Article 11 ECHR provides for, amongst other things, the right to take industrial actions against employers, including strike action (the large-scale withdrawal of labour from the workplace to put pressure on employers to improve pay or conditions, through disrupting business operations). However, the United Kingdom does not protect striking workers from dismissal by their employers if they take *secondary* strike action; that is, going on strike to support the strike of another group of workers if they themselves have not first decided to do so by way of the required ballot of their own members.

This 'solidarity' striking is therefore seen as prohibited by statute in the United Kingdom – and was the subject of the challenge in this case before the European Court of Human Rights by the RMT, a trade union body.

However, while the European Court of Human Rights agreed with the RMT that the prohibition on secondary strike action constituted an interference with the right to freedom of association, under Article 11 ECHR, it was an interference that was justified as necessary by the 'pressing social need' in the United Kingdom to protect the economy from overly aggressive strike action by large, well-organised trade unions; an economic issue that fell within a wide margin of appreciation for the UK Government on this important policy issue.

16.15.2 *Redfearn v United Kingdom* (2012) 162 NLJ 1466 (ECtHR)

Key Comment

Redfearn, a white British employee of a local authority, had been working as a shuttle bus service driver when it was discovered by the local authority, his employers, that he was a member of the British National Party (which at one time was a relatively popular anti-multicultural political Party). The local authority decided to dismiss Redfearn due to his political affiliation to the BNP, since his role at work involved providing a public service to all members and sections of a multicultural society – though he had not been involved in any behaviour, politically or in relation to his employment, which was discriminatory or otherwise warranted his dismissal.

In their *Redfearn* decision, the European Court of Human Rights held that Redfearn had been vulnerable to dismissal on the basis of political Party membership, and UK employment law had not done enough to protect his Article 11 ECHR rights. UK workers are now protected from dismissal purely because of their membership of a legitimate political Party.

16.16 ECHR rights drawn from Protocols

16.16.1 *Firth v United Kingdom* (2014) (47784/09); and *McHugh v United Kingdom* (2015) (51987/08)

Key Comment

The decision of *Hirst v United Kingdom (No. 2)* (2005) established that it was unlawful, and a breach of ECHR Protocol 1 Article 3, to institute, as the UK Government had done, a 'blanket ban' or prohibition on prisoners from voting in any elections.

However, the decision by the European Court of Human Rights in *Firth v United Kingdom* established further that now it had been settled that the prohibition on prisoner voting had been determined as unlawful by the Court itself, future applicants in similar situations who were seeking redress for this breach of their rights would not receive compensation or be entitled to the recovery of their legal costs – since simply a declaration that the voting ban was unlawful following *Hirst* would be 'just satisfaction' for the relevant infringement of their rights. The same decision was reached in *McHugh v United Kingdom*.

16.17 Overlaps between ECHR rights and the EU Charter on Fundamental Rights

16.17.1 For a discussion as to how overlaps and key differences in the manner of implementation of the European Convention on Human Rights, versus the Charter of Fundamental Rights of the European Union, have begun to manifest themselves, see the discussion of the following cases in **Chapter 6, Section 8**, on the 'EU Charter on Fundamental Rights and overlaps with European human rights law':

- *Vidal-Hall v Google Inc.* [2015] **EWCA Civ 311;** *and*
- *Benkharbouche v Embassy of Sudan* [2015] **EWCA Civ 33.**

Index

Belfast Agreement 1998 115
bias 239–240
Bill of Rights 1689 4, 10, 11, 43, 44, 47, 138, 158
broadcasting 132–3

Charter of the United Nations and the Statute of the International Court of Justice (1945) 65, 66
Civil Procedure Rules, Part 54 209
Constitutions: Classifying constitutions 3; codified constitutions 3, 7–9; 'common law constitutionalism' 184; constitutional statutes 11; constitutional conventions 55–58; Constitutional Reform Act 2005 35–6; European legal systems and the UK constitution 14; monarchical 5; sources of the constitution 10–13; UK constitution 6–10; uncodified constitutions 3, 7–9; unitary nature of UK constitution 6; unwritten constitutions 3; written constitutions 3
convention (constitutional convention) 55–8; examples 56–7; non-binding legal nature 57–8
Convention *see* European Convention on Human Rights
Courts 179–188: and Europe 186; and Government 185; and Parliament 183–85; common law 10, 13, 180; tribunals 188–89

declaration(s) (declaratory relief) 216
declaration(s) of incompatibility 99–101
devolution 111–121: 20th century history 114–15; 'English votes for English laws' (EVEL) 123; historical context 112–13; legislation 116–21; Sewel convention 121–22; Smith Commission 123
discrimination *see* rights

ECHR *see* European Convention on Human Rights
Electoral Commission 131
error of fact 224
error of law 224
European Communities Act 1972 4, 11, 14, 17, 21–23, 47–48, 69, 72, 79–82, 117, 186
European Convention on Human Rights 89–95: absolute rights 259; derogation 95; engaging; ECHR rights 259; European Court of Human Rights (Strasbourg) 96, 186–7; impact on the UK constitution 96;

limited rights 259; margin of appreciation 95, 260; positive obligations 260; proportionality principle 95

European Convention on Human Rights, Articles and Protocols of the ECHR: Article 2 90, 93, 97, 263; Article 3 90, 93, 97, 263–64; Article 4 90; Article 5 90, 93, 97, 215, 241, 265–66; Article 6 91, 94, 98, 238, 239, 241, 258, 266–68; Article 7 91; Article 8 91, 94, 98, 268–74; Article 9 91, 98, 268–69, 275; Article 10 91, 94, 268–69, 271–72, 276–77; Article 11 91, 277–78; Article 12 91; Article 13 91; Article 14 91, 275–76; Article 17 261; Article 1 First Protocol 92; Article 2 First Protocol 92; Article 3 First Protocol 92, 279; Article 1 Fourth Protocol 92; Article 2 Fourth Protocol 92; Article 3 Fourth Protocol 92; Article 4 Fourth Protocol 92; Sixth Protocol 92; Article 1 Seventh Protocol 92; Article 2 Seventh Protocol 92; Article 3 Seventh Protocol 92; Article 4 Seventh Protocol 92; Article 5 Seventh Protocol 92; Twelfth Protocol 92; Thirteenth Protocol 92; Fourteenth Protocol 92

European Court of Human Rights (Strasbourg) 96, 186–7

European Union law 72–85: Directives 76; ECJ or European Court of Justice (Court of Justice of the European Union) (Luxembourg) 75–6; EU Charter on Fundamental Rights (Charter of Fundamental Rights of the European Union) 73, 82–84; EU institutions 74–5; *Factortame* 81; Regulations 76; Supremacy of EU law in the UK constitution 78–82

European Union law, Treaties of the EU 73, 76: Treaty of Amsterdam (1997) 73; Treaty on European Union (Maastricht Treaty, TEU) (1992) 73, 74; Treaty on the Functioning of the European Union 73, 74, 75, 76, 77; Treaty of Lisbon (2007) 73, 74; Treaty of Nice (2001) 73; Treaty of Rome (1957) 72; Treaty Establishing a Constitution for Europe (2004) 73

excess of powers 223

executive 147–175: Cabinet 148; central government 148–165; Civil Service 170; local government 152–155; ministerial responsibility 149–152; police 155; Prime Minister 148; scrutiny by Parliament 166–168

fair trial *see* rights
fettering of discretion 226
freedom from discrimination *see* Rights
freedom of assembly *see* Rights
freedom of expression *see* Rights
freedom of information 173–175, 276–77
freedom of religion *see* Rights

HRA see Human Rights Act 1998
Human Rights Act 1998 96–106, 198–9: reform of the UK human rights framework 103–05;

Section 2 96; Section 3 99; Section 4 99–101; Section 6 101; Section 7 102; Section 8 103; Section 10 99

illegality (as a ground of judicial review) 222–226
implied repeal 44
improper purpose 223
inquiries 192
international law 63–70: custom in international law 65–66; enabling Acts 70; international law and national law in the UK 67–70; nature of 63–4; *opinio juris* 66; ratification in the UK 70; sources of international law 64–5; Treaties 66
irrationality *see* unreasonableness
irrelevant consideration(s) 225

judicial review 169, 196–203: amenability 199; Civil Procedure Rules, Part 54 209; comity 216; deference 216; excess of powers 222–3; grounds 221; growth in judicial review cases 197–8; human rights in judicial review 198–9, 256–261; illegality 222–226; irrationality 227; justiciability 201; leave 209–10; legitimate expectation(s) 241–244; natural justice 238; ouster clauses 201–202; permission 209–10; policy 200; pre-action protocol 210; procedural grounds 237–249; procedural fairness 245; procedural *ultra vires* 245–6; procedure 209–213; proportionality principle 95; remedies 203, 214–16; right to be heard 238; and the rule of law 196; standing 211–214; substantive grounds 221–229; time limits 211; *ultra vires* 222–3; unreasonableness 227–8; *Wednesbury* review 227–8
judiciary (and judges): Administration Court of the Queen's Bench Division of the High Court 182; circuit judges 181; Court of Appeal 182; district judges 181; High Court 181–2; and juries 181; Magistrates 181; magistrates' courts 181; Supreme Court 182–3

legal realism 184
legitimate expectation(s) 241–244
liberty *see* rights

Magistrates 181
Magistrates' Courts 181
Magna Carta 1215 10
Margin of appreciation 95, 260
Ministers 147–151: Ministerial Code 151; ministerial responsibility 149–152; special advisers 171–3

natural justice 238

ombudsmen 190
ouster clauses 201–202

Parliament 116–141: bicameral nature 126; electoral system 127; House of Commons 133–4; House of Lords 134–7; Parliament Acts 137; parliamentary standards 140–41; privilege 138–140
parliamentary privilege 138–140

parliamentary sovereignty 42–54:
limitations on parliamentary
sovereignty 45–48; European
dimensions 48; implied repeal
44; principle of legality 49
parliamentary supremacy *see*
parliamentary sovereignty
police 155–6
positive obligations 260
prerogative power(s) *see* Royal
prerogative
principle of legality 49
privacy *see* right to private and
family life
privilege *see* Parliamentary privilege
procedural fairness 245
proportionality 95, 228, 268–9
PSED *see* public sector
equality duty
public sector equality duty 246–249
public records 173–5
publication 270–72

relevant consideration(s) 225
religion *see* rights
rights: right to be heard 238; Right
to life 90, 93, 97, 263; right
to freedom from torture and
inhuman or degrading treatment
90, 93, 97, 263–64; right to
liberty and security of the person
90, 93, 97, 215, 241, 265–66;
right to a fair trial 91, 94, 98,
238, 239, 241, 258, 266–68; right
to private and family life 91, 94,
98, 268–74; right to freedom of

religion 91, 98, 268–69, 275;
right to freedom of expression
91, 94, 268–69, 271–72, 276–77;
right to freedom of assembly 91,
277–78; right to freedom from
discrimination 91, 275–76
Royal prerogative 13–14, 34,
157–66: examples of
prerogative powers 158–61;
limitations and scope of
prerogative powers 161–4;
reforms 165–6
rule of law 24–35: Bingham on
the rule of law 26; critique and
limitation of 28–9; Dicey on
the rule of law 25; and judicial
review 196; and separation of
powers 31–2

separation of powers 31–34,
169, 180
Sewel convention 121–22
Supreme Court Act 1981 209

torture *see* rights
treaty or treaties *see* international
law *or* European Union law
tribunals 188–190

ultra vires see excess of powers
United Nations Declaration of
Human Rights 1948 90
unreasonableness 227

Wednesbury unreasonableness *see*
unreasonableness